This special reprint edition originally published
in 1877 is now republished by:

Longmeadow Press
201 High Ridge Road
Stamford, CT 06904

in association with

Platinum Press Inc.
311 Crossways Park Drive
Woodbury, NY 11797

Longmeadow Press and the colophon are registered trademarks.

ISBN 0-681-10435-X

0987654321

Printed in the USA

Library of Congress Cataloging-in-Publication Data

Fowler, William Worthington, 1833 - 1881.
    [Woman on the American frontier]
    Frontier women : an authentic history of the courage and trials
    of the pioneer heroines of our American frontier. / by William
    Fowler.
        p. cm.
    Originally published : Hartford, CT: S.S. Scranton, 1877.
    ISBN 0-681-10435-X
        1. Women pioneers — United States — Biography. 2. Frontier
    and pioneer life — United States. I. Title.
    E176.F69   1995
    973'.082 — dc20   95-15729
                                                          CIP

PREFACE.

The history of our race is the record mainly of men's achievments, in war, in statecraft and diplomacy. If mention is made of woman it is of queens and intriguing beauties who ruled and schemed for power and riches, and often worked mischief and ruin by their wiles.

The story of woman's work in great migrations has been told only in lines and passages where it ought instead to fill volumes. Here and there incidents and anecdotes scattered through a thousand tomes give us glimpses of the wife, the mother, or the daughter as a heroine or as an angel of kindness and goodness, but most of her story is a blank which never will be filled up. And yet it is precisely in her position as a pioneer and colonizer that her influence is the most potent and her life story most interesting.

The glory of a nation consists in its migrations and the colonies it plants as well as in its wars of conquest. The warrior who wins a battle deserves a laurel no more rightfully than the pioneer who leads his race into the wilderness and builds there a new empire.

The movement which has carried our people from the Atlantic to the Pacific Ocean and in the short space of two centuries and a half has founded the greatest republic which the world ever saw, has already taken its place in history as one of the grandest achievments of humanity since the world began. It is a moral as well as a physical triumph, and forms an epoch in the advance of civilization. In this grand achievement, in this triumph of physical and moral endurance, woman must be allowed her share of the honor.

It would be a truism, if we were to say that our Republic would not have been founded without her aid. We need not enlarge on the necessary position which she fills in human society every where. We are to speak of her now as a soldier and laborer, a heroine and

(3)

comforter in a peculiar set of dangers and difficulties such as are met with in our American wilderness. The crossing of a stormy ocean, the reclamation of the soil from nature, the fighting with savage men are mere generalities wherein some vague idea may be gained of true pioneer life. But it is only by following woman in her wanderings and standing beside her in the forest or in the cabin and by marking in detail the thousand trials and perils which surround her in such a position that we can obtain the true picture of the heroine in so many unmentioned battles.

The recorded sum total of an observation like this would be a noble history of human effort. It would show us the latent causes from which have come extraordinary effects. It would teach us how much this republic owes to its pioneer mothers, and would fill us with gratitude and self-congratulation—gratitude for their inestimable services to our country and to mankind, self-congratulation in that we are the lawful inheritors of their work, and as Americans are partakers in their glory.

In the preparation of this work particular pains have been taken to avoid what was trite and hackneyed, and at the same time preserve historic truth and accuracy. Use has been made to a limited extent of the ancient border books, selecting the most note-worthy incidents which never grow old because they illustrate a heroism, that like "renown and grace cannot die." Thanks are due to Mrs. Ellet, from whose interesting book entitled "Women of the Revolution," a few passages have been culled. The stories of Mrs. VanAlstine, of Mrs. Slocum, Mrs. McCalla, and Dicey Langston, and of Deborah Samson, are condensed from her accounts of those heroines.

A large portion of the work is, however, composed of incidents which will be new to the reader. The eye-witnesses of scenes which have been lately enacted upon the border have furnished the writer with materials for many of the most thrilling stories of frontier life, and which it has been his aim to spread before the reader in this work.

CONTENTS

CHAPTER I: WOMAN AS A PIONEER, ... 17

America's Unnamed Heroines.
Maids and Matrons of the "Mayflower."
Woman's Work in Early Days.
Devotion and Self-sacrifice.
Strange Story of Mrs. Hendee.
Face to Face with the Indians.
A Mother's Love Triumphant.
Woman among the Savages.

The Massacre of Wyoming.
Sufferings of a Forsaken Household.
The Patriot Matron and her Children.
The Acmé of Heroism.
Adventures of an English Traveler.
Woman in the Rocky Mountains.

A Story of a Lonely Life.
Nocturnal Visitors and their Reception.
Life in the Far West.
Mrs. Manning's Home in Montana.
Female Emigrants on the Plains.
A True Heroine.

CHAPTER II: WOMAN'S WORK IN FLOODS AND STORMS, ... 34

The Frontier two Centuries ago.
The Pioneer Army.
The Pilgrim "Mothers."
Story of Margaret Winthrop.
Danger in the Wilderness.
A Reckless Husband and a Watchful Wife.
Lost in a Snow-storm.

The Beacon-fire at Midnight.
Saved by a Woman.
Mrs. Noble's Terrible Story.
Alone with Famine and Death.
A Legend of the Connecticut.
What befel the Nash Family.
Three Heroic Women.
In Flood and Storm.

A Tale of the Prairies.
A Western Settler and her Fate.
Battling with an Unseen Enemy.
Emerging from the Valley of the Shadow.
Heartbroken and Alone.

CHAPTER III: EARLY PIONEERS.—WOMAN'S ADVENTURES AND HEROISM, .. 56

In the Maine Wilderness.
Voyaging up the Kennebec.
The Huntress of the Lakes.
Extraordinary Story of Mrs. Trevor.
Two Hundred Miles from Civilization.
Sleeping in a Birch-bark Canoe.
A Fight with Five Savages.

A Victorious Heroine.
The Trail of a Lost Husband.
Only just in Time.
A Narrow Escape.
Voyaging in an Ice-boat.
Snow-bound in a Cave.
Fighting for Food.
Grappling with a Forest Monster.

Mrs. Storey, the Forester.
Alida Johnson's Thrilling Narrative.
Caught in a Death-trap.
A Desperate Measure and its Result.
The Connecticut Settlers.
Their Courage and Heroism.

CHAPTER IV: ON THE INDIAN TRAIL, ... 79

A Block-house Attacked.
Wild Pictures of Indian Warfare.
Exploits of Mrs. Howe.
A Pioneer Woman's Record.
Holding the Fort Alone.
Treacherous "Lo."
Witnessing a Husband's Tortures.
The Beautiful Victim.

Forced to Carry a Mother's Scalp.
The Fate of the Glendennings.
A Feast and a Massacre.
Led into Captivity.
Elizabeth Lane's Adventures.
In Ambush.
Siege of Bryant's Station.
Outwitting the Savages.

Mrs. Porter's Combat with the Indians.
Ghastly Trophies of her Prowess.
"Long Knife Squaw."
Smoking out Redskins.
The Widows of Innis Station.
A Daring Achievement.
The Amazon of the Stockade.

CONTENTS

CHAPTER V: CAPTIVE SCOUTS.—HEROINES OF THE MOHAWK VALLEY, ... 98

The Poetry of Border Life.
Mrs. Mack in her Forest Fort.
The Ambush in the Cornfield.
The Night-watch at the Port-hole.
A Shot in the Dark.
The Hiding Place of her Little Ones.
A Sad Discovery.

An Avenger on the Track.
Massy Herbeson's Strange Story.
On the Trail.
Miss Washburn and the Scouts.
An Extraordinary *Rencontre*.
A Wild Fight with the Savages.
Mysterious Aid.

Passing through an Indian Village.
Hairbreadth Escapes.
Courageous Conduct of Mrs. Van Alstine.
Settlements on the Mohawk.
Circumventing a Robber Band.
How she Saved him.
The Pioneer Woman at Home.

CHAPTER VI: PATRIOT WOMEN OF THE REVOLUTION, ... 121

Times that Tried Men's Souls.
The Women of Wyoming.
Silas Deane's Sister.
Mrs. Corbin, the Cannoneer.
A Heroine on the Gun-deck.
The Schoharie Girl.
Women of the Mohawk Wars.
Concerning a Curious Siege.

The Patriot Daughter and the Bloody Scouts.
What she Dared him to do.
Brave Deeds of Mary Ledyard.
Ministering Angels.
Heroism of "Mother Bailey."
Petticoats and Cartridges.
A Thrilling Incident of Valley Forge.

Ready-witted Ladies.
Miss Geiger, the Courier.
How Miss Darrah Saved the Army.
Adventures of McCalla's Wife.
Love and Constancy.
A Clergyman's Story of his Mother.

CHAPTER VII: GOING WEST.—PERILS BY THE WAY, ... 150

After the Revolution.
Starting for the Mississippi.
Curious Methods of Migration.
A Modern Exodus.
Incidents on the Route.
Wonderful Story of Mrs. Jameson.
Forsaking all for Love.
A Woman with One Idea.

That Fatal Stream.
Alone in the Wilderness.
A Glimpse of the Enemy.
Strength of a Mother's Love.
Saved from a Rattlesnake.
Individual Enterprise.
Migrating in a Flat-boat.
A Night of Peril on the Ohio River.

Terrifying Sounds and Sights.
A Fiery Scene of Savage Orgies.
Coolness and Daring of a Mother.
An Extraordinary Line of Mothers and Daughters.
A Pioneer Pedigree and its Heroines.

CHAPTER VIII: HOME LIFE IN THE BACKWOODS, ... 173

The Nomads of the West.
Romance of a Pioneer's March.
How the Cabin was Built.
Where Mrs. Graves Concealed her Babes.
Husband and Wife at Home.
Rather Rough Furniture.
Forest Fortresses.
Fighting for her Children.

Firing the Alarm Gun.
Mrs. Fulsom and the Ambushed Savage.
Domestic Life on the Border.
From a Wedding to a Funeral.
Among the Beasts and Savages.
Little Ones in the Wilds.
Woman takes Care of Herself.

Ann Bush's Sorrows.
The Bright Side of the Picture.
Western Hospitality.
A Traveler's Story.
"Evangeline" on the Frontier.
An Eden of the Wilderness and its Eve.

CONTENTS

CHAPTER IX: SOME REMARKABLE WOMEN, ... 195

Diary of a Heroine.
The Border Maid, Wife, Mother, and Widow.
Strange Vicissitudes in the Life of Mrs. W.
Adopted by an Indian Tribe.
Shrewd Plan of Escape.
The Hiding-place in the Glen.
Surprised and Surrounded, but Safe.

Successful Issue of her Enterprise.
Mrs. Marliss and her Strategy.
Combing the Wool over a Savage's Eyes.
Marking the Trail.
A Captive's Cunning Devices.
A Pursuit and a Rescue.
Extraordinary Presence of Mind.

A Robber Captured by a Woman.
A Brave, Good Girl.
Helping "the Lord's People."
A Home of Love in the Wilderness.
A Singular Courtship.
The Benevolent Matron and her Errand.
Story of the Pioneer Quakeress.

CHAPTER X: A ROMANCE OF THE BORDER, ... 217

The Honeymoon in the Mountains.
United in Life and Death.
A Devoted Lover.
Capture of Two Young Ladies.
Discovery and Rescue.
The Captain and the Maid at the Mill.
The Chase Family in Trouble.

The Romance of a Young Girl's Life.
Danger in the Wind.
Hunter and Lover.
Treacherous Savages.
Old Chase Knocked Over.
The Fight on the Plains.
An Unexpected Meeting.
Heroism of La Bonté.
The Guard of Love.

The Marriage of Mary.
Miss Rouse and her Lover.
A Bridal and a Massacre.
Brought back to Life but not to Joy.
A Fruitless Search for a Lost Bride.
Mrs. Philbrick's Singular Experience.

CHAPTER XI: PATHETIC SCENES OF PIONEER LIFE, ... 239

Grief in the Pioneer's Home.
Graves in the Wilderness.
The Returned Captive and the Nursery Song.
The Lost Child of Wyoming.
Little Francis and her Indian Captors.
Parted For Ever.
Discovery of the Lost One.

An Affecting Interview.
Striking Story of the Kansas War.
The Prairie on Fire.
Mother and Children Alone.
Homeless and Helpless.
Solitude, Famine, and Cold.
Three Fearful Days.
The Burning Cabin.

A Gathering Storm.
Affecting Scenes.
A Dream of Home and Happiness.
Return of Father and Son.
A Love Stronger than Death.
The Last Embrace.
A Desolate Household.

CHAPTER XII: THE HEROINES OF THE SOUTH WEST, ... 261

Texas and the South West.
Across the "Staked Plain."
Mrs. Drayton and Mrs. Benham.
A Perilous Journey.
Sunstrokes and Reptiles.
Death from Thirst.
Mexican Bandits.
A Night Gallop to the Rendezvous.

Escape of our Heroines.
A Ride for Life.
Saving Husband and Children.
Surrounded by Brigands on the Pecos.
Heroism of Mrs. Benham.
The Treacherous Envoy.
The Gold Hunters of Arizona.
Mrs. D. and her Dearly Bought Treasure.

Battling for Life in the California Desert.
The Last Survivor of a Perilous Journey.
Mrs. L., the Widow of the Colorado.
Among the Camanches.
A Prodigious Equestrian Feat.

CHAPTER I.

EVERY battle has its unnamed heroes. The common soldier enters the stormed fortress and, falling in the breach which his valor has made, sleeps in a nameless grave. The subaltern whose surname is scarcely heard beyond the roll-call on parade, bears the colors of his company where the fight is hottest. And the corporal who heads his file in the final charge, is forgotten in the "earthquake shout" of the victory which he has helped to win. The victory may be due as much, or more, to the patriot courage of him who is content to do his duty in the rank and file, as to the dashing colonel who heads the regiment, or even to the general who plans the campaign: and yet unobserved, unknown, and unrewarded the former passes into oblivion while the leader's name is on every tongue, and perhaps goes down in history as that of one who deserved well of his country.

Our comparison is a familiar one. There are other battles and armies besides those where thousands of disciplined men move over the ground to the sounds of the drum and fife. Life itself is a battle, and no grander army has ever been set in motion since the world began than that which for more than two centuries and a half has been moving across our continent from the Atlantic to the Pacific, fighting its way through countless hardships and dangers, bearing the

2   (17)

banner of civilization, and building a new republic in
the wilderness.

In this army WOMAN HAS BEEN TOO OFTEN THE
UNNAMED HEROINE.

Let us not forget her now. Her patience, her courage, her fortitude, her tact, her presence of mind in
trying hours; these are the shining virtues which we
have to record. Woman *as a pioneer* standing beside her rougher, stronger companion—man; first on
the voyage across a stormy ocean, from England to
America; then at Plymouth, and Jamestown, and all
the settlements first planted by Europeans on our
coast; then through the trackless wilderness, onward
across the continent, till every river has been forded,
and every chain of mountains has been scaled, the
Peaceful Ocean has been reached, and fifty thousand
cities, towns, and hamlets all over the land have been
formed from those aggregations of household life
where woman's work has been wrought out to its
fullness.

Among all the characteristics of woman there is
none more marked than the self-devotion which she
displays in what she believes is a righteous cause, or
where for her loved ones she sacrifices herself. In
India we see her wrapped in flames and burned to
ashes with the corpse of her husband. Under the
Moslem her highest condition is a life-long incarcera-
tion. She patiently places her shoulders under the
burden which the aboriginal lord of the American
forest lays upon them. Calmly and in silence she
submits to the onerous duties imposed upon her by
social and religious laws. Throughout the whole
heathen world she remained, in the words of an

elegant French writer, "anonymous, indifferent to herself, and leaving no trace of her passage upon earth."

The benign spirit of Christianity has lifted woman from the position she held under other religious systems and elevated her to a higher sphere. She is brought forward as a teacher; she displays a martyr's courage in the presence of pestilence, or ascends the deck of the mission-ship to take her part in "perils among the heathen." She endures the hardships and faces the dangers of colonial life with a new sense of her responsibility as a wife and mother. In all these capacities, whether teaching, ministering to the sick, or carrying the Gospel to the heathen, she shows the same self-devotion as in "the brave days of old;" it is this quality which peculiarly fits her to be the pioneer's companion in the new world, and by her works in that capacity she must be judged.

If all true greatness should be estimated by the good it performs, it is peculiarly desirable that woman's claims to distinction should thus be estimated and awarded. In America her presence has been acknowledged, and her aid faithfully rendered from the beginning. In the era of colonial life; in the cruel wars with the aborigines; in the struggle of the Revolution; in the western march of the army of exploration and settlement, a grateful people must now recognize her services.

There is a beautiful tradition, that the first foot which pressed the snow-clad rock of Plymouth was that of Mary Chilton, a fair young maiden, and that the last survivor of those heroic pioneers was Mary Allerton, who lived to see the planting of twelve out of the thirteen colonies, which formed the nucleus of these United States.

In the *Mayflower*, nineteen wives accompanied their husbands to a waste land and uninhabited, save by the wily and vengeful savage. On the unfloored hut, she who had been nurtured amid the rich carpets and curtains of the mother-land, rocked her new-born babe, and complained not. She, who in the home of her youth had arranged the gorgeous shades of embroidery, or, perchance, had compounded the rich venison pasty, as her share in the housekeeping, now pounded the coarse Indian corn for her children's bread, and bade them ask God's blessing, ere they took their scanty portion. When the snows sifted through the miserable roof-tree upon her little ones, she gathered them closer to her bosom; she taught them the Bible, and the catechism, and the holy hymn, though the war-whoop of the Indian rang through the wild. Amid the untold hardships of colonial life she infused new strength into her husband by her firmness, and solaced his weary hours by her love. She was to him,

> " —— an undergoing spirit, to bear up
> Against whate'er ensued."

The names of these nineteen pioneer-matrons should be engraved in letters of gold on the pillars of American history.

The Wives of the Pilgrims.

Mrs. Catharine Carver.	Mrs. Elizabeth Hopkins.
Mrs. Dorothy Bradford.	Mrs. —— Tilley.
Mrs. Elizabeth Winslow.	Mrs. —— Tilley.
Mrs. Mary Brewster.	Mrs. —— Tinker.
Mrs. Mary Allerton.	Mrs. —— Ridgdale.

Mrs. Rose Standish.   Mrs. ——— Eaton.
Mrs. ——— Martin.   Mrs. ——— Chilton.
Mrs. ——— Mullins.   Mrs. ——— Fuller.
Mrs. Susanna White.   Mrs. Helen Billington.
               Mrs. Lucretia Brewster.

Nor should the names of the daughters of these heroic women be forgotten, who, with their mothers and fathers shared the perils of that winter's voyage, and bore, with their parents, the toils, and hardships, and changes of the infant colony.

The Daughters of the Pilgrim Mothers.

Elizabeth Carver.   Sarah Allerton.
Remember Allerton.   Constance Hopkins.
Mary Allerton.   Mary Chilton.
             Priscilla Mullins.

The voyage of the *Mayflower;* the landing upon a desolate coast in the dead of winter; the building of those ten small houses, with oiled paper for windows; the suffering of that first winter and spring, in which woman bore her whole share; these were the first steps in the grand movement which has carried the Anglo-Saxon race across the American continent. The next steps were the penetration of the wilderness westward from the sea, by the emigrant pioneers and their wives. Fighting their way through dense forests, building cabins, block-houses, and churches in the clearings which they had made; warred against by cruel savages; woman was ever present to guard, to comfort, to work. The annals of colonial history teem with her deeds of love and heroism, and what are those recorded instances to those which had no chronicler? She loaded the flint-lock in the block-house while it was surrounded by yelling savages; she exposed herself to the scalping-knife to save her babe; in her forest-home she worked and watched, far from the loved ones in Old England; and by discharging a thousand duties in the household and the field, did her share in a silent way towards building up the young Republic of the West.

Sometimes she ranged herself in battle beside her husband or brother, and fought with the steadiness and bravery of a veteran. But her heroism never shone so brightly as in undergoing danger in defense of her children.

In the early days of the settlement of Royalton, Vermont, a sudden attack was made upon it by the Indians. Mrs. Hendee, the wife of one of the settlers, was working alone in the field, her husband being absent on military duty, when the Indians entered her house and capturing her children carried them across the White river, at that place a hundred yards wide and quite deep for fording, and placed them under keepers who had some other persons, thirty or forty in number, in charge.

Returning from the field Mrs. Hendee discovered the fate of her children. Her first outburst of grief was heart-rending to behold, but this was only transient; she ceased her lamentations, and like the lioness who has been robbed of her litter, she bounded on the trail of her plunderers. Resolutely dashing into the river, she stemmed the current, planting her feet firmly on the bottom and pushed across. With pallid face, flashing eyes, and lips compressed, maternal love dominating every fear, she strode into the Indian camp, regardless of the tomahawks menacingly flourished round her head, boldly demanded the release of her little ones, and persevered in her alternate upbraidings and supplications, till her request was granted. She then carried her children back through the river and landed them in safety on the other bank.

Not content with what she had done, like a patriot as she was, she immediately returned, begged for the release of the children of others, again was rewarded with success, and brought two or three more away; again returned, and again succeeded, till she had rescued the whole fifteen of her neighbors' children who had been thus snatched away from their distracted parents. On her last visit to the camp of the enemy, the Indians were so struck with her conduct that one of them declared that so brave a squaw deserved to be carried across the river, and offered to take her on his back and carry her over. She, in the same spirit, accepted the offer, mounted the back of the gallant savage, was carried to the opposite bank, where she collected her rescued troop of children, and hastened away to restore them to their overjoyed parents.

During the memorable Wyoming massacre, Mrs. Mary Gould, wife of James Gould, with the other women remaining in the village of Wyoming, sought safety in the fort. In the haste and confusion attending this act, she left her boy, about four years old, behind. Obeying the instincts of a mother, and turning a deaf ear to the admonitions of friends, she started off on a perilous search for the missing one. It was dark; she was alone; and the foe was lurking around; but the agonies of death could not exceed her agonies of suspense; so she hastened on. She traversed the fields which, but a few hours before,

"Were trampled by the hurrying crowd,"

where—

"———— fiery hearts and armed hands,
Encountered in the battle cloud,"

and where unarmed hands were now resting on cold and motionless hearts. After a search of between one and two hours, she found her child on the bank of the river, sporting with a little band of playmates. Clasping her treasure in her arms, she hurried back and reached the fort in safety.

During the struggles of the Revolution, the privations sustained, and the efforts made, by women, were neither few nor of short duration. Many of them are delineated in the present volume. Yet innumerable instances of faithful toil, and patient endurance, must have been covered with oblivion. In how many a lone home, from which the father was long sundered by a soldier's destiny, did the mother labor to perform to their little ones both his duties and her own, having no witness of the extent of her heavy burdens and sleepless anxieties, save the Hearer of prayer.

A good and hoary-headed man, who had passed the limits of fourscore, once said to me, "My father was in the army during the whole eight years of the Revolutionary War, at first as a common soldier, afterwards as an officer. My mother had the sole charge of us four little ones. Our house was a poor one, and far from neighbors. I have a keen remembrance of the terrible cold of some of those winters. The snow lay so deep and long, that it was difficult to cut or draw fuel from the woods, or to get our corn to the mill, when we had any. My mother was the possessor of a coffee-mill. In that she ground wheat, and made coarse bread, which we ate, and were thankful. It was not always we could be allowed as much, even of this, as our keen appetites craved. Many is the time that we have gone to bed, with only a drink of water for our supper, in which a little molasses had been mingled. We patiently received it, for we knew our mother did as well for us as she could; and we hoped to have something better in the morning. She was never heard to repine; and young as we were, we tried to make her loving spirit and heavenly trust, our example.

" When my father was permitted to come home, his stay was short, and he had not much to leave us, for the pay of those who achieved our liberties was slight, and irregularly given. Yet when he went, my mother ever bade him farewell with a cheerful face, and told him not to be anxious about his children, for she would watch over them night and day, and God would take care of the families of those who went forth to defend the righteous cause of their country. Sometimes we wondered that she did not mention the cold weather, or our short meals, or her hard work, that we little ones might be clothed, and fed, and taught. But she would not weaken his hands, or sadden his heart, for she said a soldier's life was harder than all. We saw that she never complained, but always kept in her heart a sweet hope, like a well of water. Every night ere we slept, and every morning when we arose, we lifted our little hands for God's blessing on our absent father, and our endangered country.

"How deeply the prayers from such solitary homes and faithful hearts were mingled with the infant liberties of our dear native land, we may not know until we enter where we see no more 'through a glass darkly, but face to face.'

"Incidents repeatedly occurred during this contest of eight years, between the feeble colonies and the strong mother-land, of a courage that ancient Sparta would have applauded.

"In a thinly settled part of Virginia, the quiet of the Sabbath eve was once broken by the loud, hurried roll of the drum. Volunteers were invoked to go forth and prevent the British troops, under the pitiless Tarleton, from forcing their way through an important mountain pass. In an old fort resided a family, all of whose elder sons were absent with our army, which at the north opposed the foe. The father lay enfeebled and sick. By his bedside the mother called their three sons, of the ages of thirteen, fifteen, and seventeen.

"'Go forth, children,' said she, "to the defence of your native clime. Go, each and all of you; I spare not my youngest, my fair-haired boy, the light of my declining years.

"'Go forth, my sons! Repel the foot of the invader, or see my face no more.'"

In order to get a proper estimate of the greatness of the part which woman has acted in the mighty onward-moving drama of civilization on this continent, we must remember too her peculiar physical constitution. Her highly strung nervous organization and her softness of fiber make labor more severe and suffering keener. It is an instinct with her to tremble at dan-

A VIRGINIA MATRON ENCOURAGING THE PATRIOTISM OF HER SONS AT THE DEATH-BED OF THEIR FATHER.   Page 26.

ger; her training from girlhood unfits her to cope with the difficulties of outdoor life. " Men," says the poet, "must work, and women must weep." But the pioneer women must both work and weep. The toils and hardships of frontier life write early wrinkles upon her brow and bow her delicate frame with care. We do not expect to subject our little ones to the toils or dangers that belong to adults. Labor is pain to the soft fibers and unknit limbs of childhood, and to the impressible minds of the young, danger conveys a thousand fears not felt by the firmer natures of older persons. Hence it is that all mankind admire youthful heroism. The story of Casabianca on the deck of the burning ship, or of the little wounded drummer, borne on the shoulders of a musketeer and still beating the *rappel*—while the bullets are flying around him—thrill the heart of man because these were great and heroic deeds performed by striplings. It is the bravery and firmness of the weak that challenges the highest admiration. This is woman's case: and when we see her matching her strength and courage against those of man in the same cause, with equal results, what can we do but applaud?

A European traveler lately visited the Territory of Montana—abandoning the beaten trail, in company only with an Indian guide, for he was a bold and fearless explorer. He struck across the mountains, traveling for two days without seeing the sign of a human being. Just at dusk, on the evening of the second day, he drew rein on the summit of one of those lofty hills which form the spurs of the Rocky Mountains. The solitude was awful. As far as the eye could see stretched an unbroken succession of mountain

peaks, bare of forest—a wilderness of rocks with
stunted trees at their base, and deep ravines where no
streams were running.   In all this desolate scene there
was no sign of a living thing.   While they were teth-
ering their horses and preparing for the night, the
sharp eyes of the Indian guide caught sight of a gleam
of light at the bottom of a deep gorge beneath them.

Descending the declivity, they reached a cabin
rudely built of dead wood, which seemed to have been
brought down by the spring rains from the hill-sides to
the west.   Knocking at the door, it was opened by a
woman, holding in her arms a child of six months.
The woman appeared to be fifty years of age, but she
was in reality only thirty.   Casting a searching look
upon the traveler and his companion, she asked them
to enter.

The cabin was divided into two apartments, a
kitchen, which also served for a store-room, dining-
room, and sitting-room; the other was the chamber,
or rather bunk-room, where the family slept.   Five
children came tumbling out from this latter apartment
as the traveler entered, and greeted him with a stare
of childlike curiosity.   The woman asked them to be
seated on blocks of wood, which served for chairs, and
soon threw off her reserve and told them her story,
while they awaited the return of her husband from
the nearest village, some thirty miles distant, whither
he had gone the day before to dispose of the gold-dust
which he had "panned out" from a gulch near by.
He was a miner.   Four years before he had come
with his family from the East, and pushing on in
advance of the main movement of emigration in the
territory, had discovered a rich gold placer in this

lonely gorge. While he had been working in this placer, his wife had with her own hands turned up the soil in the valley below and raised all the corn and potatoes required for the support of the family; she had done the housework, and had made all the clothes for the family. Once when her husband was sick, she had ridden thirty miles for medicine. It was a dreary ride, she said, for the road, or rather trail, was very rough, and her husband was in a burning fever. She left him in charge of her oldest child, a girl of eleven years, but she was a bright, helpful little creature, able to wait upon the sick man and feed the other children during the two days' absence of her mother.

Next summer they were to build a house lower down the valley and would be joined by three other families of their kindred from the East. "Have you never been attacked by the Indians?" inquired the traveler.

"Only three times," she replied. "Once three prowling red-skins came to the door, in the night, and asked for food. My husband handed them a loaf of bread through the window, but they refused to go away and lurked in the bushes all night; they were stragglers from a war-party, and wanted more scalps. I saw them in the moonlight, armed with rifles and tomahawks, and frightfully painted. They kindled a fire a hundred yards below our cabin and stayed there all night, as if they were watching for us to come out, but early in the morning they disappeared, and we saw them no more.

"Another time, a large war-party of Indians encamped a mile below us, and a dozen of them came up and surrounded the house. Then we thought we were lost: they amused themselves aiming at marks in the logs, or at the chimney and windows; we could hear their bullets rattle against the rafters, and you can see the holes they made in the doors. One big brave took a large stone and was about to dash it against the door, when my husband pointed his rifle at him through the window, and he turned and ran away. We should have all been killed and scalped if a company of soldiers had not come up the valley that day with an exploring party and driven the red-skins away.

"One afternoon as my husband was at work in the diggings, two red-skins came up to him and wounded him with arrows, but he caught up his rifle and soon made an end of them.

"When we first came there was no end of bears and wolves, and we could hear them howling all night long. Winter nights the wolves would come and drum on the door with their paws and whine as if they wanted to eat up the children. Husband shot ten and I shot six, and after that we were troubled no more with them.

"We have no schools here, as you see," continued she; "but I have taught my three oldest children to read since we came here, and every Sunday we have family prayers. Husband reads a verse in the Bible, and then I and the children read a verse in turn, till we finish a whole chapter. Then I make the children, all but baby, repeat a verse over and over till they have it by heart; the Scripture promises do comfort us all, even the littlest one who can only lisp them.

"Sometimes on Sunday morning I take all the chil-

dren to the top of that hill yonder and look at the
sun as it comes up over the mountains, and I think
of the old folks at home and all our friends in the
East. The hardest thing to bear is the solitude. We
are awful lonesome. Once, for eighteen months, I
never saw the face of a white person except those of
my husband and children. It makes me laugh and
cry too when I see a strange face. But I am too
busy to think much about it daytimes. I must wash,
and boil, and bake, or look after the cows which wander off in search of pasture; or go into the valley
and hoe the corn and potatoes, or cut the wood; for
husband makes his ten or fifteen dollars a day panning
out dust up the mountain, and I know that whenever
I want him I have only to blow the horn and he will
come down to me. So I tend to business here and
let him get gold. In five or six years we shall
have a nice house farther down and shall want for
nothing. We shall have a saw-mill next spring started
on the run below, and folks are going to join us from
the States."

The woman who told this story of dangers and
hardships amid the Rocky Mountains was of a slight,
frail figure. She had evidently been once possessed
of more than ordinary attractions; but the cares of
maternity and the toils of frontier life had bowed her
delicate frame and engraved premature wrinkles upon
her face: she was old before her time, but her spirit
was as dauntless and her will to do and dare for her
loved ones was as firm as that of any of the heroines
whom history has made so famous. She had been
reared in luxury in one of the towns of central New

York, and till she was eighteen years old had never known what toil and trouble were.

Her husband was a true type of the American explorer and possessed in his wife a fit companion; and when he determined to push his fortune among the Western wilds she accompanied him cheerfully; already they had accumulated five thousand dollars, which was safely deposited in the bank; they were rearing a band of sturdy little pioneers; they had planted an outpost in a region teeming with mineral wealth, and around them is now growing up a thriving village of which this heroic couple are soon to be the patriarchs. All honor to the names of Mr. and Mrs. James Manning, the pioneers of Montana.

The traveler and his guide, declining the hospitality which this brave matron tendered them, soon returned to their camp on the hill-top; but the Englishman made notes of the pioneer woman's story, and pondered over it, for he saw in it an epitome of frontier life.

If a tourist were to pass to-day beyond the Mississippi River, and journey over the wagon-roads which lead Westward towards the Rocky Mountains, he would see moving towards the setting sun innumerable caravans of emigrants' canvas-covered wagons, bound for the frontier. In each of these wagons is a man, one or two women with children, agricultural tools, and household gear. At night the horses or oxen are tethered or turned loose on the prairie; a fire is kindled with buffalo chips, or such fuel as can be had, and supper is prepared. A bed of prairie grass suffices for the man, while the women and children rest in the covered wagon. When the morning dawns they resume their Westward journey. Weeks, months, sometimes, roll by before the wagon reaches its destination; but it reaches it at last. Then begin the struggle, and pains, the labors, and dangers of border life, in all of which woman bears her part. While the primeval forest falls before the stroke of the man-pioneer, his companion does the duty of both man and woman at home. The hearthstone is laid, and the rude cabin rises. The virgin soil is vexed by the ploughshare driven by the man; the garden and house, the dairy and barns are tended by the woman, who clasps her babe while she milks, and fodders, and weeds. Danger comes when the man is away; the woman must meet it alone. Famine comes, and the woman must eke out the slender store, scrimping and pinching for the little ones; sickness comes, and the woman must nurse and watch alone, and without the sympathy of any of her sex. Fifty miles from a doctor or a friend, except her weary and perhaps morose husband, she must keep strong under labor, and be patient under suffering, till death. And thus the household, the hamlet, the village, the town, the city, the state, rise out of her "homely toils, and destiny obscure." Truly she is one of the founders of the Republic.

CHAPTER II.

THE American Frontier has for more than two centuries been a vague and variable term. In 1620–21 it was a line of forest which bounded the infant colony at Plymouth, a few scattered settlements on the James River, in Virginia, and the stockade on Manhattan Island, where Holland had established a trading-post destined to become one day the great commercial city of the continent.

Seventy years later, in 1690, the frontier-line had become greatly extended. In New England it was the forest which still hemmed in the coast and river settlements: far to the north stretched the wilderness covering that tract of country which now comprises the states of Maine, New Hampshire, and Vermont. In New York the frontier was just beyond the posts on the Hudson River; and in Virginia life outside of the oldest settlements was strictly "*life on the border.*" The James, the Rappahannock, and the Potomac Rivers made the Virginia frontier a series of long lines approaching to a parallel. But the European settlements were still sparse, as compared with the area of uninhabited country. The villages, hamlets, and single homesteads were like little islands in a wild green waste; mere specks in a vast expanse of wilderness. Every line beyond musket-shot was a frontier-line.

(34)

Every settlement, small or large, was surrounded by a dark circle, outside of which lurked starvation, fear, and danger. The sea and the great rivers were perilous avenues of escape for those who dwelt thereby, but the interior settlements were almost completely isolated and girt around as if with a wall built by hostile forces to forbid access or egress.

The grand exodus of European emigrants from their native land to these shores, had vastly diminished by the year 1690, but the westward movement from the sea and the rivers in America still went forward with scarcely diminished impetus: and as the pioneers advanced and established their outposts farther and farther to the west, woman was, as she had been from the landing, their companion on the march, their ally in the presence of danger, and their efficient co-worker in establishing homes in the wilderness.

The heroic enterprises recorded in the history of man have generally been remarkable in proportion to their apparent original weakness. This is true in an eminent degree of the settlement of European colonies on the western continent. The sway which woman's influence exercised in these colonial enterprises is all the more wonderful when we contemplate them from this point of view. Three feeble bands of men and women;—the first at Jamestown, Virginia, in 1609–1612; the second at Plymouth, in 1620; the third on the Island of Manhattan, in 1624;—these were the dim nuclei from which radiated those long lines of light which stretch to-day across a continent and strike the Pacific ocean. This is a simile borrowed from astronomy. To adopt the language of the naturalist, those three little colonies were the puny

germs which bore within themselves a vital force vastly
more potent and wonderful than that which dwells in
the heart of the gourd seed, and the acorn whose
nascent swelling energies will lift huge boulders and
split the living rock asunder: vastly more potent because it was not the blind motions of nature merely,
but a force at once physical, moral, and intellectual.

These feeble bands of men and women took foot-
hold and held themselves firmly like a hard-pressed
garrison waiting for re-enforcements. Re-enforcements
came, and then they went out from their works, and
setting their faces westward moved slowly forward.
The vanguard were men with pikes and musketoons
and axes; the rearguard were women who kept watch
and ward over the household treasures. Sometimes
in trying hours the rearguard ranged itself and fought
in the front ranks, falling back to its old position when
the crisis was past.

In order to appreciate the actual value of woman
as a component part of that mighty impulse which set
in motion, and still impels the pioneers of our country, we must remember that she is really the cohesive
power which cements society together; that when the
outward pressure is greatest, the cohesive power is
strongest; that in times of sore trial woman's native
traits of character are intensified; that she has greater
tact, quicker perceptions, more enduring patience, and
greater capacity for suffering than man; that motherly,
and wifely, and sisterly love are strongest and brightest when trials, labors, and dangers impend over the
loved ones.

We must bear in mind too, that woman and man
were possessed of the same convictions and impulses

in their heroic enterprise—the sense of duty, the spirit
of liberty, the desire to worship God after their own
ideas of truth, the desire to possess, though in a wilderness, homes where no one could intrude or call
them vassals; and deep down below all this, the instincts, the gifts, and motive power of the most energetic race the world has ever seen—the Anglo-Saxon;
thus we come to see how in each band of pioneers and
in each household were centered that solid and constant moving force which made each man a hero and
each woman a heroine in the struggle with hostile nature, with savage man more cruel than the storm or the
wild beasts, with solitude which makes a desert in the
soul; with famine, with pestilence, that "wasteth at
noon-day,"—a struggle which has finally been victorious over all antagonisms, and has made us what we
are in this centennial year of our existence as an independent republic.

Another powerful influence exercised by woman as
a pioneer was the influence of religion. The whole
nature certainly of the Puritan woman was transfused
with a deep, glowing, unwavering religious faith. We
picture those wives, mothers, and daughters of the
New England pioneers as the saints described by the
poet,

"Their eyes are homes of silent prayer."

How the prayers of these good and honorable women were answered events have proved.

Hardly had the Plymouth Colony landed before they
were called upon to battle with their first foes—the
cold, the wind, and the storms on the bleak New England coast. Famine came next, and finally pestilence.
The blast from the sea shook their frail cabins; the

frost sealed the earth, and the snow drifted on the pillow of the sick and dying. Five kernels of corn a day were doled out to such as were in health, by those appointed to this duty. Woman's heart was full then, but it kept strong though it swelled to bursting.

Within five months from the landing on the Rock, forty-six men, women, and children, or nearly one-half of the *Mayflower's* passengers had perished of disease and hardships, and the survivors saw the vessel that brought them sail away to the land of their birth. To the surviving women of that devoted Pilgrim band this departure of the *Mayflower* must have added a new pang to the grief that was already rending their hearts after the loss of so many dear ones during that fearful winter. As the vessel dropped down Plymouth harbor, they watched it with tearful eyes, and when they could see it no more, they turned calmly back to their heroic labors.

Mrs. Bradford, Rose Standish, and their companions were the original types of women on our American frontier. Nobly, too, were they seconded by the matrons and daughters in the other infant colonies. Who can read the letters of Margaret Winthrop, of the Massachusetts Colony, without recognizing the loving, devoted woman sharing with her noble husband the toils and privations of the wilderness, in order that God's promise might be justified and an empire built on this Western Continent.

In her we have a noble type of the Puritan woman of the seventeenth century, representing, as she did, a numerous class of her sex in the same condition. Reared in luxury, and surrounded by the allurements of the superior social circle in which she moved in her native England, she nevertheless preferred a life of self-denial with her husband on the bleak shores where the Puritans were struggling for existence. She had fully prepared her mind for the heroic undertaking. She did not overlook the trials, discouragements, and difficulties of the course she was about to take. For years she had been habituated to look forward to it as one of the eventualities of her life. She was now beyond the age of romance, and cherished no golden dreams of earthly happiness to be realized in that far-off western clime.

Two traits are most prominent in her letters: her religious faith, and her love for and trust in her husband. She placed a high estimate on the wisdom, the energy, and the talents of her husband, and felt that he could best serve God and man by helping to lay broad and deep the foundations of a new State, and to secure the present and future prosperity, both temporal and spiritual, of the colony. With admiration and esteem she blended the ardent but balanced fondness of the loving wife and the sedate matron. In no less degree do her letters show the power and attractiveness of genuine religion. The sanctity of conjugal affection tallies with and is hallowed by the Spirit of Grace. The sense of duty is harmoniously mingled with the impulses of the heart. That religion was the dominant principle of thought and action with Margaret Winthrop, no one can doubt who reflects how severely it was tested in the trying enterprise of her life. A sincere, deep, and healthful piety formed in her a spring of energy to great and noble actions.

There are glimpses in the correspondence between her and her husband of a kind of prophetic vision,

that the planting of that colony was the laying of one
of the foundation-stones of a great empire. May we
not suppose that by the contemplation of such a vision
she was buoyed up and soothed amid the many trials
and privations, perils and uncertainties that surrounded her in that rugged colonial life.

The influence of Puritanism to inspire with uncon-
querable principle, to infuse public spirit, to purify the
character from frivolity and feebleness, to lift the soul
to an all-enduring heroism and to exalt it to a lofty
standard of Christian excellence, is grandly illustrated
by the life of Margaret Winthrop, one of the pioneer-
matrons of the Massachusetts colony.

The narrations which we set forth in this book must
of course be largely concerning families and individuals.
The outposts of the advancing army of settlement
were most exposed to the dangers and hardships of
frontier life. Every town or village, as soon as it was
settled, became a garrison against attack and a mutual
Benefit-Aid-Society, leagued together against every
enemy that threatened the infant settlement; it was
also a place of refuge for the bolder pioneers who had
pushed farther out into the forest.

But as time rolled on many of these more adventurous settlers found themselves isolated from the villages
and stockades. Every hostile influence they had to
meet alone and unaided. Cold and storm, fire and
flood, hunger and sickness, savage man and savage
beast, these were the foes with which they had to con-
tend. The battle was going on all the time while the
pioneer and his wife were subjugating the forest,
breaking the soil, and gaining shelter and food for
themselves and their children.

It is easy to see what were the added pains, privations, and hardships of such a situation to the mind and heart of woman, craving, as she does, companionship and sympathy from her own sex. It is a consoling reflection to us who are reaping the fruits of her self-sacrifice that the very multiplicity of her toils and cares gave her less time for brooding over her hard and lonely lot, and that she found in her religious faith and hope a constant fountain of comfort and joy.

One of the greatest hardships endured by the first settlers in New England was the rigorous and changeable climate, which bore most severely, of course, on the weaker sex. This makes the fortitude of Mrs. Shute all the more admirable. Her story is only one of innumerable instances in early colonial life where wives were the preservers of their husbands.

In the spring of 1676, James Shute, with his wife and two small children, set out from Dorchester for the purpose of settling themselves on a tract of land in the southern part of what is now New Hampshire, but which then was an unbroken forest. The tract where they purposed making their home was a meadow on a small affluent of the Connecticut.

Taking their household goods and farming tools in an ox-cart drawn by four oxen and driving two cows before them, they reached their destination after a toilsome journey of ten days. The summer was spent in building their cabin, and outhouses, planting and tending the crop of Indian corn which was to be their winter's food, and in cutting the coarse meadow-grass for hay.

Late in October they found themselves destitute of many articles which even in those days of primitive

housewifery and husbandry, were considered of prime
necessity. Accordingly, the husband started on foot
for a small trading-post on the Connecticut River,
about ten miles distant, at which point he expected to
find some trading shallop or skiff to take him to Springfield, thirty-eight miles further south. The weather
was fine and at nightfall Shute had reached the river,
and before sunrise the next morning was floating down
the stream on an Indian trader's skiff.

Within two days he made his purchases, and hiring a
skiff rowed slowly up the river against the sluggish
current on his return. In twelve hours he reached
the trading-post. It was now late in the evening.
The sky had been lowering all day, and by dusk it began to snow. Disregarding the admonitions of the
traders, he left his goods under their care and struck
out boldly through the forest over the trail by which
he came, trusting to be able to find his way, as the
moon had risen, and the clouds seemed to be breaking.
The trail lay along the stream on which his farm was
situated, and four hours at an easy gait would, he
thought, bring him home.

The snow when he started from the river was already
nearly a foot deep, and before he had proceeded a mile
on his way the storm redoubled in violence, and the
snow fell faster and faster. At midnight he had only
made five miles, and the snow was two feet deep.
After trying in vain to kindle a fire by the aid of flint
and steel, he prayed fervently to God, and resuming
his journey struggled slowly on through the storm.
It had been agreed between his wife and himself that
on the evening of this day on which he told her he
should return, he would kindle a fire on a knoll about

two miles from his cabin as a beacon to assure his wife of his safety and announce his approach.

Suddenly he saw a glare in the sky.

During his absence his wife had tended the cattle, milked the cows, cut the firewood, and fed the children. When night came she barricaded the door, and saying a prayer, folded 'her little ones in her arms and lay down to rest. Three suns had risen and set since she saw her husband with gun on his shoulder disappear through the clearing into the dense undergrowth which fringed the bank of the stream, and when the appointed evening came, she seated herself at the narrow window, or, more properly, opening in the logs of which the cabin was built, and watched for the beacon which her husband was to kindle. She looked through the falling snow but could see no light. Little drifts sifted through the chinks in the roof upon the bed where her children lay asleep; the night grew darker, and now and then the howling of the wolves could be heard from the woods to the north.

Seven o'clock struck—eight—nine—by the old Dutch clock which ticked in the corner. Then her woman's instinct told her that her husband must have started and been overtaken by the storm. If she could reach the knoll and kindle the fire it would light him on his way. She quickly collected a small bundle of dry wood in her apron and taking flint, steel, and tinder, started for the knoll. In an hour, after a toilsome march, floundering through the snow, she reached the spot. A large pile of dry wood had already been collected by her husband and was ready for lighting, and in a few moments the heroic woman was warming her shivering limbs before a fire which blazed far up through the crackling branches and lighted the forest around it.

For more than two hours the devoted woman watched beside the fire, straining her eyes into the gloom and catching every sound. Wading through the snow she brought branches and logs to replenish the flames. At last her patience was rewarded : she heard a cry, to which she responded. It was the voice of her husband which she heard, shouting. In a few moments he came up staggering through the drifts, and fell exhausted before the fire. The snow soon ceased to fall, and after resting till morning, the rescued pioneer and his brave wife returned in safety to their cabin.

Mrs. Frank Noble, in 1664, proved herself worthy of her surname. She and her husband, with four small children, had established themselves in a log-cabin eight miles from a settlement in New Hampshire, and now known as the town of Dover.

Their crops having turned out poorly that autumn, they were constrained to put themselves on short allowance, owing to the depth of the snow and the distance from the settlement. As long as Mr. Noble was well, he was able to procure game and kept their larder tolerably well stocked. But in mid-winter, being naturally of a delicate habit of body, he sickened, and in two weeks, in spite of the nursing and tireless care of his devoted wife, he died. The snow was six feet deep, and only a peck of musty corn and a bushel of potatoes were left as their winter supply. The fuel also was short, and most of the time Mrs. Noble could only keep herself and her children warm by huddling in the bedclothes on bundles of straw, in the loft which served

LOST IN A SNOW-STORM.

Page 44.

them for a sleeping room. Below lay the corpse of Mr. Noble, frozen stiff. Famine and death stared them in the face. Two weeks passed and the supply of provisions was half gone. The heroic woman had tried to eke out her slender store, but the cries of her children were so piteous with hunger that while she denied herself, she gave her own portion to her babes, lulled them to sleep, and then sent up her petitions to Him who keeps the widow and the fatherless. She prayed, we may suppose, from her heart, for deliverance from her sore straits for food, for warmth, for the spring to come and the snow to melt, so that she might lay away the remains of her husband beneath the sod of the little clearing.

Every morning when she awoke, she looked out from the window of the loft. Nothing was to be seen but the white surface of the snow stretching away into the forest. One day the sun shone down warmly on the snow and melted its surface, and the next morning there was a crust which would bear her weight. She stepped out upon it and looked around her. She would then have walked eight miles to the settlement but she was worn out with anxiety and watching, and was weak from want of food. As she gazed wistfully toward the east, her ears caught the sound of a crashing among the boughs of the forest. She looked toward the spot from which it came and saw a dark object floundering in the snow. Looking more closely she saw it was a moose, with its horns entangled in the branches of a hemlock and buried to its flanks in the snow.

Hastening back to the cabin she seized her husband's gun, and loading it with buckshot, hurried out

and killed the monstrous brute. Skilled in woodcraft, like most pioneer women, she skinned the
animal and cutting it up bore the pieces to the cabin.
Her first thought then was of her children, and after
she had given them a hearty meal of the tender
moose-flesh she partook of it herself, and then, re-
freshed and strengthened, she took the axe and cut
a fresh supply of fuel. During the day a party came
out from the settlement and supplied the wants of the
stricken household. The body of the dead husband
was borne to the settlement and laid in the graveyard
beneath the snow.

Nothing daunted by this terrible experience, this
heroic woman kept her frontier cabin and, with friendly
aid from the settlers, continued to till her farm. In
ten years, when her oldest boy had become a man, he
and his brothers tilled two hundred acres of meadow
land, most of it redeemed from the wilderness by the
skill, strength, and industry of their noble mother.

The spring season must have been to the early
settlers, particularly to the women, even more trying
than the winter. In the latter season, except after
extraordinary falls of snow, transit from place to place
was made by means of sledges over the snow or on
ox-carts over the frozen ground. Traveling could also
be done across or up and down rivers on the ice, and as
bridges were rare in those days the crossing of rivers
on the ice was much to be preferred to fording them in
other seasons of the year. Fuel too was more easily
obtained in the winter than in the spring, and as roads
were generally little more than passage-ways or cow-
paths through the meadows or the woods, the depth
of the mud was often such as to form a barrier to the

locomotion of the heavy vehicles of the period or even to prevent travel on horseback or on foot.

Other dangers and hardships in the spring of the year were the freshets and floods to which the river dwellers were exposed. Woman, be it remembered, is naturally as alien to water as a mountain-fowl, which flies over a stream for fear of wetting its feet. We can imagine the discomfort to which a family of women and children were exposed who lived, for example, on the banks of the Connecticut in the olden time. In some seasons families were, as they now are, driven to the upper stories of their houses by the overflow of the river. But it should be remembered that the houses of those days were not the firm, well-built structures of modern times. Sometimes the settler found himself and family floating slowly down stream, cabin and all, borne along by the freshet caused by a sudden. thaw: as long as his cabin held together, the family had always hopes of grounding as the flood subsided and saving their lives though with much loss of property, besides the discomfort if not positive danger to which they had been exposed.

But sometimes the flood was so sudden and violent that the cabin would be submerged or break to pieces, and float away, drowning some or all of the family. It might be supposed that the married portion of the pioneers would select other sites than on the borders of a large river subject every year to overflow, but the richness of the alluvial soil on the banks of the Connecticut was so tempting that other considerations were overlooked, and to no part of New England was the tide of emigration turned so strongly as to the Connecticut Valley.

In the year 1643, an adventurous family of eight persons embarked on a shallop from Hartford (to which place they had come shortly before from Watertown, Mass.), and sailing or rowing up the river made a landing on a beautiful meadow near the modern town of Hatfield.

The family consisted of Peter Nash and Hannah his wife, David, their son, a youth of seventeen, Deborah and Mehitabel, their two daughters, aged respectively nineteen and fourteen, Mrs. Elizabeth Nash, the mother of Peter, aged sixty-four, and Mr. and Mrs. Jacob Nash. They found the land all ready for ploughing, and after building a spacious cabin and barns, they had nothing to do but to plant and harvest their crops and stock their farm with cattle which they brought from Springfield, driving them up along the river. For four years everything went on prosperously. They harvested large crops, added to their barns, and had a great increase in stock. Although the wolves and wild cats had made an occasional foray in their stock and poultry yard and the spring freshets had made inroads into their finest meadow, their general course had been only one of prosperity.

Their house and barns were built upon a tongue of land where the river made a bend, and were on higher ground than the surrounding meadow, which every spring was submerged by the freshets. Year after year the force of the waters had washed an angle into this tongue of land and threatened some time to break through and leave the houses and barns of the pioneers upon an island. But the inroads of the waters were gradual, and the Nashes flattered themselves that it would be at least two generations before the river would break through.

Mrs. Peter Nash and her daughter were women of almost masculine courage and firmness. They all handled axe and gun as skilfully as the men of the household; they could row a boat, ride horseback, swim, and drag a seine for shad; and Mehitabel, the younger daughter, though only fourteen years old, was already a woman of more than ordinary size and strength. These three women accompanied the men on their hunting and fishing excursions and assisted them in hoeing corn, in felling trees, and dragging home fuel and timber.

The winter of 1647–8 was memorable for the amount of snow that fell, and the spring for its lateness. The sun made some impression on the snow in March, but it was not till early in April that a decided change came in the temperature. One morning the wind shifted to the southwest, the sun was as hot as in June; before night it came on to rain, and, before the following night, nearly the whole vast body of snow had been dissolved into water which had swelled all the streams to an unprecedented height. The streams poured down into the great river, which rose with fearful rapidity, converting all the alluvial meadows into a vast lake.

All this took place so suddenly that the Nash family had scarcely a warning till they found themselves in the midst of perils. When the rain ceased, on the evening of the second day, the water had flooded the surrounding meadows and risen high up into the first story of their house. The force of the current had already torn a channel across the tongue of land on

4

which the house stood and had washed away the barns and live-stock. One of their two boats had been floated off but had struck broadside against a clump of bushes and was kept in its place by the force of the current. The other boat had been fastened by a short rope to a stout sapling, but this latter boat was ten feet under water, held down by the rope.

The water had now risen to the upper story, and the family were driven to the roof. If the house would stand they might yet be saved. It was firmly built but it shook with the force and weight of the waters. If either of the boats could be secured they might reach dry land by rowing out of the current and over the meadows where the water was stiller. The oars of the submerged boat had been floated away, but in the other boat they could be seen from the roof of the house lying safely on the bottom.

It was decided that Jacob Nash should swim out and row the boat up to the house. He was a strong swimmer, and though the water was icy cold it was thought the swift current would soon enable him to reach the skiff which lay only a few rods below the house. Accordingly, he struck boldly out, and in a moment had reached the boat, when he suddenly threw up his hands and sank, the current whirling him out of sight in an instant, amid the shrieks of his young wife, who was then a nursing mother and holding her babe in her arms as her husband went down. Mrs. Nash, the elder, gazed for a moment speechless at the spot where her son had sunk, and then fell upon her knees, the whole family following her example, and prayed fervently to Almighty God for deliverance from their awful danger. Then rising from her kneeling posture, she bade her other son make one more trial to reach the boat.

Peter Nash and his son Daniel then plunged into the water, reached the boat, and took the oars, but the force of the current was such that they could make, by rowing, but little headway against it. The two daughters then leaped into the flood, and in a few strokes reached and entered the boat. By their united force it was brought up and safely moored to the chimney of the cabin. In two trips the family were conveyed to the hillside. Then the brave girls returned and brought away a boat-load of household gear. Not content with that they rowed to the submerged boat, and diving down, cut the rope, baled out the water, and in company with their mother, father, and brother, brought away all the moveables in the upper stories of the house. Their courage appeared to have been rewarded in another way, since the house stood through the flood, and in ten days they were assisting to tear down the house and build another on a hill where the floods never came.

As soldiers fall in battle, so in the struggles and hardships of border life, the delicate frame of woman often succumbs, leaving the partner of her toils to mourn her loss and meet the onset of life alone. Such a loss necessarily implies more than when it occurs in the comfortable homes of refined life, since it removes at once a loving wife, a companion in solitude, and an efficient co-worker in the severe tasks incident to life in frontier settlements. Sometimes the husband's career is broken off when he loses his wife under such circumstances, and he gives up both hope and effort.

About sixty years since, and while the rich prairies
of Indiana began to be viewed as the promised land of
the adventurous pioneer, among the emigrants who
were attracted thither by the golden dreams of happiness and fortune, was a Mr. H., a young man from an
eastern city, who came accompanied by his newly married wife, a dark-eyed girl of nineteen.   Leaving his
bride at one of the westernmost frontier-settlements,
he pushed on in search of a favorable location for their
new home.   Near the present town of LaFayette he
found a tract which pleased his eye and promised
abundant harvests, and after his wife had been brought
to view it and expressed her satisfaction and delight
at the happy choice he had made, the site was selected
and the house was built.

They moved into their prairie-home in the first flush
of summer.   Their cabin was built upon a knoll and
faced the south.   Sitting at the door at eventide they
contemplated a prospect of unrivaled beauty.   The
sun-bright soil remained still in its primeval greatness
and magnificence, unchecked by human hands, covered with flowers, protected and watched by the eye
of the sun.   The days were glorious; the sky of the
brightest blue, the sun of the purest gold, and the air
full of vitality, but calm; and there, in that brilliant
light, stretched itself far, far out into the infinite, as
far as the eye could discern, an ocean-like extent, the
waves of which were sunflowers, asters, and gentians,
nodding and beckoning in the wind, as if inviting mil-
lions of beings to the festival set out on the rich table
of the earth.   Mrs. H. was an impressible woman with
poetic tastes, and a strong admiration for the beautiful
in nature; and as she gazed upon the glorious ex-

panse her whole face lighted up and glowed with pleasure. Here she thought was the paradise of which she had long dreamed.

As the summer advanced a plenteous harvest promised to reward the labors of her husband. Nature was bounteous and smiling in all her aspects, and the young wife toiled faithfully and patiently to make her rough house a pleasant home for her husband. She had been reared like him amid the luxuries of an eastern city, and her hands had never been trained to work. But the influences of nature around her, and the almost idolatrous love which she cherished for her husband, cheered and sweetened the homely toils of her prairie life.

Eight months sped happily and prosperously away; the winter had been mild, and open, and spring had come with its temperate breezes, telling of another summer of brightness and beauty.

Soon after the middle of April in that year, commenced an extraordinary series of storms. They occurred daily, and sometimes twice a day, accompanied by the most vivid lightning, and awful peals of thunder; the rain poured down in a deluge until it seemed as if another flood was coming to purify the earth. For more than sixty days those terrible scenes recurred, and blighted the whole face of the country for miles around the lonely cabin. The prairies, saturated with moisture, refused any longer to drink up the showers. Every hollow and even the slightest depression became a stagnant pool, and when the rains ceased and the sun came out with the heat of the summer solstice, it engendered pestilence, which rose from the green plain that smiled beneath him, and stalked resistless among the dwellers throughout that vast expanse.

Of all the widely isolated and remote cabins which sent their smoke curling into the dank morning air of the region thereabouts, there was not one in which disease was not already raging with fearful malignity. Doctors or hired nurses there were none ; each stricken household was forced to battle single-handed with the destroyer who dealt his blows stealthily, suddenly, and alas! too often, effectually. The news of the dreadful visitation soon reached the family of Mr. H—— and for a period they were in a fearful suspense. They were surrounded by the same malarial influences that had made such havoc among their neighbors, and why should they escape ? They were living directly over a noisome cess-pool ; their cellar was filled with water which could not be drained away, nor would the saturated earth drink it up. Centuries of vegetable accumulations forming the rich mould in which the cellar was dug, gave out their emanations to the water, and the fiery rays of the sun made the mixture a decoction whose steams were laden with death.

There was no escape unless they abandoned their house, and this they were reluctant to do, hoping that the disease would pass by them. But this was a vain hope ; in a few days Mr. H. was prostrated by the fever. Mrs. H. had preserved her courage and energy till now, but her impressible nature began to yield before the onset of this new danger. Her life had been sunny and care-free from a child ; her new home had till recently been the realization of her dreams of happiness ; but the loss of her husband would destroy at once every fair prospect for the future. All that a loving wife could do as a nurse or watcher or doctress, was done by her, but long before her husband had turned the sharp corner between death and life, Mrs. H. was attacked and both lay helpless, dependent upon the care of their only hired man. Neighbors whose hearts had been made tender and sympathetic by their own bereavements, came from their far-off cabins and for several weeks watched beside their bedside. The attack of the wife commenced with a fever which continued till after the birth of her child. For three days longer she lingered in pain, sinking slowly till the last great change came, and Mr. H., now convalescent, saw her eyes closed for ever.

The first time he left the house was to follow the remains of his wife and child to their last resting place, beneath an arbor of boughs which her own hands had tended. We cannot describe the grief of that bereaved husband. His very appearance was that of one who had emerged from the tomb. Sickness had blanched his dark face to a ghastly hue, and drawn great furrows in his cheeks, which were immovable, and as if chiseled in granite. During his sickness he had seen little of her before she was stricken down, for his mind was clouded. When the light of reason dawned he was faintly conscious that she lay near him suffering, first from the fever, and then from woman's greatest pain and trial, but that he was unable to soothe and comfort her; and finally that her last hours were hours of intense agony, which he could not alleviate. He was as one in a trance; a confused consciousness of his terrible loss slowly took possession of him. When at length his weakened intellect comprehended the truth with all its sad surrounding, a great cloud of desolation settled down over his whole life.

That cloud, sad to say, never lifted. As he stood by the open grave, he lifted the lid, gazed long and intently on that sweet pale face, bent and kissed the marble brow, and as the mother and child were lowered into the grave, he turned away a broken-hearted man.

CHAPTER III.

EARLY PIONEERS—WOMAN'S ADVENTURES AND HEROISM.

FOR nearly one hundred years after the settlement of Plymouth, the whole of the territory now known as the State of Maine was, with the exception of a few settlements on the coast and rivers, a howling wilderness. From the sea to Canada extended a vast forest, intersected with rapid streams and dotted with numerous lakes. While the larger number of settlers were disinclined to attempt to penetrate this trackless waste, some few hardy pioneers dared to advance far into the unknown land, tempted by the abundance of fish in the streams and lakes or by the variety of game which was to be found in the forests. It was the land for hunters rather than for tillers of the soil, and most of its early explorers were men who were skillful marksmen, and versed in forest lore. But occasionally women joined these predatory expeditions against the denizens of the woods and waters.

In the history of American settlements too little credit has been given to the hunter. He is often the first to penetrate the wilderness; he notes the general features of the country as he passes on his swift course; he ascertains the fertility of the soil and the capabilities of different regions; he *reconnoiters* the Indian tribes, and learns their habits and how they are affected towards the white man. When he returns to the settlements he makes his report concerning the region which he has explored, and by means of the knowledge thus obtained the permanent settlers were and are enabled to push forward and establish themselves in the wilderness. In the glory and usefulness of these discoveries woman not unfrequently shared. Some of the most interesting narratives are those in which she was the companion and coadjutor of the hunter in his explorations of the trackless mazes of our American forests.

In the year 1672 a small party of hunters arrived at the mouth of the Kennebec in two canoes. The larger one of the canoes was paddled up stream by three men, the other was propelled swiftly forward by a man and a woman. Both were dressed in hunters' costume; the woman in a close-fitting tunic of deerskin reaching to the knees, with leggins to match, and the man in hunting-shirt and trowsers of the same material. Edward Pentry, for this was the name of the man, was a stalwart Cornishman who had spent ten years in hunting and exploring the American wilderness. Mrs. Pentry, his wife, was of French extraction, and had passed most of her life in the settlements in Canada, where she had met her adventurous husband on one of his hunting expeditions. She was of manly stature and strength, and like her husband, was a splendid shot and skillful fisher. Both were passionately fond of forest life, and perfectly fearless of its dangers, whether from savage man or beast.

It was their purpose to explore thoroughly the region watered by the upper Kennebec, and to establish a trading-post which would serve as the headquarters of fur-traders, and ultimately open the country for settlement. Their outfit was extremely simple: guns, traps, axes, fishing-gear, powder, and bullets, &c., with an assorted cargo of such trinkets and other articles as the Indians desired in return for peltry.

In three weeks they reached the head-waters of the Kennebec, at Moosehead Lake. There they built a large cabin, divided into two compartments, one of which was occupied by three of the men, the other by Mr. and Mrs. Pentry. All of the party were versed in the Indian dialect of the region, and as Mrs. Pentry could speak French, no trouble was anticipated from the Indians, who in that part of the country were generally friendly to the French.

The labors of the men in felling trees and shaping logs for the cabin, as well as in framing the structure, were shared in by Mrs. Pentry, who in addition did all the necessary cooking and other culinary offices. They decided to explore the surrounding country for the purpose of discovering the lay of the land and the haunts of game. No signs of any Indians had yet been seen, and it was thought best that the four men should start, each in a different direction, and having explored the neighboring region return to the cabin at night, Mrs. Pentry meanwhile being left alone—a situation which she did not in the least dread. Accordingly, early in the morning, after eating a hunter's breakfast of salt pork, fried fish, and parched corn, the quartette selected their several routes, and started, taking good care to mark their trail as they went, that they could the more readily find the way back.

It was agreed that they should return by sunset, which would give them twelve good hours for exploration, as it was the month of July, and the days were long. After their departure Mrs. P. put things to rights about the house, and barring the door against intruders, whether biped or quadruped, took her gun and fishing-tackle and went out for a little sport in the woods.

The cabin stood on the border of Moosehead Lake. Unloosing the canoes, she embarked in one, and towing the other behind her, rowed across a part of the lake which jutted in shore to the southwest; she soon reached a dense piece of woods which skirted the lake, and there mooring her canoe, watched for the deer which came down to that place to drink. A fat buck before long made his appearance, and as he bent down his head to quaff the water, a brace of buck-shot planted behind his left foreleg laid him low, and his carcase was speedily deposited in the canoe.

The sun was now well up, and as Mrs. P. had provided for the wants of the party by her lucky shot, and no more deer made their appearance, she lay down in the bottom of the boat, and soon fell fast asleep. Hunters and soldiers should be light sleepers, as was Mrs. Pentry upon this occasion.

How long she slept she never exactly knew, but she was awakened by a splash; lifting her head above the edge of the boat, she saw nothing but a muddy spot on the water some thirty feet away, near the shore. This was a suspicious sign. Looking more closely, she saw a slight motion beneath the lily-pads, which covered closely, like a broad green carpet, the surface of the lake. Her hand was on her gun, and as she leveled the barrel towards the turbid spot, she saw a head suddenly lifted, and at the same moment a huge Indian sprang from the water and struggled up through the dense undergrowth that lined the edge of the lake.

It was a sudden impulse rather than a thought, which made Mrs. P. level the gun at his broad back and pull the trigger. The Indian leaped into the air, and fell back in the water dead, with half a dozen buck-shot through his heart. At the same moment she felt a strong grasp on her shoulder, and heard a deep guttural "ugh!" Turning her head she saw the malignant face of another Indian standing waist-deep in the water, with one hand on the boat which he was dragging towards the shore.

A swift side-blow from the gun-barrel, and he tumbled into the water; before he could recover, the brave woman had snatched the paddle, and sent the canoe spinning out into the lake. Then dropping the paddle and seizing her gun she dashed in a heavy charge of powder, dropped a dozen buck-shot down the muzzle, rammed in some dry grass, primed the pan, and leveled it again at the savage, who having recovered from the blow, was floundering towards the shore, turning and shaking his tomahawk at her, meanwhile, with a ferocious grin. Again the report of her gun awakened the forest echoes, and before the echoes had died away, the savage's corpse was floating on the water.

She dared not immediately approach the shore, fearing that other savages might be lying in ambush; but after closely scrutinizing the bushes, she saw no signs of others, besides the two whom she had shot. She then cut long strips of raw hide from the dead buck, and towing the bodies of the Indians far out into the lake sunk them with the stones that served to anchor the canoes. Returning to the shore, she took their guns which lay upon the shelving bank, and rapidly paddled the canoe homeward.

It was now high noon. She reached the cabin, entered, and sat down to rest. She supposed that the savages she had just killed were stragglers from a war-party who had lagged behind their comrades, and attracted by the sound made by her gun when she shot the buck, had come to see what it was. The thought that a larger body might be in the vicinity, and that they would capture and perhaps kill her beloved husband and his companions, was a torture to her. She sat a few moments to collect her thoughts and resolve what course to pursue.

Her resolution was soon taken. She could not sit longer there, while her husband and friends were exposed to danger or death. Again she entered the canoe and paddled across the arm of the lake to the spot where the waters were still stained with the blood of the Indians. Hastily effacing this bloody trace, she moored the canoes and followed the trail of the savages for four miles to the northwest. There she found in a ravine the embers of a fire, where, from appearances as many as twenty redskins had spent the pre-

ceding night. Their trail led to the northwest, and
by certain signs known to hunters, she inferred that
they had started at day-break and were now far on
their way northward.

When her four male associates selected their respective routes in the morning, her husband had,
she now remembered, selected one which led directly
in the trail of the Indian war-party, and by good cal-
culation he would have been about six miles in their
rear. Not being joined by the two savages whose
bodies lay at the bottom of the lake, what was more
likely than that they would send back a detachment
to look after the safety of their missing comrades?

The first thing to be done was to strike her husband's trail and then follow it till she overtook him or
met him returning. Swiftly, and yet cautiously, she
struck out into the forest in a direction at right angles
with the Indian camp. Being clad in trowsers of deer
skin and a short tunic and moccasins of the same material, she made her way through the woods as easily
as a man, and fortunately in a few moments discovered
a trail which she concluded was that of her husband.
Her opinion was soon verified by finding a piece of
leather which she recognized as part of his accoutre-
ments. For two hours she strode swiftly on through
the forest, treading literally in her husband's tracks.

The sun was now three hours above the western
horizon; so taking her seat upon a fallen tree, she
waited, expecting to see him soon returning on his
trail, when she heard faintly in the distance the report
of a gun; a moment after, another and still another
report followed in quick succession. Guided by the
sound she hurried through the tangled thicket from

THE HUNTRESS OF THE LAKE SURPRISED BY INDIANS.   Page 60.

which she soon emerged into a grove of tall pine trees, and in the distance saw two Indians with their backs turned toward her and shielding themselves from some one in front by standing behind large trees. Without being seen by them she stole up and sheltered herself in a similar manner, while her eye ranged the forest in search of her husband who she feared was under the fire of the red-skins.

At length she descried the object of their hostility behind the trunk of a fallen tree. It was clearly a white man who crouched there, and he seemed to be wounded. She immediately took aim at the nearest Indian and sent two bullets through his lungs. The other Indian at the same instant had fired at the white man and then sprang forward to finish him with his tomahawk. Mrs. Pentry flew to the rescue and just as the savage lifted his arm to brain his foe, she drove her hunting knife to the haft into his spine.

Her husband lay prostrate before her and senseless with loss of blood from a bullet-wound in the right shoulder. Staunching the flow of blood with styptics which she gathered among the forest shrubs, she brought water and the wounded man soon revived. After a slow and weary march she brought him back to the cabin, carrying him part of the way upon her shoulders. Under her careful nursing he at length recovered his strength though he always carried the bullet in his shoulder. It appears he had met three Indians who told him they were in search of their two missing companions. One of them afterwards treacherously shot him from behind through the shoulder, and in return Pentry sent a ball through his heart. Then becoming weak from loss of blood he could only point his gun-barrel at the remaining Indians, and this was his situation when his wife came up and saved his life.

After receiving such an admonition it is natural to suppose the whole party were content to remain near their forest home for a season, extending their rambles only far enough to enable them to procure game and fish for their table; and this was not far, for the lake was alive with fish; and wild turkeys, deer, and other game could be shot sometimes even from the cabin door.

The party were also deterred by this experience from attempting to drive any trade with the Indians until the following spring, when they expected to be joined by a large party of hunters.

The summer soon passed away, and the cold nights of September and October admonished our hardy pioneers that they must prepare for a rigorous winter. Mrs. Pentry made winter clothing for the men and for herself out of the skins of animals which they had shot, and snow-shoes from the sinews of deer stretched on a frame composed of strips of hard wood. She also felled trees for fuel and lined the walls of the cabin with deer and bear skins; she was the most skilful mechanic of the party, and having fitted runners of hickory to one of the boats she rigged a sail of soft skins sewed together, and once in November, after the river was frozen, and when the wind blew strongly from the northwest, the whole party undertook to reach the mouth of the river by sailing down in their boat upon the ice. A boat of this kind, when the ice is smooth and the wind strong, will make fifteen miles an hour.

They were interrupted frequently in their course by the falls and rapids, making portages necessary; nevertheless in three days and two nights they reached the mouth of the river.

Here they bartered their peltry for powder, bullets, and various other articles most needed by frontiersmen, and catching a southeast wind started on their return. In a few hours they had made seventy miles, and at night, as the sky threatened snow, they prepared a shelter in a hollow in the bank of the river. Before morning a snow-storm had covered the river-ice and blocked their passage. For three days, the snow fell continuously. They were therefore forced to abandon all hopes of reaching their cabin at the head-waters of the Kennebec. The hollow or cave in the bank where they were sheltered they covered with saplings and branches cut from the bluff, and banked up the snow round it. Their supply of food was soon exhausted, but by cutting holes in the ice they caught fish for their subsistence.

The depth of the snow prevented them from going far from their place of shelter, and the nights were bitter cold. The ice on the river was two feet in thickness; and one day, in cutting through it to fish, their only axe was broken. No worse calamity could have befallen them, since they were now unable to cut fuel or to procure fish. Mr. Pentry, who was still suffering from the effects of his wound, contracted a cold which settled in his lame shoulder, and he was obliged to stay in doors, carefully nursed and tended by his devoted wife. The privations endured by these unfortunates are scarcely to be paralleled. Short of food, ill-supplied with clothing, and exposed to the howling sever-

5

ity of the climate, the escape of any one of the number appears almost a miracle.

A number of bear-skins, removed from the boat to the cave, served them for bedding. Some days, when there was nothing to eat and no means of making a fire, they passed the whole time huddled up in the skins. Daily they became weaker and less capable of exertion. Wading through the snow up to the waist, they were able now and then to shoot enough small game to barely keep them alive.

After the lapse of a fortnight there came a thaw, succeeded by a cold rain, which froze as it fell. The snow became crusted over, to the depth of two inches, with ice that was strong enough to bear their weight. They extricated their ice-boat and prepared for departure. One of the party had gone out that morning on the crust, hoping to secure some larger game to stock their larder before starting; the rest awaited his return for two hours, and then, fearing some casualty had happened to him, followed his trail for half a mile from the river and found him engaged in a desperate struggle with a large black she-bear which he had wounded.

The ferocious animal immediately left its prey and rushed at Mrs. Pentry with open mouth, seizing her left arm in its jaws, crunched it, and then, rising on its hind legs, gave her a terrible hug. The rest of the party dared not fire, for fear of hitting the woman. Twice she drove her hunting knife into the beast's vitals and it fell on the crust, breaking through into the snow beneath, where the two rolled over in a death-struggle. The heroic woman at length arose victorious, and the carcase of the bear was dragged forth, skinned, and cut up. A fire was speedily kindled, Mrs. Pentry's wounds were dressed, and after refreshing themselves with a hearty meal of bearsteak, the remainder of the meat was packed in the boat.

The party then embarked, and by the aid of a stiff easterly breeze, were enabled, in three days, to reach their cabin on the head-waters of the Kennebec. The explorations made along the Kennebec by Mrs. Pentry and her companions attracted thither an adventurous class of settlers, and ultimately led to the important settlements on the line of that river.

The remainder of Mrs. Pentry's life was spent mainly on the northern frontier. She literally lived and died in the woods, reaching the advanced age of ninety-six years, and seeing three generations of her descendants grow up around her. Possessing the strength and courage of a man, she had also all a woman's kindness, and appears to have been an estimable person in all the relations of life—a good wife and mother, a warm friend, and a generous neighbor. In fact, she was a representative woman of the times in which she lived.

The toils of a severer nature, such as properly belong to man, often fall upon woman from the necessities of life in remote and isolated settlements; she is seen plying strange vocations and undertaking tasks that bear hardly on the soft and gentle sex. Sometimes a hunter and trapper; and again a mariner; now we see her performing the rugged work of a farm, and again a fighter, stoutly defending her home. The fact that habit and necessity accustom her, in frontier life, to those employments which in older and more conventional communities are deemed unfitting and ungraceful for woman to engage in, makes it none the less striking and admirable, because in doing so she serves a great and useful purpose; she is thereby doing her part in forming new communities in the places that are uninhabited and waste.

Vermont was largely settled by the soldiers who had served in the army of the Revolution. The settlers, both men and women, were hardy and intrepid, and seem to have been peculiarly adapted to subjugate that rugged region in our New England wilderness. The women were especially noted for the strength and courage with which they shared the labors of the men and encountered the hardships and dangers of frontier life.

When sickness or death visited the men of the family, the mothers, wives, or widows filled their places in the woods, or on the farm, or among the cattle. Often, side by side with the men, women could be seen emulating their husbands in the severe task of felling timber and making a clearing in the forest.

In the words of Daniel P. Thompson, author of "The Green Mountain Boys":—

"The women of the Green Mountains deserve as much credit for their various displays of courage, endurance, and patriotism, in the early settlement of their State, as was ever awarded to their sex for similar exhibitions in any part of the world. In the controversy with New York and New Hampshire, which took the form of war in many instances; in the predatory Indian incursions, and in the War of the Revolution, they often displayed a capacity for labor and endurance, a spirit and firmness in the hour of danger, a resolution and hardihood in defending

their families and their threatened land against all
enemies, whether domestic or foreign, that would have
done honor to the dames of Sparta."

The first man who commenced a settlement in the
town of Salisbury, Vermont, on the Otter Creek, was
Amos Storey, who, in making an opening in the heart
of the wilderness on the right of land to which the
first settler was entitled, was killed by the fall of a
tree. His widow, who had been left in Connecticut,
immediately resolved to push into the wilderness with
her ten small children, to take his place and preserve
and clear up his farm. This bold resolution she
carried out to the letter, in spite of every difficulty,
hardship, and danger, which for years constantly beset
her in her solitary location in the woods. Acre after
acre of the dense and dark forest melted away before
her axe, which she handled with the dexterity of the
most experienced chopper. The logs and bushes
were piled and burnt by her own strong and untiring hand; crops were raised, by which, with the
fruits of her fishing and unerring rifle, she supported
herself and her hardy brood of children. As a place
of refuge from the assaults of Indians or dangerous
wild beasts, she dug out an underground room, into
which, through a small entrance made to open under
an overhanging thicket on the bank of the stream,
she nightly retreated with her children.

Frequently during the dreary winter nights she was
kept awake by the howling of the wolves, and sometimes, looking through the chinks in the logs, she
could see them loping in circles around the cabin,
whining and snuffing the air as if they yearned for
human blood. They were gaunt, fierce-looking crea-

tures, and in the winter-time their hunger made them so bold that they would come up to the door and scratch against it. The barking of her mastiff would soon drive the cowardly beasts away but only a few rods, to the edge of the clearing where, sitting on their haunches, they frequently watched the house all night, galloping away into the woods when day broke.

Here she continued to reside, thus living, thus laboring, unassisted, till, by her own hand and the help which her boys soon began to afford her, she cleared up a valuable farm and placed herself in independent circumstances.

Miss Hannah Fox tells the following thrilling story of an adventure that befel her while engaged in felling trees in her mother's woods in Rhode Island, in the early colonial days.

We were making fine progress with our clearing and getting ready to build a house in the spring. My brother and I worked early and late, often going without our dinner, when the bread and meat which we brought with us was frozen so hard that our teeth could make no impression upon it, without taking too much of our time. My brother plied his axe on the largest trees, while I worked at the smaller ones or trimmed the boughs from the trunks of such as had been felled.

The last day of our chopping was colder than ever. The ground was covered by a deep snow which had crusted over hard enough to bear our weight, which was a great convenience in moving from spot to spot in the forest, as well as in walking to and from our cabin, which was a mile away. My brother had gone to the nearest settlement that day, leaving me to do my work alone.

As a storm was threatening, I toiled as long as I could see, and after twilight felled a sizeable tree which in its descent lodged against another. Not liking to leave the job half finished, I mounted the almost prostrate trunk to cut away a limb and let it down. The bole of the tree was forked about twenty feet from the ground, and one of the divisions of the fork would have to be cut asunder. A few blows of my axe and the tree began to settle, but as I was about to descend, the fork split and the first joints of my left-hand fingers slid into the crack so that for the moment I could not extricate them. The pressure was not severe, and as I believed I could soon relieve myself by cutting away the remaining portion, I felt no alarm. But at the first blow of the axe which I held in my right hand, the trunk changed its position, rolling over and closing the split, with the whole force of its tough oaken fibers crushing my fingers like pipe-stems; at the same time my body was dislodged from the trunk and I slid slowly down till I hung suspended with the points of my feet just brushing the snow. The air was freezing and every moment growing colder; no prospect of any relief that night; the nearest house a mile away; no friends to feel alarmed at my absence, for my mother would suppose that I was safe with my brother, while the latter would suppose I was by this time at home.

The first thought was of my mother. "It will kill her to know that I died in this death-trap so near home, almost within hearing of her voice! There must be some escape! but how?" My axe had fallen below me and my feet could almost touch it. It was impossible to imagine how I could cut myself loose unless I could reach it. My only hope of life rested on that keen blade which lay glittering on the snow.

Within reach of my hand was a dead bush which towered some eight feet above me, and by a great exertion of strength I managed to break it. Holding it between my teeth I stripped it of its twigs, leaving two projecting a few inches at the lower end to form a hook. With this I managed to draw towards me the head of the axe until my fingers touched it, when it slipped from the hook and fell again upon the snow, breaking through the crust and burying itself so that only the upper end of the helve could be seen.

Up to that moment the recollection of my mother and the first excitement engendered by hope had almost made me unconscious of the excruciating pain in my crushed fingers, and the sharp thrills that shot through my nerves, as my body swung and twisted in my efforts to reach the axe. But now, as the axe fell beyond my reach, the reaction came, hope fled, and I shuddered with the thought that I must die there alone like some wild thing caught in a snare. I thought of my widowed mother, my brother, the home which we had toiled to make comfortable and happy. I prayed earnestly to God for forgiveness of my sins, and then calmly resigned myself to death, which I now believed to be inevitable. For a time, which I afterwards found to be only five minutes, but which then seemed to me like hours, I hung motionless. The pain had ceased, for the intense cold blunted my sense of feeling. A numbness stole over me, and I seemed to be falling into a trance, from which I was roused by a sound of bells borne to me as if from a great distance. Hope again awoke, and I screamed loud and long; the woods echoed my cries, but no voice replied. The bells grew fainter and fainter, and at last died away. But the sound of my voice had broken the spell which cold and despair were fast throwing over me. A hundred devices ran swiftly through my mind, and each device was dismissed as impracticable. The helve of the axe caught my eye, and in an instant by an association of ideas it flashed across me that in the pocket of my dress there was a small knife—another sharp instrument by which I could extricate myself. With some difficulty I contrived to open the blade, and then withdrawing the knife from my pocket and griping it as one who clings to the last hope of life, I strove to cut away the wood that held my fingers in its terrible vise. In vain! the wood was like iron. The motion of my arm and body brought back the pain which the cold had lulled, and I feared that I should faint.

After a moment's pause I adopted a last expedient. Nerving myself to the dreadful necessity, I disjointed my fingers and fell exhausted to the ground. My life was saved, but my left hand was a bleeding stump. The intensity of the cold stopped the flow of blood. I tore off a piece of my dress, bound up my fingers, and started for home. My complete exhaustion and the bitter cold made that the longest mile I had ever traveled. By nine o'clock that evening I had managed to drag myself, more dead than alive, to my mother's door, but it was more than a week before I could again leave the house.

The difficulties encountered by the first emigrant-bands from Massachusetts, on their journey to Con-

necticut, may be understood best when we consider
the face of the country between Massachusetts Bay
and Hartford. It was a succession of ridges and deep
valleys with swamps and rapid streams, and covered
with forests and thickets where bears, wolves, and
catamounts prowled. The journey, which occupies
now but a few hours, then generally required two
weeks to perform. The early settlers, men, women,
and children, pursued their toilsome march over this
rough country, picking their way through morasses,
wading through rivers and streams, and climbing
mountains; driving their cattle, sheep, and swine
before them. Some came on horseback; the older
and feebler in ox-carts, but most of them traveled on
foot. At night aged and delicate women slept under
trees in the forest, with no covering but the foliage
and the cope of heaven.

The winter was near at hand, and the nights were
already cold and frosty. Many of the women had
been delicately reared, and yet were obliged to travel
on foot for the whole distance, reaching their destination in a condition of exhaustion that ill prepared
them for the hardships of the ensuing winter. Some
were nursing mothers, who sheltered themselves and
their babes in rude huts where the wind, rain, and
snow drove in through yawning fissures which there
were no means to close. Others were aged women,
who in sore distress sent up their prayers and rolled
their quavering hymns to the wintry skies, their only
canopy. The story of these hapless families is told in
the simple but effective language of the old historian.

" On the 15th of October [1632] about sixty men,
women, and children, with their houses, cattle, and

swine, commenced their journey from Massachusetts, through the wilderness, to Connecticut River. After a tedious and difficult journey through swamps and rivers, over mountains and rough grounds, which were passed with great difficulty and fatigue, they arrived safely at their respective destinations. They were so long on their journey, and so much time and pains were spent in passing the river, and in getting over their cattle, that after all their exertions, winter came upon them before they were prepared. This was an occasion of great distress and damage to the plantation. The same autumn several other parties came from the east—including a large number of women and children—by different routes, and settled on the banks of the Connecticut river.

" The winter set in this year much sooner than usual, and the weather was stormy and severe. By the 15th of November, the Connecticut river was frozen over, and the snow was so deep, and the season so tempestuous, that a considerable number of the cattle which had been driven on from the Massachusetts, could not be brought across the river. The people had so little time to prepare their huts and houses, and to erect sheds and shelter for their cattle, that the sufferings of man and beast were extreme. Indeed the hardships and distresses of the first planters of Connecticut scarcely admit of a description. To carry much provision or furniture through a pathless wilderness was impracticable. Their principal provisions and household furniture were therefore put on several small vessels, which, by reason of delays and the tempestuousness of the season, were cast away. Several vessels were wrecked on the coast of New England, by the violence of the storms. Two shallops laden with goods from Boston to Connecticut, were cast away in October, on Brown's Island, near the Gurnet's Nose; and the men with every thing on board were lost. A vessel with six of the Connecticut people on board, which sailed from the river for Boston, early in November, was, about the middle of the month, cast away in Manamet Bay. The men and women got on shore, and after wandering ten days in deep snow and a severe season, without meeting any human being, arrived, nearly spent with cold and fatigue, at New Plymouth.

" By the last of November, or beginning of December, provisions generally failed in the settlements on the river, and famine and death looked the inhabitants sternly in the face. Some of them driven by hunger attempted their way, in that severe season, through the wilderness, from Connecticut to Massachusetts. Of thirteen, in one company, who made this attempt, one in passing the river fell through the ice and was drowned. The other twelve were ten days on their journey, and would all have perished, had it not been for the assistance of the Indians.

"Indeed, such was the distress in general, that by the 3d and 4th of December, a considerable part of the new settlers were obliged to abandon their habitations. Seventy persons, men, women, and children, were compelled, in the extremity of winter, to go down to the mouth of the river to meet their provisions, as the only expedient to preserve their lives. Not meeting with the vessels which they expected, they all went on board the Rebecca, a vessel of about sixty tons. This, two days before, was frozen in, twenty miles up the river; but by the falling of a small rain,

and the influence of the tide, the ice became so broken
and was so far removed, that she made a shift to get
out. She ran, however, upon the bar, and the people
were forced to unlade her to get off. She was released, and in five days reached Boston. Had it not
been for these providential circumstances, the people
must have perished with famine.

" The people who kept their stations on the river
suffered in an extreme degree. After all the help
they were able to obtain, by hunting, and from the
Indians, they were obliged to subsist on acorns, malt,
and grains.

" Numbers of the cattle which could not be got
over the river before winter, lived through without
anything but what they found in the woods and meadows. They wintered as well, or better than those
which were brought over, and for which all the provision was made and pains taken of which the owners
were capable. However, a great number of cattle
perished. The Dorchester or Windsor people, lost in
this way alone about two hundred pounds sterling.
Their other losses were very considerable."

It is difficult to describe, or even to conceive, the
apprehensions or distresses of a people in the circumstances of our venerable ancestors, during this doleful
winter. All the horrors of a dreary wilderness spread
themselves around them. They were compassed with
numerous fierce and cruel tribes of wild and savage
men, who could have swallowed up parents and children at pleasure, in their feeble and distressed condition. They had neither bread for themselves nor
children ; neither habitation nor clothing convenient
for them. Whatever emergency might happen, they
were cut off, both by land and water, from any succor

or retreat. What self-denial, firmness, and magnanimity are necessary for such enterprises! How distressing, in the beginning, was the condition of those now fair and opulent towns on Connecticut River!

Under the most favorable circumstances, the lives of the pioneer-women must have been one long ordeal of hardship and suffering. The fertile valleys were the scenes of the bloodiest Indian raids, while the remote and sterile hill country, if it escaped the attention of the hostile savage, was liable to be visited by other ills. Famine in such regions was always imminent, and the remoteness and isolation of those frontier-cabins often made relief impossible. A failure in the little crop of corn, which the thin soil of the hillside scantily furnished, and the family were driven to the front for game and to the streams for fish, to supply their wants. Then came the winter, and the cabin was often blockaded with snow for weeks. The fuel and food consumed, nothing seemed left to the doomed household but to struggle on for a season, and then lie down and die. Fortunately the last sad catastrophe was of rare occurrence, owing to the extraordinary resolution and hardihood of the settlers.

It is a striking fact that in all the records, chronicles, and letters of the early settlers that have come down to us, there are scarcely to be found any complaining word from woman. She simply stated her sufferings, the dangers she encountered, the hardships she endured, and that was all. No querulous or peevish complaints, no moanings over her hard lot. She bore her pains and sorrows and privations in silence, looking forward to her reward, and knowing that she was making homes in the wilderness, and that future generations would rise up and call her blessed.

CHAPTER IV.

THE BLOCK-HOUSE, AND ON THE INDIAN TRAIL.

THE axe and the gun, the one to conquer the forces of wild nature, the other to battle against savage man and beast—these were the twin weapons that the pioneer always kept beside him, whether on the march or during a halt. In defensive warfare the axe was scarcely less potent than the gun, for with its keen edge the great logs were hewed which formed the block-house, and the tall saplings shaped, which were driven into the earth to make the stockade. We know too that woman could handle the gun and ply the axe when required so to do.

In one of our historical galleries there was exhibited not long since a painting representing a party of Indians attacking a block-house in a New England settlement. The house is a structure framed, and built of enormous logs, hexagonal in shape, the upper stories over-hanging those beneath, and pierced with loop-holes. There is a thick parapet on the roof, behind which are collected the children of the settlement guarded by women, old and young, some of whom are firing over the parapet at the yelling fiends who have just emerged from their forest-ambush. A glimpse of the interior of the block-house shows us women engaged in casting bullets and loading fire-arms which they are handing to the men. In the background a brave girl is returning swiftly to the garri-

(79)

son, with buckets of water which she has drawn from the spring, a few rods away from the house. A crouching savage has leveled his gun at her, and she evidently knows the danger she is in, but moves steadily forward without spilling a drop of her precious burden.

The block-house is surrounded by the primeval forest, which is alive with savages. Some are shaking at the defenders of the block-house fresh scalps, evidently just torn from the heads of men and women who have been overtaken and tomahawked before they could reach their forest-citadel: others have fired the stack of corn. A large fire has been kindled in the woods and a score of savages are wrapping dry grass around the ends of long poles, with which to fire the wooden walls of the block-house.

Thirty or forty men women and children in a wooden fort, a hundred miles, perhaps, from any settlement, and surrounded by five times their number of Pequots or Wampanoags thirsting for their blood! This is indeed a faithful picture of one of the frequent episodes of colonial life in New England!

Every new settlement was brought face to face with such dangers as we have described. The red-man and the white man were next door neighbors. The smokes of the wigwam and the cabin mingled as they rose to the sky. From the first there was more or less antagonism. Life among the white settlers was a kind of picket-service in which woman shared.

At times, as for example in the wars with the Pequots and King Philip, there was safety nowhere. Men went armed to the field, to meeting, and to bring home their brides from their father's house where they

had married them. Women with muskets at their
side lulled their babes to sleep. Like the tiger of the
jungles, the savage lay in ambush for the women and
children: he knew he could strike the infant colony
best by thus desolating the homes.

The captivities of Mrs. Williams and her children,
of Mrs. Shute, of Mrs. Johnson, of Mrs. Howe, and of
many other matrons, as well as of unmarried women,
are well-conned incidents of New England colonial
history. The story of Mrs. Dustin's exploit and escape reads like a romance. "At night," to use the
concise language of Mr. Bancroft, "while the household slumbers, the captives, each with a tomahawk,
strike vigorously, and fleetly, and with division of labor,—and of the twelve sleepers, ten lie dead; of one
squaw the wound was not mortal; one child was
spared from design. The love of glory next asserted
its power; and the gun and tomahawk of the mur-
derer of her infant, and a bag heaped full of scalps
were choicely kept as trophies of the heroine. The
streams are the guides which God has set for the stranger in the wilderness: in a bark canoe the three
descend the Merrimac to the English settlement,
astonishing their friends by their escape and filling
the land with wonder at their successful daring."

The details of Mrs. Rowlandson's sufferings after her
capture at Lancaster, Mass., in 1676, are almost too
painful to dwell upon. When the Indians began their
march the day after the destruction of that place,
Mrs. Rowlandson carried her infant till her strength
failed and she fell. Toward night it began to snow;
and gathering a few sticks, she made a fire. Sitting
beside it on the snow, she held her child in her arms,

6

through the long and dismal night. For three or four days she had no sustenance but water; nor did her child share any better for nine days. During this time it was constantly in her arms or lap. At the end of that period, the frost of death crept into its eyes, and she was forced to relinquish it to be disposed of by the unfeeling sextons of the forest.

She went through almost every suffering but death. She was beaten, kicked, turned out of doors, refused food, insulted in the grossest manner, and at times almost starved. Nothing but experience can enable us to conceive what must be the hunger of a person by whom the discovery of six acorns and two chestnuts was regarded as a rich prize. At times, in order to make her miserable, they announced to her the death of her husband and her children.

On various occasions they threatened to kill her. Occasionally, but for short intervals only, she was permitted to see her children, and suffered her own anguish over again in their miseries. She was obliged, while hardly able to walk, to carry a heavy burden, over hills, and through rivers, swamps, and marshes; and in the most inclement seasons. These evils were repeated daily; and, to crown them all, she was daily saluted with the most barbarous and insolent accounts of the burning and slaughter, the tortures and agonies, inflicted by them upon her countrymen. It is to be remembered that Mrs. Rowlandson was tenderly and delicately educated, and ill fitted to encounter such distresses; and yet she bore them all with a fortitude truly wonderful.

Instances too there were, where a single woman infused her own dauntless spirit into a whole garrison,

and prevented them from abandoning their post. Mrs.
Heard, "a widow of good estate, a mother of many
children, and a daughter of Mr. Hull, a revered minister formerly settled in Piscataqua," having escaped
from captivity among the Indians, about 1689, returned
to one of the garrisons on the extreme frontier of New
Hampshire. By her presence and courage this out-
post was maintained for ten years and during the
whole war, though frequently assaulted by savages.
It is stated that if she had left the garrison and retired
to Portsmouth, as she was solicited to do by her friends,
the out-post would have been abandoned, greatly to
the damage of the surrounding country.

Long after the New England colonies rested in comparative security from the attacks of the aboriginal
tribes, the warfare was continued in the Middle, Southern, and Western States; and even at this hour, sitting
in our peaceful homes we read in the journals of the
day reports of Indian atrocities perpetrated against
the families of the pioneers on our extreme western
frontier.

Our whole history from the earliest times to the
present, is full of instances of woman's noble achievements. East, west, north, south, wherever we wander, we tread the soil which has been wearily trodden
by her feet as a pioneer, moistened by her tears as a
captive, or by her blood as a martyr in the cause of
civilization on this western continent.

The sorrows of maidens, wives, and mothers in the
border wars of our colonial times, have furnished
themes for the poet, the artist, and the novelist, but
the reality of these scenes as described in the simple

words of the local historians, often exceeds the most vivid dress in which imagination can clothe it.

One of the most deeply rooted traits of woman's nature is sympathy, and the outflow of that emotion into action is as natural as the emotion itself. When a woman witnesses the sufferings of others it is instinctive with her to try and relieve them, and to be thwarted in the exercise of this faculty is to her a positive pain.

We may judge from this of what her feelings must have been when she saw, as she often did, those who were dearest to her put to torture and death without being permitted to rescue them or even alleviate their agonies.

Such was the position in which Mrs. Waldron was placed, on the northern border, during the French and Indian war of the last century. She and her husband occupied a small block-house which they had built a few miles from Cherry Valley, New York, and here she was doomed to suffer all that a wife could, in witnessing the terrible fate of her husband and being at the same time powerless to rescue him.

" One fatal evening," to use the quaint words of our heroine, " I was all alone in the house, when I was of a sudden surprised with the fearful war-whoop and a tremendous attack upon the door and the palisades around. I flew to the upper window and seizing my husband's gun, which I had learned to use expertly, I leveled the barrel on the window-sill and took aim at the foremost savage. Knowing their cruelty and merciless disposition, and wishing to obtain some favor, I desisted from firing ; but how vain and fruitless are the efforts of one woman against the united

force of so many, and of such merciless monsters as
I had here to deal with! One of them that could
speak a little English, threatened me in return, 'that
if I did not come out, they would burn me alive in
the house.' My terror and distraction at hearing this
is not to be expressed by words nor easily imagined
by any person unless in the same condition. Distracted as I was in such deplorable circumstances, I
chose to rely on the uncertainty of their protection,
rather than meet with certain death in the house;
and accordingly went out with my gun in my hand,
scarcely knowing what I did. Immediately on my
approach, they rushed on me like so many tigers, and
instantly disarmed me. Having me thus in their
power, the merciless villians bound me to a tree near
the door.

"While our house and barns were burning, sad to
relate, my husband just then came through the woods,
and being spied by the barbarians, they gave chase
and soon overtook him. Alas! for what a fate was
he reserved! Digging a deep pit, they tied his arms
to his side and put him into it and then rammed and
beat the earth all around his body up to his neck,
his head only appearing above ground. They then
scalped him and kindled a slow fire near his head.

"I broke my bonds, and running to him kissed his
poor bleeding face, and threw myself at the feet of
his barbarous tormentors, begging them to spare his
life. Deaf to all my tears and entreaties and to the
piercing shrieks of my unfortunate husband, they
dragged me away and bound me more firmly to the
tree, smiting my face with the dripping scalp and
laughing at my agonies.

Thank God! I then lost all consciousness of the dreadful scene; and when I regained my senses the monsters had fled after cutting off the head of the poor victim of their cruel rage."

When the British formed an unholy alliance with the Indians during the Revolutionary War and turned the tomahawk and scalping knife against their kinsmen, the beautiful valley of Wyoming became a dark and bloody battle-ground. The organization and disciplined valor of the white man, leagued with the cunning and ferocity of the red man, was a combination which met the patriots at every step in those then remote settlements, and spread rapine, fire, and murder over that lovely region.

The sufferings of the captive women, the dreadful scenes they witnessed, and the fortitude and courage they displayed, have been rescued from tradition and embodied in a permanent record by more than one historian. The names of Mrs. Bennet, Mrs. Myers, Mrs. Marcy, Mrs. Franklin, and a host of others, are inseparably associated with the household legends of the Wyoming Valley.

Miss Cook, after witnessing the barbarous murder and mutilation of a beautiful girl, whose rosy cheeks were gashed and whose silken tresses were torn from her head with the scalping knife, was threatened with instant death unless she would assist in dressing a bundle of fresh, reeking scalps cut from the heads of her friends and relatives. As she handled the gory trophies, expecting every moment that her own locks would be added to the ghastly heap, she saw something in each of those sad mementos that reminded her of those who were near and dear to her. At last

she lifted one which she thought was her mother's;
she gazed at the long tresses sprinkled with gray and
called to mind how often she had combed and caressed
them in happier hours: shuddering through her whole
frame, the wretched girl burst into a passion of tears.
The ruthless savage who stood guard over her with
brandished tomahawk immediately forced her to resume and complete her horrible task.

In estimating the heroism of American women displayed in their conflicts with the aborigines, we must
take into account her natural repugnance to repulsive
and horrid spectacles. The North American savage
streaked with war-paint, a bunch of reeking scalps at
his girdle, his snaky eyes gleaming with malignity,
was a direful sight for even a hardened frontiers-man;
how much more, then, to his impressionable and
delicate wife and daughter. The very appearance of
the savage suggested thoughts of the tomahawk, the
scalping knife, the butchered relations, the desolated
homestead. Nothing can better illustrate the hardihood of these bold spirited women than the fact that
they showed themselves not seldom superior to these
feelings of dread and abhorrence, daring even in the
midst of scenes of blood to denounce personally and
to their face the treachery and cruelty of their foes.

*In the year 1763 a party of Shawnees visited the
Block-House at Big Levels, Virginia, and after being
hospitably entertained by the inhabitants, turned
treacherously upon them and massacred every white
man in the house. The women and children were
carried away as captives, including Mrs. Glendenning,
the late wife, and now the widow of one of the leading settlers. Notwithstanding the dreadful scenes

---

* DeHass.

through which she had passed, Mrs. Glendenning was not intimidated. Her husband and friends had been butchered before her eyes; but though possessed of keen sensibilities, her spirit was undaunted by the awful spectacle. Filled with indignation at the treachery and cruelty of the Indians, she loudly denounced them, and tauntingly told them that they lacked the hearts of great warriors who met their foes in fair and open conflict. The savages were astounded at her audacity; they tried to frighten her into silence by flapping the bloody scalp of her husband in her face and by flourishing their tomahawks above her head. The intrepid woman still continued to express her indignation and detestation. The savages, admiring her courage, refrained from inflicting any injury upon her. She soon after managed to effect her escape and returned to her desolate home, where she gave decent interment to the mangled remains of her husband. During all the trying scenes of the massacre and captivity Mrs. Glendenning proved herself worthy of being ranked with the bravest women of our Colonial history.

The region watered by the upper Ohio and its tributary streams was for fifty years the battle-ground where the French and their Indian allies, and afterwards the Indians alone, strove to drive back the Anglo-Saxon race as it moved westward. The country there was rich and beautiful, but what made its possession especially desirable was the fact that it was the strategic key to the great West. The French, understanding its importance, established their fortresses and trading-posts as bulwarks against the army of

English settlers advancing from the East, and also instructed their savage allies in the art of war.

The Indian tribes in that region were warlike and powerful, and for some years it seemed as if the country would be effectually barred against the access of the Eastern pioneer. But the same school that reared and trained the daughters and grand-daughters of the Pilgrims, and of the settlers of Jamestown, and fitted them to cope with the perils and hardships of the wilderness, and to battle with hostile aboriginal tribes, also fitted their descendants for new struggles on a wider field and against more desperate odds. The courage and fortitude of men and women alike rose to the occasion, and in those scenes of danger and carnage, the presence of mind displayed by women especially, have been frequent themes of panegyric by the border annalists.

* The scene wherein Miss Elizabeth Zane, one of these heroines, played so conspicuous a part, was at Fort Henry, near the present city of Wheeling, Virginia, in the latter part of November, 1782. Of the forty-two men who originally composed the garrisons, nearly all had been drawn into an ambush and slaughtered. The Indians, to the number of several hundred, surrounded the garrison which numbered no more than twelve men and boys.

A brisk fire upon the fort was kept up for six hours by the savages, who at times rushed close up to the palisades and received the reward of their temerity from the rifles of the frontiersmen. In the afternoon the stock of powder was nearly exhausted. There was a keg in a house ten or twelve rods from the gate of the fort, and the question arose, who shall attempt

* DeHass.

to seize this prize? Strange to say, every soldier proffered his services, and there was an ardent contention among them for the honor. In the weak state of the garrison, Colonel Shepard, the commander, deemed it advisable that only one person could be spared; and in the midst of the confusion, before any one could be designated, Elizabeth Zane interrupted the debate, saying that her life was not so important at that time as any one of the soldiers, and claiming the privilege of performing the contested services. The Colonel would not at first listen to her proposal, but she was so resolute, so persevering in her plea, and her argument was so powerful, that he finally suffered the gate to be opened, and she passed out. The Indians saw her before she reached her brother's house, where the keg was deposited; but for some cause unknown, they did not molest her until she reappeared with the article under her arm. Probably, divining the nature of her burden, they discharged a volley as she was running towards the gate, but the whizzing balls only gave agility to her feet, and herself and the prize were quickly safe within the gate.

The successful issue of this perilous enterprise infused new spirit into the garrison; re-enforcements soon reached them, the assailants were forced to beat a precipitate retreat, and Fort Henry and the whole frontier was saved, thanks to the heroism of Elizabeth Zane!

* The heroines of Bryant's Station deserve a place on the roll of honor, beside the name of the preserver of Fort Henry, since like her their courage preserved a garrison from destruction. We condense the story

---

* McClung's Sketches of Western Adventure.

A HEROIC EXPLOIT IN SUPPLYING WITH POWDER A BLOCK HOUSE BESIEGED BY INDIANS.   Page 90.

from the several sources from which it has come down to us.

The station, consisting of about forty cabins ranged in parallel lines, stood upon a gentle rise on the southern banks of the Elkhorn, near Lexington, Kentucky. One morning in August, 1782, an army of six hundred Indians appeared before it as suddenly as if they had risen out of the earth. One hundred picked warriors made a feint on one side of the fort, trying to entice the men out from behind the stockade, while the remainder were concealed in ambush near the spring with which the garrison was supplied with water. The most experienced of the defenders understood the tactics of their wily foes, and shrewdly guessed that an ambuscade had been prepared in order to cut off the garrison from access to the spring. The water in the station was already exhausted, and unless a fresh supply could be obtained the most dreadful sufferings were apprehended. It was thought probable that the Indians in ambush would not unmask themselves until they saw indications that the party on the opposite side of the fort had succeeded in enticing the soldiers to an open engagement.

*Acting upon this impression, and yielding to the urgent necessity of the case, they summoned all the women, without exception, and explaining to them the circumstances in which they were placed, and the improbability that any injury would be done them, until the firing had been returned from the opposite side of the fort, they urged them to go in a body to the spring, and each to bring up a bucket full of water. Some, as was natural, had no relish for the undertaking; they observed they were not bullet-

* McClung's Sketches of Western Adventure.

proof, and asked why the men could not bring the water as well as themselves; adding that the Indians made no distinction between male and female scalps.

To this it was answered, that women were in the habit of bringing water every morning to the fort, and that if the Indians saw them engaged as usual, it would induce them to believe that their ambuscade was undiscovered, and that they would not unmask themselves for the sake of firing at a few women, when they hoped, by remaining concealed a few moments longer to obtain complete possession of the fort; that if men should go down to the spring, the Indians would immediately suspect that something was wrong, would despair of succeeding by ambuscade, and would instantly rush upon them, follow them into the fort, or shoot them down at the spring. The decision was soon made.

A few of the boldest declared their readiness to brave the danger, and the younger and more timid rallying in the rear of these veterans, they all marched down in a body to the spring, within point blank shot of more than five hundred Indian warriors! Some of the girls could not help betraying symptoms of terror, but the married women, in general, moved with a steadiness and composure which completely deceived the Indians. Not a shot was fired. The party were permitted to fill their buckets, one after another, without interruption, and although their steps became quicker and quicker, on their return, and when near the gate of the fort, degenerated into a rather un-military celerity, attended with some little crowding in passing the gate, yet only a small portion of the water was spilled. The brave water carriers were received with open arms and loud cheers by the garrison, who hailed them as their preservers, and the Indians shortly after retired, baffled and cursing themselves for being outwitted by the " white squaws."

The annals of the border-wars in the region of which we have been speaking abound in stories where women have been the victors in hand-to-hand fights with savages. In all these combats we may note the spirit that inspired those brave women with such wonderful strength and courage, transforming them from gentle matrons into brave soldiers. It was love for their children, their husbands, their kindred, or their homes rather than the selfish instinct of self-preservation which impelled Mrs. Porter, the two Mrs. Cooks, Mrs. Merrill, and Mrs. Bozarth to perform those feats of prowess and daring which will make their names live for ever in the thrilling story of border-warfare.

The scene where Mrs. Porter acted her amazing part was in Huntingdon county, Pennsylvania, and the time was during the terrible war instigated by the great Pontiac. While sitting by the window of her cabin, awaiting the return of her husband, who had gone to the mill, she caught sight of an Indian approaching the door. Taking her husband's sword from the wall where it hung, she planted herself behind the door; and when the Indian entered she struck with all her might, splitting his skull and stretching him a corpse upon the floor. Another savage entered and met the same fate. A third seeing the slaughter of his companions prudently retired.

Dropping the bloody weapon, she next seized the loaded gun which stood beside her and retreated to the upper story looking for an opportunity to shoot the savage from the port-holes. The Indian pursued her and as he set foot upon the upper floor received the contents of her gun full in the chest and fell dead in his tracks. Cautiously reconnoitering in all directions and seeing the field clear she fled swiftly toward the mill and meeting her husband, both rode to a neighboring block-house where they found refuge and aid. The next morning it was discovered that other Indians had burned their cabin, partly out of revenge and partly to conceal their discomfiture by a woman. The bones of the three savages found among the ashes were ghastly trophies of Mrs. Porter's extraordinary achievement.

In Nelson county, Kentucky, on a midsummer night, in 1787, just before the gray light of morning, John Merrill, attracted by the barking of his dog, went to the door of his cabin to reconnoiter. Scarcely had he left the threshold, when he received the fire of six or seven Indians, by which his arm and thigh were both broken. He managed to crawl inside the cabin and shouted to his wife to shut the door. Scarcely had she succeeded in doing so when the tomahawks of the enemy were hewing a breach into the apartment.

* Mrs. Merrill, with Amazonian courage and strength, grasped a large axe and killed, or badly wounded, four of the enemy in succession as they attempted to force their way into the cabin.

The Indians then ascended the roof and attempted to enter by way of the chimney, but here, again, they were met by the same determined enemy. Mrs. Merrill seized the only feather-bed which the cabin afforded, and hastily ripping it open, poured its contents upon the fire. A furious blaze and stifling smoke ascended the chimney, and quickly brought down two

* McClung's Sketches of Western Adventure.

of the enemy, who lay for a few moments at the mercy of the lady. Seizing the axe, she despatched them, and was instantly summoned to the door, where the only remaining savage appeared, endeavoring to effect an entrance, while Mrs. Merrill was engaged at the chimney. He soon received a gash in the cheek which compelled him with a loud yell to relinquish his purpose, and return hastily to Chillicothe, where, from the report of a prisoner, he gave an exaggerated account of the fierceness, strength, and courage of the "Long knife squaw!"

The wives of Jesse and Hosea Cook, the "heroines of Innis station" (Kentucky), as they have been styled, are shining examples of a firmness of spirit which sorrow could not blench nor tears dim.

While the brothers Cook were peacefully engaged in the avocations of the farm beside their cabins, in April, 1792, little dreaming of the proximity of the savages, a sharp crack of rifles was heard and they both lay weltering in their blood. The elder fell dead, the younger was barely able to reach his cabin.

The two Mrs. Cooks with three children were instantly collected in the house and the door made fast. The thickness of the door resisted the hail of rifleballs which fell upon it, and the Indians tried in vain to cut through it with their tomahawks.

While the assault was being made on the outside of the cabin, within was heart-rending sorrow mingled with fearless determination and high resolve. The younger Cook while the door was being barred breathed his last in the arms of his wife, and the two Mrs. Cooks, thus sadly bereaved of their partners, were left the sole defenders of the cabin and the three children.

There was a rifle in the house but no balls could be found. In this extremity one of the women took a musket-ball and placing it between her teeth bit it into pieces. Her eyes streaming with tears, she loaded the rifle and took her position at an aperture from which she could watch the motions of the savages. She dried her tears and thought of vengeance on her husband's murderers and of saving the innocent babes which she was guarding.

After the failure of the Indians to break down the door, one of them seated himself upon a log, apprehending no danger from the "white squaws" who, he knew, were the only defenders of the cabin. A ball sped from the rifle in the hands of Mrs. Cook, and with a loud yell the savage bounded into the air and fell dead.

The Indians, infuriated at the death of their comrade, threatened, in broken English, the direst vengeance on the inmates of the cabin. A half dozen of the yelling fiends instantly climbed to the roof of the cabin and kindled a fire upon the dry boards around the chimney. As the flames began to take effect the destruction of the cabin and the doom of the unfortunate inmates seemed certain.

But the self-possession and intrepidity of the brave women were equal to the occasion. While one stood in the loft the other handed her water with which she extinguished the fire. Again and again the roof was fired, and as often extinguished. When the water was exhausted, the dauntless pair held the flames at bay by breaking eggs upon them. The Indians, at length fatigued by the obstinacy and valor of the brave defenders, threw the body of their comrade into the creek and precipitately fled.

The exploits of Mrs. Bozarth in defending her home and family against superior numbers, has scarcely been paralleled in ancient or modern history. Relying upon her firmness and courage, two or three families had gathered themselves for safety at her house, on the Pennsylvania border, in the spring of 1779. The forest swarmed with savages, who soon made their appearance near the stockade, severely wounding one of the only two men in the house. * The Indian who had shot him, springing over his prostrate body, engaged with the other white man in a struggle which ended in his discomfiture. A knife was wanting to dispatch the savage who lay writhing beneath his antagonist. Mrs. Bozarth seized an axe and with one blow clove the Indian's skull. Another entered and shot the white man dead. Mrs. Bozarth, with unflinching boldness, turned to this new foe and gave him several cuts with the axe, one of which laid bare his entrails. In response to his cries for help, his comrades, who had been killing some children out of doors, came rushing to his relief. The head of one of them was cut in twain by the axe of Mrs. Bozarth, and the others made a speedy retreat through the door. Rendered furious by the desperate resistance they had met, the Indians now beseiged the house, and for several days they employed all their arts to enter and slay the weak garrison. But all their efforts were futile. Mrs. Bozarth and her wounded companion employed themselves so vigorously and vigilantly that the enemy were completely baffled. At length a party of white men arrived, put the Indians to flight, and relieved Mrs. Bozarth from her perilous situation.

---

* Doddridge's Notes.

7

CHAPTER V.

THE CAPTIVE SCOUTS:—THE GUARDIAN MOTHER OF THE
MOHAWK.

THE part that woman has taken in so many ways
and under so many conditions, in securing the
ultimate results represented by our present status as
a nation, is given too small a place in the general estimate of those who pen the record of civilization on the
North American continent. This is no doubt partly due
to her own distaste for notoriety. While man stands
as a front figure in the temple of fame, and celebrates
his own deeds with pen and voice, she takes her place
in the background, content and happy so long as her
father, or husband, or son, is conspicuous in the glory
to which she has largely contributed. Thus it is that
in the march of grand events the historian of the Republic often passes by the woman's niche without
dwelling upon its claims to our attention. But notwithstanding the self-chosen position of the weaker
sex, their names and deeds are not all buried in oblivion. The filial, proud, and patriotic fondness of sons
and daughters have preserved in their household traditions the memory of brave and good mothers; the
antiquarian and the local historian, with loving zeal
have wiped the dust from woman's urn, and traced
anew the names and inscriptions which time has half
effaced.

As we scan the pages of Woman's Record the roll

(98)

of honor lengthens, stretching far out like the line of
Banquo's phantom-kings. Their names become impressed on our memory; their acts dilate, and their
whole lives grow brighter the more closely we study
them.

Among the many duties which from necessity or
choice were assigned to woman in the remote and
isolated settlements, was that of standing guard. She
was *par excellence* the vigilant member of the household, a sentinel ever on the alert and ready to give
alarm at the first note of danger. The pioneers were
the pickets of the army of civilization: woman was
a picket of pickets, a sentinel of sentinels, watchful of danger and the quickest to apprehend it. She
was always a guardian, and not seldom the preserver
of her home and of the settlement. Such duties as
these, faithfully performed, contribute perhaps to the
success of a campaign more even than great battles.
As soon as the front line or picket-force of the pioneers
was fairly established in the enemies' country, the
work was more than half done, and the whole army—
center, right, and left wings—could move forward
with little danger, though labor, hard and continuous,
was still required. In successive regions the same
sentinel and picket duties were performed; in New
England and on the Atlantic coast first; then in the
interior districts, in the middle States; and already,
a hundred years ago, the flying skirmish-line had
crossed the great Appalachian range, and was fording
the rivers of the western basin. On the march, on
the halt, in the camp, that is, in the permanent settlement, woman was a sentinel keeping perpetual guard
over the household treasures.

What materials for romance—for epic and tragic poetry—in the lives of those pioneer women! The lonely cabin in the depths of the forest; the father away; the mother rocking her babe to sleep; the howling of the wolves; the storm beating on the roof; the crafty savage lying in ambush; the war-whoop in the night; the attack and the repulse; or perchance the massacre and the cruel captivity; and all the thousand lights and shadows of border life!

During the French and Indian war, and while the northern border was being desolated by savage raids, a hardy settler named Mack, with his wife and two children, occupied a cabin and clearing in the forest a few miles south of Lake Pleasant, in Hamilton County, New York. For some months after the breaking out of the war no molestation was offered to Mr. Mack or his family, either owing to the sequestered situation in which they lived, or from the richer opportunities for plunder offered in the valleys some distance below the lonely and rock-encompassed forest where the Mack homestead lay. Encouraged by this immunity from attack, and placing unbounded confidence in the vigilance and courage of his wife, Mr. Mack, when summoned to accompany Sir William Johnson's forces on one of their military expeditions, obeyed the call and prepared to join his fellow-borderers. Mrs. Mack cheerfully and patriotically acquiesced in her husband's resolution, assuring him that during his absence she would protect their home and children or perish in the attempt.

The cabin was a fortress, such as befitted the exposed situation in which it lay, and was supplied by the provident husband before his departure with provisions and ammunition sufficient to stand a siege: it was furnished on each side with a loop-hole through which a gun could be fixed or a reconnoisance made in every direction.

Yielding to the dictates of prudence and desirous of redeeming the pledge which she had made to her husband, Mrs. Mack stayed within doors most of the time for some days after her husband had bade her farewell, keeping a vigilant look-out on every side for the prowling foe. No sound but the voices of nature disturbed the stillness of the forest. Everything around spoke of peace and repose. Lulled into security by these appearances and urged by the necessities of her out-door duties, she gradually relaxed her vigilance until she pursued the labors of the farm with as much regularity as she would have done if her husband had been at home.

One day while plucking ears of corn for roasting, she caught a glimpse of a moccasin and a brawny limb fringed with leggins, projecting behind a clump of bushes not twenty paces from her. Repressing the shriek which rose to her lips, she quietly and leisurely strolled back to the house with her basket of ears. Once she thought she heard the stealthy tread of the savage behind her and was about to break into a run; but a moment's reflection convinced her that her fears were groundless. She steadily pursued her course till she reached the cabin. With a vast weight of fear taken from her mind she now turned and cast a rapid glance towards the bushes where the foe lay in ambush; nothing was visible there, and having closed and barred the door she made a reconnoisance from each of the four loop-holes of her fortress, but saw nothing to alarm her.

It seemed to her probable that it was only a single prowling savage who was seeking an opportunity to plunder the cabin. Accordingly with a loaded gun by her side, she sat down before the loop-hole which commanded the spot where the savage lay concealed and watched for further developments. For two hours all was still and she began to imagine that he had left his hiding place, when she noticed a rustling in the bushes and soon after descried the savage crawling on his belly and disappearing in the cornfield. Night found her still watching, and as soon as her children had been lulled to sleep, she returned to her post and straining her eyes into the darkness, listened for the faintest sound that might give note of the approach of the enemy. It was near midnight when overcome with fatigue she leaned against the log wall and fell asleep with her gun in her hand.

She was conscious in her slumbers of some mesmeric power exerting an influence upon her, and awakening with a start saw for an instant by the faint light, a pair of snaky eyes looking directly into hers through the loop-hole. They were gone before she was fairly awake, and she tried to convince herself that she had been dreaming. Not a sound was audible, and after taking an observation from each of the loop-holes she became persuaded that the fierce eyes that seemed to have been watching her was the figment of a brain disturbed by anxiety and vigils.

Once more sleep overcame her and again she was awakened by a rattling sound followed by heavy breathing. The noise seemed to proceed from the chimney to which she had scarcely began to direct her attention, when a large body fell with a thud into the ashes of the fire-place, and a deep guttural "ugh" was uttered by an Indian who rose and peered around the roon..

The first flickering light which follows the blackness of midnight, gave him a glimpse of the heroic matron who stood with her piece cocked and leveled directly at his breast. Brandishing his tomahawk he rushed towards her yelling so as to disconcert her aim. The brave woman with unshaken nerves pulled the trigger, and the savage fell back with a screech, dead upon the floor. Almost simultaneously with the report of the gun, a triumphant warwhoop was sounded outside the cabin, and peering through the aperture in the direction from which it proceeded she saw three savages rushing toward the door. Rapidly loading her piece she took her position at the loop-hole that commanded the entrance to the cabin, and taking aim, shot one savage dead, the ball passing completely through his body and wounding another who stood in range. The third made a precipitate retreat, leaving his wounded comrade who crawled into the cornfield and there died.

After the occurrence of these events we may well suppose that the life of Mrs. Mack was one of constant vigilance. For some days and nights she stood sentinel over her little ones, and then in her dread lest the Indians should return and take vengeance upon her and her children for the slaughter of their companions, she concluded the wisest course would be to take refuge in the nearest fort thirty miles distant. Accordingly the following week she made all her preparations and carrying her gun started for the fort with her children.

Before they had proceeded a mile on their course she had the misfortune to drop her powder-horn in a stream: this compelled her to return to the cabin for ammunition. Hiding her children in a dense copse and telling them to preserve silence during her absence, she hastened back, filled her powder-horn and returned rapidly upon her trail.

But what was her agony on discovering that her children were missing from the place where she left them! A brief scrutiny of the ground showed her the tracks of moccasins, and following them she soon ascertained that her children had been carried away by two Indians. Like the tigress robbed of her young, she followed the trail swiftly but cautiously and soon came up with the savages, whose speed had been retarded by the children. Stealing behind them she shot one of them and clubbing her gun rushed at the other with such fierceness that he turned and fled.

Pursuing her way to the fort she met her husband returning home from the war. The family then retraced their steps and reached their home, the scene of Mrs. Mack's heroic exploit.

It was during their captivities that women often learned the arts and practiced the perilous profession of a scout. Their Indian captors were sometimes the first to suffer from the knowledge which they themselves had taught their captive pupils. In this rugged school of Indian life was nurtured a brave girl of New England parentage, who acted a conspicuous part in protecting an infant settlement in Ohio.

* In the year 1790, the block-house and stockade

---

* Finley's Autobiography.

above the mouth of the Hockhocking river in Ohio, was a refuge and rallying point for the hardy frontiersmen of that region. The valley of the Hockhocking was preëminent for the richness and luxuriance of nature's gifts, and had been from time immemorial the seat of powerful and warlike tribes of Indians, which still clung with desperate tenacity to a region which had been for so many years the chosen and beloved abode of the red man.

The little garrison, always on the alert, received intelligence early in the autumn that the Indian tribes were gathering in the north for the purpose of striking a final and fatal blow on this or some other important out-post. A council was immediately held by the garrison, and two scouts were dispatched up the Hockhocking, in order to ascertain the strength of the foe and the probable point of attack.

The scouts set out one balmy day in the Indian summer, and threading the dense growth of plum and hazel bushes which skirted the prairie, stealthily climbed the eastern declivity of Mount Pleasant, and cast their eyes over the extensive prairie-country which stretches from that point far to the north. Every movement that took place upon their field of vision was carefully noted day by day. The prairie was the *campus martius* where an army of braves had assembled, and were playing their rugged games and performing their warlike evolutions. Every day new accessions of warriors were hailed by those already assembled, with terrific war-whoops, which, striking the face of Mount Pleasant, were echoed and re-echoed till it seemed as if a myriad of yelling demons were celebrating the orgies of the infernal pit.

To the hardy scouts these well-known yells, so terrible to softer ears, were only martial music which woke a keener watchfulness and strung their iron nerves to a stronger tension. Though well aware of the ferocity of the savages, they were too well practiced in the crafty and subtle arts of their profession to allow themselves to be circumvented by their wily foes.

On several occasions small parties of warriors left the prairies and ascended the mount. At these times the scouts hid themselves in fissures of the rocks or beneath sere leaves by the side of some prostrate tree, leaving their hiding places when the unwelcome visitors had taken their departure. Their food was jerked beef and cold corn-bread, with which their knapsacks had been well stored. Fire they dared not kindle for the smoke would have brought a hundred savages on their trail. Their drink was the rain-water remaining in the excavations in the rocks. In a few days this water was exhausted, and a new supply had to be obtained, as their observations were still incomplete. McClelland, the elder of the two, accordingly set out alone in search of a spring or brook from which they could replenish their canteens. Cautiously descending the mount to the prairie, and skirting the hills on the north, keeping as much as possible within the hazel-thickets, he reached at length a fountain of cool limpid water near the banks of the Hockhocking river. Filling the canteens he rejoined his companion.

The daily duty of visiting the spring and obtaining a fresh supply, was after this performed alternately by the scouts. On one of these diurnal visits, after

White had filled his canteens, he sat watching the
limpid stream that came gurgling out of the bosom of
the earth. The light sound of footsteps caught his
practiced ear, and turning round he saw two squaws
within a few feet of him. The elder squaw at the
same moment spying White, started back and gave a
far-reaching war-whoop. He comprehended at once
his perilous situation. If the alarm should reach the
camp, he and his companion must inevitably perish.

A noiseless death inflicted upon the squaws, and in
such a manner as to leave no trace behind, was the
only sure course which the instinct of self-preservation
suggested. With men of his profession action follows
thought as the bolt follows the flash. Springing upon
his victims with the rapidity and power of a tiger, he
grasped the throat of each and sprang into the Hockhocking river. The head of the elder squaw he easily
thrust under the water, and kept it in that position;
but the younger woman powerfully resisted his efforts
to submerge her. During the brief struggle she ad-
dressed him to his amazement in the English language,
though in inarticulate sounds. Relaxing his hold she
informed him that she had been made a prisoner ten
years before, on Grave Creek Flats, that the Indians
in her presence had butchered her mother and two
sisters, and that an only brother had been captured
with her, but had succeeded on the second night in
making his escape, since which time she had never
heard of him.

During this narrative, White, unobserved by the
girl, had released his grip on the throat of the squaw,
whose corpse floated slowly down stream, and, directing the girl to follow him, he pushed for the Mount

with the greatest speed and energy. Scarcely had
they proceeded two hundred yards from the spring
before an Indian alarm-cry was heard some distance
down the river. A party of warriors returning from
a hunt had seen the body of the squaw as it floated
past. White and the girl succeeded in reaching the
Mount where they found McClelland fully awake to the
danger they were in. From his eyrie he had seen
parties of warriors strike off in every direction on
hearing the shrill note of alarm first sounded by the
squaw, and before White and the girl had joined him,
twenty warriors had already gained the eastern accliv-
ity of the Mount and were cautiously ascending, keeping their bodies under cover. The scouts soon caught
glimpses of their swarthy faces as they glided from
tree to tree and from rock to rock, until the hiding
place of the luckless two was surrounded and all hope
of escape was cut off.

The scouts calmly prepared to sell their lives as
dearly as they could, but strongly advised the girl to
return to the Indians and tell them that she had been
captured by scouts. This she refused to do, saying
that death among her own people was preferable to
captivity such as she had been enduring. "Give me
a rifle," she continued," and I will show you that I
can fight as well as die! On this spot will I remain,
and here my bones shall bleach with yours! Should
either of you escape, you will carry the tidings of my
fate to my remaining relatives."

All remonstrances with the brave girl proving useless, the two scouts prepared for a vigorous defense.
The attack by the Indians commenced in front, where
from the nature of the ground they were obliged to

advance in single file, sheltering themselves as they best could, behind rocks and trees. Availing themselves of the slightest exposure of the warriors' bodies, the scouts made every shot tell upon them, and succeeded for a time in keeping them in check.

The Indians meanwhile made for an isolated rock on the southern hillside, and having reached it, opened fire upon the scouts at point blank range. The situation of the defenders was now almost hopeless; but the brave never despair. They calmly watched the movements of the warriors and calculated the few chances of escape which remained. McClelland saw a tall, swarthy figure preparing to spring from cover to a point from which their position would be completely commanded. He felt that much depended upon one lucky shot, and although but a single inch of the warrior's body was exposed, and at a distance of one hundred yards, yet he resolved to take the risk of a shot at this diminutive target. Coolly raising the rifle to his eye, and shading the sight with his hand, he threw a bead so accurately that he felt perfectly confident that his bullet would pierce the mark; but when the hammer fell, instead of striking fire, it crushed his flint into a hundred fragments. Rapidly, but with the utmost composure, he proceeded to adjust a new flint, casting meantime many a furtive glance towards the critical point. Before his task was completed he saw the warrior strain every muscle for the leap, and, with the agility of a deer, bound towards the rock; but instead of reaching it, he fell between and rolled fifty feet down hill. He had received a death-shot from some unseen hand, and the mournful whoops of the savages gave token that they had lost a favorite warrior.

The advantage thus gained was only momentary. The Indians slowly advanced in front and on the flank, and only the incessant fire of the scouts sufficed to keep them in check. A second savage attempted to gain the eminence which commanded the position where the scouts were posted, but just as he was about to attain his object, McClelland saw him turn a summerset, and, with a frightful yell, fall down the hill, a corpse. The mysterious agent had again interposed in their behalf. The sun was now disappearing behind the western hills, and the savages, dismayed by their losses, retired a short distance for the purpose of devising some new mode of attack. This respite was most welcome to the scouts, whose nerves had been kept in a state of severe tension for several hours. Now for the first time they missed the girl and supposed that she had either fled to her old captors or had been killed in the fight. Their doubts were soon dispelled by the appearance of the girl herself, advancing toward them from among the rocks, with a rifle in her hand.

During the heat of the fight she had seen a warrior fall, who had advanced some fifty yards in front of the main body; she at once resolved to possess herself of his rifle, and crouching in the undergrowth, she crept to the spot and succeeded in her enterprise, being all the time exposed to the cross-fire of the defenders and assailants; her practiced eye had early noticed the fatal rock, and hers was the mysterious hand by which the two warriors had fallen—the last being the most wary, untiring, and bloodthirsty brave of the

Shawanese tribe. He it was who ten years before had scalped the family of the girl, and had led her into captivity. The clouds which had been gathering now shrouded the whole heavens, and, night coming on, the darkness was intense. It was feared that in the contemplated retreat they might lose their way or accidentally fall in with the enemy, which latter contingency was highly probable, if not almost inevitable. After consultation it was agreed that the girl, from her intimate knowledge of the localities, should lead the way, a few paces in advance.

Another advantage might be derived from this arrangement, for in case they should fall in with an outpost of savages, the girl's knowledge of the Indian tongue might enable them to deceive and elude the sentinel. The event proved the wisdom of the plan, for they had scarcely descended an hundred feet from their eyrie when a low "hush!" from the girl warned them of the presence of danger. The scouts threw themselves silently upon the earth, where by previous agreement they were to remain until another signal was given them by the girl, who glided away in the darkness. Her absence for more than a quarter of an hour had already begun to excite serious apprehensions for her safety, when she reappeared and told them that she had succeeded in removing two sentinels who were directly in their route, to a point one hundred feet distant.

The descent was noiselessly resumed, the scouts following their brave guide for half a mile in profound silence, when the barking of a small dog, almost at their feet, apprised them of a new danger. The click of the scout's rifle caught the ear of the girl, who quickly approached and warned them against making the least noise, as they were now in the midst of an Indian village, and their lives depended upon their implicitly following her instructions.

A moment afterwards the head of a squaw was seen at an opening in a wigwam, and she was heard to accost the girl, who replied in the Indian language, and without stopping pressed forward. At length she paused and assured the scouts that the village was cleared, and that they were now in safety. She had been well aware that every pass leading out through the prairies was guarded, and resolved to push boldly through the midst of the village as the safest route.

After three days rapid marching and great suffering from hunger, the trio succeeded in reaching the block-house in safety. The Indians finding that the scouts had escaped, and that their plan of attack was discovered, soon after withdrew to their homes; the girl, who by her courage, fortitude, and skill, thus preserved the little settlement from destruction, proved to be a sister of Neil Washburn, one of the most renowned scouts upon the frontier.

The situation of the earlier pioneers who settled on the outskirts of the Mississippi basin was one of peculiar peril. In their isolation and weakness, they were able to keep their position rather by incessant watchfulness, than by actual combat. How to extricate themselves from the snares and escape from the dangers that beset them, was the constant study of their lives. The knowledge and the arts of a scout were a part of the education, therefore, of the women as well as of the men.

Massy Herbeson and her husband were of those

bold pioneers who crossed the Alleghany Mountains and joined the picket-line, whose lives were spent in reconnoitering and watching the motions of the savage tribes which roamed over Western Pennsylvania.

* They lived near Reed's block-house, about twenty-five miles from Pittsburgh. Mr. Herbeson, being one of the spies, was from home ; two of the scouts had lodged with her that night, but had left her house about sunrise, in order to go to the block-house, and had left the door standing wide open. Shortly after the two scouts went away, a number of Indians came into the house, and drew her out of bed, by the feet.

The Indians then scrambled to secure the articles in the house. Whilst they were at this work, Mrs. Herbeson went out of the house, and hallooed to the people in the block-house. One of the Indians then ran up and stopped her mouth, another threatened her with his tomahawk, and a third seized the tomahawk as it was about to fall upon her head, and called her his squaw.

Hurried rapidly away by her captor, she remembered the lessons taught by her husband, the scout, and marked the trail as she went on. Now breaking a bush, now dropping a piece of her dress, and when she crossed a stream, slyly turning over a stone, she hoped thus to guide her husband in pursuit or enable herself to find her way back to the block-house. The vigilance of the Indians was relaxed by the nonchalance with which she bore her captivity, and in a few days she succeeded in effecting her escape and pursuing the trail which she had marked, reached home after a weary march of two days and nights, during which it rained incessantly.

---

*Massey Herbeson's Deposition.

These and countless other instances illustrate the watchfulness and courage of woman when exposed to dangers of such a description. In the west especially, the distances to be traversed, the sparseness of the population, and the perils to which settlers are exposed, render the profession of a scout a useful and necessary one, and woman's versatility of character enables her, when necessary, to practice the art.

The traveler of to-day, passing up the Mohawk Valley will be struck by its fertility, beauty, and above all by the air of quiet repose that broods over it. One hundred years ago how different the scene! It was then the battle-ground where the fierce Indian waged an incessant warfare with the frontier settlers. Every rood of that fair valley was trodden by the wily and sanguinary foe. The people who then inhabited that region were a mixture of adventurous New Englanders and of Dutch, with a preponderance of the latter, who were a brave, steadfast, hardy race; the women vieing with the men in deeds of heroism and devotion.

Womanly tact and presence of mind was often as serviceable amid those scenes of danger and carnage, as valor in combat; and when woman combined these traits of her sex with courage and firmness she became the "guardian angel" of the settlement.

Such preëminently was the title deserved by Mrs. Van Alstine, the "Patriot mother of the Mohawk Valley."

All the early part of her long life, (for she counted nearly a century of years before she died,) was passed on the New York frontier, during the most trying period of our colonial history. Here, dwelling in the midst of alarms, she reared her fifteen children ; here more than once she saved the lives of her husband and family, and by her ready wit, her daring courage, and her open-handed generosity shielded the settlement from harm.

Born near Canajoharie, about the year 1733, and married to Martin J. Van Alstine, at the age of eighteen, she settled with her husband in the valley of the Mohawk, where the newly wedded pair occupied the Van Alstine family mansion.

In the month of August, 1780, an army of Indians and Tories, led on by Brant, rushed into the Mohawk Valley, devastated several settlements, and killed many of the inhabitants; during the two following months, Sir John Johnson made a descent and finished the work which Brant had begun. The two almost completely destroyed the settlements throughout the valley. It was during those trying times that Mrs. Van Alstine performed a portion of her exploits.

During these three months, and while the hostile forces were making their headquarters at Johnstown, the neighborhood in which Mrs. Van Alstine lived enjoyed a remarkable immunity from attack, although in a state of continual alarm. Intelligence at length came that the enemy, having ravaged the surrounding country, was about to fall upon the little settlement, and the inhabitants, for the most part women and children, were almost beside themselves with terror.

Mrs. Van Alstine's coolness and intrepidity, in this critical hour, were quickly displayed. Calling her neighbors together, she tried to relieve their fears and urged them to remove with their effects to an island belonging to her husband, near the opposite side of the

river, believing that the savages would either not discover their place of refuge or would be in too great
haste to cross the river and attack them.

Her suggestion was speedily adopted, and in a few
hours the seven families in the neighborhood were removed to their asylum, together with a store of provisions and other articles essential to their comfort.
Mrs. Van Alstine was the last to cross and assisted to
place out of reach of the enemy, the boat in which
the passage had been made. An hour after they had
been all snugly bestowed in their bushy retreat, the
war-whoop was heard and the Indians made their appearance. Gazing from their hiding place the unfor-
nate women and children soon saw their loved homes
in flames, Van Alstine's house alone being spared, owing to the friendship borne the owner by Sir John
Johnson.

The voices and even the words of the Indian raid-
ers could be distinctly heard on the island, and as
Mrs. Van Alstine gazed at the mansion untouched by
the flames she rejoiced that she would now be able to
give shelter to the homeless families by whom she was
surrounded. In the following year the Van Alstine
mansion was pillaged by the Indians, and although
the house was completely stripped of furniture and
provisions and clothing, none of the family were killed
or carried away as prisoners.

The Indians came upon them by surprise, entered
the house without ceremony, and plundered and destroyed everything in their way. "Mrs. Van Alstine
saw her most valued articles, brought from Holland,
broken one after another, till the house was strewed
with fragments. As they passed a large mirror with-

DARING EXPLOIT OF MISS VAN ALSTINE.   Page 117.

out demolishing it, she hoped it might be saved; but presently two of the savages led in a colt from the stables and the glass being laid in the hall, compelled the animal to walk over it. The beds which they could not carry away they ripped open, shaking out the feathers and taking the ticks with them. They also took all the clothing. One young Indian, attracted by the brilliancy of a pair of inlaid buckles on the shoes of the aged grandmother seated in the corner, rudely snatched them from her feet, tore off the buckles, and flung the shoes in her face. Another took her shawl from her neck, threatening to kill her if resistance was offered."

The eldest daughter, seeing a young savage carrying off a basket containing a hat and cap her father had brought her from Philadelphia, and which she highly prized, followed him, snatched her basket, and after a struggle succeeded in pushing him down. She then fled to a pile of hemp and hid herself, throwing the basket into it as far as she could. The other Indians gathered round, and as the young girl rose clapped their hands, shouting "Brave girl," while he skulked away to escape their derision. During the struggle Mrs. Van Alstine had called to her daughter to give up the contest; but she insisted that her basket should not be taken.

Winter coming on, the family suffered severely from the want of bedding, woolen clothes, cooking utensils, and numerous other articles which had been taken from them. Mrs. Van Alstine's arduous and constant labors could do but little toward providing for so many destitute persons. Their neighbors were in no condition to help them; the roads were almost impassable besides being infested with the Indians, and all their best horses had been driven away.

This situation appealing continually to Mrs. Van Alstine as a wife and a mother, so wrought upon her as to induce her to propose to her husband to organize an expedition, and attempt to recover their property from the Indian forts eighteen or twenty miles distant, where it had been carried. But the plan seemed scarcely feasible at the time, and was therefore abandoned.

The cold soon became intense and their necessities more desperate than ever. Mrs. Van Alstine, incapable longer of witnessing the sufferings of those dependent upon her, boldly determined to go herself to the Indian country and bring back the property. Firm against all the entreaties of her husband and children who sought to move her from her purpose, she left home with a horse and sleigh accompanied by her son, a youth of sixteen.

Pushing on over wretched roads and through the deep snow she arrived at her destination at a time when the Indians were all absent on a hunting excursion, the women and children only being left at home. On entering the principal house where she supposed the most valuable articles were, she was met by an old squaw in charge of the place and asked what she wanted. "Food," she replied; the squaw sullenly commenced preparing a meal and in doing so brought out a number of utensils that Mrs. Van Alstine recognized as her own. While the squaw's back was turned she took possession of the articles and removed them to her sleigh. When the custodian of the plunder discovered that it was being reclaimed, she was about to interfere forcibly with the bold intruders and take the property into her possession. But Mrs. Van Alstine showed her a paper which she averred was an order signed by "Yankee Peter," a man of great influence among the savages, and succeeded in convincing the squaw that the property was removed by his authority.

She next proceeded to the stables and cut the halters of the horses belonging to her husband: the animals recognized their mistress with loud neighs and bounded homeward at full speed. The mother and son then drove rapidly back to their house. Reaching home late in the evening they passed a sleepless night, dreading an instant pursuit and a night attack from the infuriated savages.

The Indians came soon after daylight in full war-costume armed with rifles and tomahawks. Mrs. Van Alstine begged her husband not to show himself but to leave the matter in her hands. The Indians took their course to the stables when they were met by the daring woman alone and asked what they wanted. "Our horses," replied the marauder. "They are ours," she said boldly, "and we mean to keep them."

The chief approached in a threatening manner, and drawing her away pulled out the plug that fastened the door of the stable, but she immediately snatched it from his hand, and pushing him away resumed her position in front of the door. Presenting his rifle, he threatened her with instant death if she did not immediately move. Opening her neck-handkerchief she told him to shoot if he dared.

The Indians, cowed by her daring, or fearing punishment from their allies in case they killed her, after some hesitation retired from the premises. They afterwards related their adventure to one of the settlers, and said that were fifty such women as she in the settlement, the Indians never would have molested the inhabitants of the Mohawk Valley.

On many subsequent occasions Mrs. Van Alstine exhibited the heroic qualities of her nature. Twice by her prudence, courage, and address, she saved the lives of her husband and family. Her influence in settling difficulties with the savages was acknowledged throughout the region, and but for her it may well be doubted whether the little settlement in which she lived would have been able to sustain itself, surrounded as it was by deadly foes.

Her influence was felt in another and higher way. She was a Christian woman, and her husband's house was opened for religious worship every Sunday when the weather would permit. She was able to persuade many of the Indians to attend, and as she had acquired their language she was wont to interpret to them the word of God and what was said by the minister. Many times their rude hearts were touched, and the tears rolled down their swarthy faces, while she dwelt on the wondrous story of our Redeemer's life and death, and explained how the white man and the red man alike could be saved by the grace of the Lord Jesus Christ. In after years the savages blessed her as their benefactress.

Nearly a hundred summers have passed since the occurrence of the events we have been describing. The war-whoop of the cruel Mohawk sounds no more from the forest-ambush, nor in the clearing; the dews and rains have washed away the red stains on the soft sward, and green and peaceful in the sunshine lies the turf by the beautiful river and on the grave where the patriot mother is sleeping; but still in the memory of the sons and daughters of the region she once blessed, lives the courage, the firmness, and the goodness of Nancy Van Alstine, the guardian of the Mohawk Valley.

CHAPTER VI.

PATRIOT WOMEN OF THE REVOLUTION.

DURING the dangers and trials of early colonial life, the daughters learned from the example of their mothers the lesson and the power of self-trust; they learned to endure what their parents endured, to face the perils which environed the settlement or the household, and grew up to woman's estate versed in that knowledge and experience of border-life which well fitted them to repeat, in wilder and more perilous scenes, the heroism of their forefathers and foremothers.

The daughters again taught these, and added other lessons, to their children. The grand-daughters of the first emigrants seemed to possess—with the traits and virtues of woman—the wisdom, courage, and strength of their fathers and brothers. Each succeeding generation seemed to acquire new features of character, added force, and stronger virtues, and thus woman became a heroine endowed with manly vigor and capable of performing deeds of masculine courage and resolution.

The generation of daughters, fourth in descent from the first settlers, lived during the stormy days of the Revolution; and right worthily did they perform their part on that stage of action, and prove by their deeds that they were lineal descendants of the first mothers of the Republic.

If we were to analyze the characters and motives of the women who lived and acted in that great crisis of our history, we should better understand and appreciate, in its nature, height, and breadth, their singular patriotism. Untainted by selfish ambition, undefiled by greed of gain, and purged of the earthy dross that too often alloys the lofty impulses of soldiers and statesmen in the path of fame, hers was a love of country that looked not for gain or glory, imperiled much, and was locked fast in a bitter companionship with anxiety, fear, and grief. Her heroism was not sordid or secular. Dearly did she prize the blessings of peace—household calm, the security of her loved ones, and the comforts and amenities of an unbroken social status. But she cheerfully surrendered them all at the call of her country in its hour of peril. For one hundred and fifty years she had toiled and suffered. She had won the right to repose, but this was not yet to be hers. A new ordeal awaited her which would test her courage and fortitude still more keenly, especially if her lot was cast in the frontier settlements.

It is easy to see that border-life in—

—"the times that tried men's souls"—

was surrounded by double dangers and hardships. Indeed it is difficult to conceive of a more trying situation than that of woman in the outlying settlements in the days of the Revolution. Left alone by her natural protector, who had gone far away to fight the battles of his country; exposed to attacks from the red men who lurked in the forest, or from the British soldiers marching up from the coast; wearied by the labors of the farm and the household; harassed by the cares of motherhood; for long years in the midst of dangers, privations, and trials; with serene patience, and with dauntless courage, she went on nobly doing her part in the great work which resulted in the glorious achievement of American Independence.

The wonder is that the American wives and mothers of that day did not sink under their burdens. Their patient endurance of accumulated hardships did not arise from a slavish servility or from insensibility to their rights and comforts. They justly appreciated the situation and nobly encountered the difficulties which could not be avoided.

Possessing all the affections of the wife, the tenderness of the mother, and the sympathies of the woman, their tears flowed freely for others' griefs, while they bore their own with a fortitude that none but a woman could display. In the absence of the father the entire education devolved upon the mother, who, in the midst of the labors and sorrows of her isolated existence, taught them to read, and instructed them in the principles of Christianity.

The countless roll of these unnamed heroines is inscribed in the Book of the Most Just. Their record is on high. But the names and deeds of not a few are preserved as a bright example to the men and women of to-day.

While the husbands and fathers of Wyoming were on public duty the wives and daughters cheerfully assumed a large portion of the labor which women could perform. They assisted to plant, to make hay, to husk, and to garner the corn. The settlement was mainly dependent on its own resources for powder. To meet the necessary demand, the women boiled together a ley of wood-ashes, to which they added the earth scraped from beneath the floors of their house, and thus manufactured saltpeter, one of the most essential ingredients. Charcoal and sulphur were then mingled with it, and powder was produced " for the public defense."

One of the married sisters of Silas Deane, that eminent Revolutionary patriot, while her husband, Captain Ebenezer Smith, was with the army, was left alone with six small children in a hamlet among the hills of Berkshire, Massachusetts. Finding it difficult to eke out a subsistence from the sterile soil of their farm, and being quick and ingenious with her needle, she turned tailoress and made garments for her little ones, and for all the families in that region. She wrote her husband, telling him to be of good cheer, and not to give himself anxiety on his wife's or his children's account, adding that as long as her fingers could hold a needle, food should be provided for them. " Fight on for your country," she said; " God will give us deliverance."

Each section of the country had its special burdens, trials, and dangers. The populous districts bore the first brunt of the enemy's attack; the thinly settled regions were drained of men, and the women were left in a pitiable condition of weakness and isolation. This was largely the condition of Massachusetts and Connecticut, where nearly every family sent some, if not all, of its men to the war. In the South the patriots were forced to practice continual vigilance in consequence of the divided feeling upon the question of the propriety of separation from the mother-country. New York, New Jersey, and Pennsylvania were battle grounds, and here, perhaps more fully than elsewhere, were experienced war's woes and desolation. But in every State throughout the thirteen colonies, and in every town, hamlet, or household, where there were patriot wives, mothers, or daughters, woman's claims to moral greatness in that crisis were gloriously vindicated.

If we were to search for traits and incidents to illustrate the whole circle of both the stronger and the gentler virtues, we might find them in woman's record during the American Revolution.

In scenes of carnage and death women not seldom displayed a cool courage which made them peers of the bravest soldiers who bore flint-locks at Bunker Hill or Trenton. Of such bravery, the following quartette of heroines will serve as examples.

During the attack on Fort Washington, Mrs. Margaret Corbin, seeing her husband, who was an artillery man, fall, unhesitatingly took his place and heroically performed his duties. Her services were appreciated by the officers of the army, and honorably noticed by Congress. This body passed the following resolution in July, 1779:

Resolved, That Margaret Corbin, wounded and disabled at the battle of Fort Washington while she heroically filled the post of her husband, who was killed by her side, serving a piece of artillery, do receive during her natural life, or continuance of said disability, one half the monthly pay drawn by a soldier in the service of these States; and that she now receive out of public store one suit of clothes, or value thereof in money.

Soon after the commencement of the Revolutionary War, the family of a Dr. Channing, being in England, removed to France, and shortly afterwards sailed for the United States. The vessel, said to be stout and well armed, was attacked on the voyage by a privateer, and a fierce engagement ensued. During its continuance, Mrs. Channing stood on the deck, exhorting the crew not to give up, encouraging them with words of cheer, handing them cartridges and aiding such of them as were disabled by wounds. When at length the colors of the vessel were struck, she seized her husband's pistol and side arms and flung them into the sea, declaring that she would prefer death to the spectacle of their surrender into the hands of the foe.

At the siege of one of the forts of the Mohawk Valley, it is related by the author of the "Border Wars of the American Revolution," that an interesting young woman, whose name yet lives in story among her own mountains, perceiving, as she thought, symptoms of fear in a soldier who had been ordered to fetch water from a well, without the ranks and within range of the enemy's fire, snatched the bucket from his hands and ran to the well herself. Without changing color or giving the slightest evidence of fear, she drew and brought back bucket after bucket to the thirsty soldiers, and providentially escaped without injury.

Four or five miles north of the village of Herkimer, N. Y., stood the block-house of John Christian Shell, whose wife acted a heroic part when attacked by the Tories, in 1781. From two o'clock in the afternoon until twilight, the besieged kept up an almost incessant firing, Mrs. Shell loading the guns for her husband and older sons to discharge. During the siege, McDonald, the leader of the Tories, attempted to force the door with a crow-bar, and was shot in the leg, seized by Shell, and drawn within doors. Exasperated by this bold feat, the enemy soon attempted to carry the fortress by assault; five of them leaping upon the walls and thrusting their guns through the loop-holes. At that moment the cool courageous woman, Mrs. Shell, seized an axe, smote the barrels, bent and spoiled them. The enemy soon after shouldered their guns, crooked barrels and all, and quickly buried themselves in the dense forest.

Heroism in those days was confined to no section of our country. Moll Pitcher, at Monmouth, battle-stained, avenged her husband by the death-dealing cannon which she loaded and aimed. Cornelia Beekman, at Croton, faced down the armed Tories with the fire of her eye; Angelica Vrooman, at Schoharie, moulded bullets amid the war and carnage of battle, while Mary Hagidorn defended the fort with a pike; Mrs. Fitzhugh, of Maryland, accompanied her blind and decrepit husband when taken prisoner at midnight and carried into the enemy's lines.

Dicey Langston, of South Carolina, also showed a "soul of love and bravery." Living in a frontier settlement, and in the midst of Tories, and being patriotically inquisitive, she often learned by accident, or discovered by strategy, the plottings so common in

those days against the Whigs. Such intelligence she
was accustomed to communicate to the friends of freedom on the opposite side of the Ennosee river.

Learning one time that a band of loyalists—known
in those days as the " Bloody Scouts "—were about to
fall upon the " Elder Settlement," a place where a
brother of hers and other friends were residing, she
resolved to warn them of their danger. To do this
she must hazard her own life. Regardless of danger
she started off alone, in the darkness of the night;
traveled several miles through the woods, over marshes,
across creeks, through a country where foot-logs and
bridges were then unknown; came to the Tyger, a
rapid and deep stream, into which she plunged and
waded till the water was up to her neck. She then
became bewildered, and zigzagged the channel for
some time, finally reaching the opposite shore, for a
helping hand was beneath, a kind Providence guided
her. She then hastened on, reached the settlement,
and her brother and the whole community were
saved.

She was returning one day from another settlement
of Whigs, in the Spartanburg district, when a company
of Tories met her and questioned her in regard to the
neighborhood she had just left; but she refused to
communicate the desired information. The leader of
the band then put a pistol to her breast, and threatened to shoot her if she did not make the wished-for
disclosure.

"Shoot me if you dare! I will not tell you!" was
her dauntless reply, as she opened a long handkerchief
that covered her neck and bosom, thus manifesting a

willingness to receive the contents of the pistol, if the officer insisted on disclosure or life.

The dastard, enraged at her defying movement, was in the act of firing, but one of the soldiers threw up the hand holding the weapon, and the uncovered heart of the girl was permitted to beat on.

The brothers of Dicey were no less patriotic than she; and they having, by their active services on the side of freedom, greatly displeased the loyalists, these latter were determined to be revenged. A desperate band accordingly went to the house of their father, and finding the sons absent, were about to wreak vengeance on the old man, whom they hated for the sons' sake. With this intent one of the party drew a pistol; but just as it was aimed at the breast of the aged and infirm old man, Dicey rushed between the two, and though the ruffian bade her get out of the way or receive in her own breast the contents of the pistol, she regarded not his threats, but flung her arms round her father's neck and declared she would receive the ball first, if the weapon must be discharged. Such fearlessness and willingness to offer her own life for the sake of her parent, softened the heart of the "Bloody Scout," and Mr. Langston lived to see his noble daughter perform other heroic deeds.

At one time her brother James, while absent, sent to the house for a gun which he had left in Dicey's care, with orders to deliver it to no one, except by his direction. On reaching the house one of the party who were directed to call for it, made known their errand. Whereupon she brought and was about to deliver the weapon. At this moment it occurred to her that she had not demanded the countersign agreed on between herself and brother. With the gun still in her hand, she looked the company sternly in the face, and remarking that they wore a suspicious look, called for the countersign. Thereupon one of them, in jest, told her she was too tardy in her requirements; that both the gun and its holder were in their possession. " Do you think so," she boldly asked, as she cocked the disputed weapon and aimed it at the speaker. " If the gun is in your possession," she added, " take charge of it !" Her appearance indicated that she was in earnest, and the countersign was given without further delay.

In these women of the Revolution were blended at once the heroine and the " Ministering Angel." To defend their homes they were men in courage and resolution, and when the battle was over they showed all a woman's tenderness and devotion. Love was the inspiring principle which nerved their arm in the fight, and poured balm into the wounds of those who had fallen. Should we have ever established our Independence but for the countless brave, kind, and self-sacrificing acts of woman ?

After the massacre of Fort Griswold, when it was found that several of the prisoners were still alive, the British soldiers piled their mangled bodies in an old cart and started it down the steep and rugged hill, towards the river, in order that they might be there drowned. Stumps and stones however obstructed the passage of the cart, and when the enemy had retreated —for the aroused inhabitants of that region soon compelled them to that course—the friends of the wounded came to their aid, and thus several lives were saved.

One of those heroic women who came the next morning to the aid of the thirty-five wounded men, who lay all night freezing in their own blood, was Mrs. Mary Ledyard, a near relative of the Colonel. "She brought warm chocolate, wine, and other refreshments, and while Dr. Downer, of Preston, was dressing the wounds of the soldiers, she went from one to another, administering her cordials, and breathing gentle words of sympathy and encouragement into their ears. In these labors of kindness she was assisted by another relative of the lamented Colonel Ledyard—Mrs. John Ledyard—who had also brought her household stores to refresh the sufferers, and lavished on them the most soothing personal attentions. The soldiers who recovered from their wounds, were accustomed, to the day of their death, to speak of these ladies in terms of fervent gratitude and praise."

Another "heroine and ministering angel" at the same massacre was Anna Warner, wife of Captain Bailey. She received from the soldiers the affectionate *sobriquet* of "Mother Bailey." Had "Mother Bailey" lived in the palmy days of ancient Roman glory no matron in that mighty empire would have been more highly honored. Hearing the British guns, at the attack on Fort Griswold, she hurried to the scene of carnage, where she found her uncle, one of the brave defenders, mortally wounded. With his dying lips he prayed to see his wife and child—once more; hastening home, she caught and saddled a horse for the feeble mother, and taking the child in her arms ran three miles and held it to receive the kisses and blessing of its dying father. At a later period flannel being needed to use for cartridges, she gave her own undergarment for that purpose. This patriotic surrender showed the noble spirit which always actuated "Mother Bailey" and was an appropriation to her country of which she might justly be proud.

The combination of manly daring and womanly kindness was admirably displayed in the deeds of a maiden, Miss Esther Gaston, and of a married lady, Mrs. Slocum, whose presence upon battlefields gave aid and comfort, in several ways, to the patriot cause.

On the morning of July 30th, 1780, the former, hearing the firing, rode to the scene of conflict in company with her sister-in-law. Meeting three skulkers retreating from the fight, Esther rebuked them sharply, and, seizing the gun from the hands of one of them, exclaimed, " Give us your guns, and we will stand in your places! " The cowards, abashed and filled with shame, thereupon turned about, and, in company with the females, hurried back to face the enemy.

While the battle was raging, Esther and her companion busied themselves in dressing and binding up the wounds of the fallen, and in quenching their thirst, not even forgetting their helpless enemies, whose bodies strewed the ground.

During another battle, which occurred the following week, she converted a church into a hospital, and administered to the wants of the wounded.

Our other heroine, Mrs. Slocum, of Pleasant Green, North Carolina, having a presentiment that her husband was dead or wounded in battle, rose in the night, saddled her horse. and rode to the scene of conflict. We continue the narrative in the words of our heroine.

" The cool night seemed after a gallop of a mile or

two, to bring reflection with it, and I asked myself where I was going, and for what purpose. Again and again I was tempted to turn back; but I was soon ten miles from home, and my mind became stronger every mile I rode that I should find my husband dead or dying —this was as firmly my presentiment and conviction as any'fact of my life. When day broke I was some thirty miles from home. I knew the general route our army expected to take, and had followed them without hesitation. About sunrise I came upon a group of women and children, standing and 'sitting by the road-side, each one of them showing the same anxiety of mind which I felt.

" Stopping a few minutes I enquired if the battle had been fought. They knew nothing, but were assembled on the road-side to catch intelligence. They thought Caswell had taken the right of the Wilmington road, and gone toward the northwest (Cape Fear). Again was I skimming over the ground through a country thinly settled, and very poor and swampy; but neither my own spirit nor my beautiful nag's failed in the least. We followed the well-marked trail of the troops.

" The sun must have been well up, say eight or nine o'clock, when I heard a sound like thunder, which I knew must be a cannon. It was the first time I ever heard a cannon. I stopped still; when presently the cannon thundered again. The battle was then fighting. What a fool! my husband could not be dead last night, and the battle only fighting now! Still, as I am so near, I will go on and see how they come out. So away we went again, faster than ever; and I soon found, by the noise of the guns, that I was near the fight. Again I stopped. I could hear muskets, rifles, and shouting. I spoke to my horse and dashed on in the direction of the firing and the shouts, which were louder than ever.

"The blind path I had been following, brought me into the Wilmington road leading to Moore's creek bridge, a few hundred yards below the bridge. A few yards from the road, under a cluster of trees, were lying perhaps twenty men. They were wounded. I knew the spot; the very tree; and the position of the men I knew as if I had seen it a thousand times. I had seen it all night! I saw *all* at once; but in an instant my whole soul centered in one spot; for there wrapped in a bloody guard cloak, was my husband's body! How I passed the few yards from my saddle to the place I never knew. I remember uncovering his head and seeing a face crusted with gore from a dreadful wound across the temple. I put my hand on the bloody face; 'twas warm; and an *unknown voice* begged for water; a small camp-kettle was lying near, and a stream of water was close by. I brought it; poured some in his mouth, washed his face; and behold—it was not my husband but Frank Cogdell. He soon revived and could speak. I was washing the wound in his head. Said he, 'It is not that; it is the hole in my leg that is killing me.' A puddle of blood was standing on the ground about his feet. I took the knife, and cut away his trousers and stockings, and found the blood came from a shot hole through and through the fleshy part of his leg. I looked about and could see nothing that looked as if it would do for dressing wounds, but some heart-leaves. I gathered a handful and bound them tight to the holes; and the bleeding stopped. I then went to others; I dressed the wounds of many a brave fellow who did good service long after that day! I had not enquired for my husband; but while I was busy Caswell came up. He appeared very much surprised to see me; and was with his hat in hand about to pay some compliment; but I interrupted him by asking—'Where is my husband?'

"'Where he ought to be, madam; in pursuit of the enemy. But pray,' said he, 'how came you here?'

"'O, I thought,' replied I, 'you would need nurses as well as soldiers. See! I have already dressed many of these good fellows; and here is one—and going up to Frank and lifting him up with my arm under his head so that he could drink some more water—'would have died before any of you men could have helped him.'

"Just then I looked up, and my husband, as bloody as a butcher, and as muddy as a ditcher, stood before me.

'Why, Mary!' he exclaimed, 'what are you doing there? Hugging Frank Cogdell, the greatest reprobate in the army?'

'I don't care,' I said. 'Frank is a brave fellow, a good soldier, and a true friend of Congress.'

'True, true! every word of it!' said Caswell. 'You are right, madam,' with the lowest possible bow.

"I would not tell my husband what brought me there. I was so happy; and so were all! It was a glorious victory; I came just at the height of the enjoyment. I knew my husband was surprised, but I could see he was not displeased with me. It was night again before our excitement had at all subsided.

Many prisoners were brought in, and among them some very obnoxious; but the worst of the Tories were not taken prisoners. They were, for the most part, left in the woods and swamps wherever they were overtaken. I begged for some of the poor prisoners, and Caswell told me none should be hurt but, such as had been guilty of murder and house-burning.

"In the middle of the night I again mounted my horse and started for home. Caswell and my husband wanted me to stay till next morning, and they would send a party with me; but no! I wanted to see my child, and I told them they could send no party who could keep up with me. What a happy ride I had back! and with what joy did I embrace my child as he ran to meet me!"

The winter at Valley Forge was the darkest season in the Revolutionary struggle. The American army were sheltered by miserable huts, through which the rain and sleet found their way upon the wretched cots where the patriots slept. By day the half-famished soldiers in tattered regimentals wandered through their camp, and the snow showed the bloody tracks of their shoeless feet. Mutinous mutterings disturbed the sleep of Washington, and one dark, cold day, the soldiers at dusk were on the point of open revolt. Nature could endure no more, and not from want of patriotism, but from want of food and clothes, the patriotic cause seemed likely to fail. Pinched with cold and wasted with hunger, the soldiers pined beside their dying camp-fires. Suddenly a shout was heard from the sentinels who paced the outer lines, and at the same time a cavalcade came slowly through the snow up the valley. Ten women in carts, each cart

FOOD AND CLOTHING SUPPLIED TO THE REVOLUTIONARY ARMY BY PATRIOTIC WOMEN. Page 136.

drawn by ten pairs of oxen, and bearing tons of meal and other supplies, passed through the lines amid cheers that rent the air. Those devoted women had preserved the army, and Independence from that day was assured.

Fortitude and patience were exemplified in a thousand homes from which members of the family had gone to battle for Independence. Straitened for means wherewith to keep their strong souls in their feeble bodies, worn with toil, tortured with anxiety for the safety of the soldier-father or son, or husband or brother, and fighting the conflict of life alone, woman proved in that great ordeal her claim to those virtues which are by common consent assigned to her as her peculiar characteristics.

We may well suppose, too, that ready wit and address had ample scope for their exercise in those perilous times. And who but woman could best display those qualities?

While Ann Elliott, styled by her British admirers, "the beautiful rebel," was affianced to Col. Lewis Morris, of New York, the house where he was visiting her was suddenly surrounded by a detachment of "Black Dragoons." They were in pursuit of the Colonel, and it was impossible for him to escape by flight. What to do he knew not, but, quick as thought, she ran to the window, opened it, and, fearlessly putting her head out, in a composed manner demanded what was wanted. The reply was, "We want the rebel." "Then go," said she, "and look for him in the American army;" adding, "how dare you disturb a family under the protection of both armies?" She was so cool, self-possessed, firm, and resolute, as to triumph over the dragoons, who left without entering the house.

While the conflict was at its height in South Carolina, Captain Richardson, of Sumter district, was obliged to conceal himself for a while in the thickets of the Santee swamp. One day he ventured to visit his family—a perilous movement, for the British had offered a reward for his apprehension, and patrolling parties were almost constantly in search of him. Before his visit was ended a small party of soldiers presented themselves in front of the house. Just as they were entering, with a great deal of composure and presence of mind, Mrs. Richardson appeared at the door, and found so much to do there at the moment, as to make it inconvenient to leave room for the uninvited guests to enter. She was so calm, and appeared so unconcerned, that they did not mistrust the cause of her wonderful diligence, till her husband had rushed out of the back door, and safely reached the neighboring swamp.

The bearing of important dispatches through an enemy's country is an enterprise that always requires both courage and address. Such a feat was performed by Miss Geiger, under circumstances of peculiar difficulty.

At the time General Greene retreated before Lord Rawdon from Ninety-Six, when he passed Broad river, he was desirous to send an order to General Sumter, who was on the Wateree, to join him, that they might attack Rawdon, who had divided his force. But the General could find no man in that part of the state who was bold enough to undertake so dangerous mission. The country to be passed through for many miles was full of blood-thirsty Tories, who, on every occasion that offered, imbrued their hands in the blood of the Whigs. At length Emily Geiger presented herself to General Greene, and proposed to act as his messenger: and the general, both surprised and delighted, closed with her proposal. He accordingly wrote a letter and delivered it, and at the same time communicated the contents of it verbally, to be told to Sumter in case of accidents.

She pursued her journey on horseback, and on the second day was intercepted by Lord Rawdon's scouts. Coming from the direction of Greene's army and not being able to tell an untruth without blushing, Emily was suspected and confined to a room; and the officer sent for an old Tory matron to search for papers upon her person. Emily was not wanting in expedients, and as soon as the door was closed and the bustle a little subsided, she *ate up the letter*, piece by piece. After a while the matron arrived, and upon searching carefully, nothing was found of a suspicious nature about the prisoner, and she would disclose nothing. Suspicion being then allayed, the officer commanding the scouts suffered Emily to depart. She then took a route somewhat circuitous to avoid further detentions and soon after struck into the road leading to Sumter's camp, where she arrived in safety. Emily told her adventure, and delivered Greene's verbal message to Sumter, who in consequence, soon after joined the main army at Orangeburgh.

The salvation of the army was due more than once to the watchfulness and tact of woman.

When the British army held possession of Philadelphia, a superior officer supposed to have been the Adjutant General, selected a back chamber in the house of Mrs. Lydia Darrah, for private conference. Suspecting that some important movement was on foot, she took off her shoes, and putting her ear to the key-hole of the door, overheard an order read for all the British troops to march out, late in the evening of the fourth, and attack General Washington's army, then encamped at White Marsh. On hearing this, she returned to her chamber and laid herself down. Soon after, the officers knocked at her door, but she rose only at the third summons, having feigned to be asleep. Her mind was so much agitated that, from this moment, she could neither eat nor sleep, supposing it to be in her power to save the lives of thousands of her countrymen, but not knowing how she was to carry the necessary information to General Washington, nor daring to confide it even to her husband. The time left was short, and she quickly determined to make her way as soon as possible, to the American outposts. She informed her family, that, as they were in want of flour, she would go to Frankfort for some; her husband insisted that she should take with her the servant maid; but, to his surprise, she positively refused. Gaining access to General Howe, she solicited what he readily granted—a pass through the British troops on the lines. Leaving her bag at the mill, she hastened towards the American lines, and encountered on her way an American, Lieutenant Colonel Craig, of the light horse, who, with some of his men, was on the lookout for information. He knew her, and inquired whither she was going. She answered, in quest of her son, an officer in the American army; and prayed the Colonel to alight and walk with her. He did so, ordering his troops to keep in sight. To him she disclosed her momentous secret, after having obtained from him the most solemn promise never to betray her individually, since her life might be at stake. He conducted her to a house near at hand, directed a female in it to give her something to eat, and hastened to head-quarters, where he made General Washington acquainted with what he had heard. Washington made, of course, all preparation for baffling the meditated surprise, and the contemplated expedition was a failure.

Mrs. Murray of New York, the mother of Lindley Murray, the grammarian, by her ceremonious hospitality detained Lord Howe and his officers, while the British forces were in pursuit of General Putnam, and thus prevented the capture of the American army. In fine, not merely the lives of many individuals, but the safety of the whole patriot army, and even the cause of independence was more than once due to feminine address and strategy.

Patriotic generosity and devotion were displayed without stint, and women were ready to submit to any sacrifice in behalf of their country.

These qualities are well illustrated by the three following instances.

Mrs. William Smith, when informed that in order to dislodge the enemy then in possession of Fort St. George, Long Island, it would be necessary to burn or batter down her dwelling-house, promptly told Major Tallmadge to proceed without hesitation in the work of destruction, if the good of the country demanded the sacrifice.

While General Greene was retreating, disheartened

and penniless, from the enemy, after the disastrous defeat at Camden, he was met at Catawba ford by Mrs. Elizabeth Steele, who, in her generous ardor in the cause of freedom, drew him aside, and, taking two bags of specie from under her apron, presented them to him, saying, " Take these, for you will want them, and I can do without them."

While Fort Motte, on the Congaree River, was in the hands of the British, in order to effect its surrender, it became necessary to burn a large mansion standing near the center of the trench. The house was the property of Mrs. Motte. Lieut. Colonel Lee communicated to her the contemplated work of destruction with painful reluctance, but her smiles, half anticipating his proposal, showed at once that she was willing to sacrifice her property if she could thereby aid in the least degree towards the expulsion of the enemy and the salvation of the land.

Pennsylvania had the honor of being the native State of Mrs. McCalla, whose affectionate and devoted efforts to liberate her invalid husband, languishing in a British dungeon, have justly given her a high rank among the patriot women of the Revolution.

Weeks elapsed after the capture of Mr. McCalla, before she was able, with the most assiduous inquiries, to ascertain the place of his confinement. In the midst of her torturing anxiety and suspense her children fell sick of small-pox. She nursed them alone and unaided, and as soon as they were out of danger, resumed her search for her husband.

Mounting her horse, she succeeded in forcing her way to the head-quarters of Lord Rawdon, at Camden, and obtained reluctant permission to visit her husband for ten minutes only in his wretched prison-pen. Though almost overcome by the interview, she hastened home, having altogether ridden through the wilderness one hundred miles in twenty-four hours.

She proceeded immediately to prepare clothing and provisions for her husband and the other prisoners. Her preparations having been completed, she set out on her return to Camden, in company with one of her neighbors, Mrs. Mary Nixon. Each of the brave women drove before her a pack-horse, laden with clothes and provisions for the prisoners. These errands of mercy were repeated every month, often in company with other women who were engaged in similar missions, and sometimes alone.

Meanwhile she did not relax her efforts to effect the release of her husband. After many months she succeeded in procuring an order for the discharge of her husband with ten other prisoners, whose handcuffs and ankle chains were knocked off, and who left the prison in company with their heroic liberator.

Examples are not wanting, in our Revolutionary annals, of a stern and lofty spirit of self-sacrifice in behalf of country, that will vie with that displayed by the first Brutus.

We are told by the orator of the Society of the Cincinnati that when the British officers presented to Mrs. Rebecca Edwards the mandate which arrested her sons as " objects of retaliation, less sensitive of private affection than attached to her honor and the interest of her country, she stifled the tender feelings of the mother and heroically bade them despise the threats of their enemies, and steadfastly persist to support the glorious cause in which they had engaged—

that if the threatened sacrifice should follow they would carry a parent's blessing, and the good opinion of every virtuous citizen with them, to the grave; but if from the frailty of human nature — of the possibility of which she would not suffer an idea to enter her mind—they were disposed to temporize and exchange this liberty for safety, they must forget her as a mother, nor subject her to the misery of ever beholding them again."

As among the early Puritan settlers, so among the women of the Revolution, nothing was more remarkable than their belief in the efficacy of prayer.

In the solitude of their homes, in the cool and silence of the forest, and in the presence of the foe, Christian women knelt down and prayed for peace, for victory, for rescue from danger, and for deliverance from the enemies which beset them. Can we doubt that the prayers of these noble patriot women were answered?

Early in the Revolutionary War, the historian of the border relates that "the inhabitants of the frontier of Burke County, North Carolina, being apprehensive of an attack by the Indians, it was determined to seek protection in a fort in a more densely populated neighborhood, in an interior settlement. A party of soldiers was sent to protect them on their retreat. The families assembled; the line of march was taken towards their place of destination, and they proceeded some miles unmolested—the soldiers forming a hollow square with the refugee families in the center. The Indians had watched these movements, and had laid a plan for the destruction of the migrating party. The road to be traveled lay through a dense forest in the fork of a river, where the Indians concealed themselves and waited till the travelers were in the desired spot.

Suddenly the war-whoop sounded in front and on either side; a large body of painted warriors rushed in, filling the gap by which the whites had entered, and an appalling crash of fire-arms followed. The soldiers, however, were prepared. Such as chanced to be near the trees darted behind them, and began to ply the deadly rifle; the others prostrated themselves upon the earth, among the tall grass, and crawled to trees. The families screened themselves as best they could. The onset was long and fiercely urged ; ever and anon, amid the din and smoke, the braves would rush out, tomahawk in hand, towards the center; but they were repulsed by the cool intrepidity of the backwoods riflemen. Still they fought on, determined on the destruction of the destined victims who offered such desperate resistance. All at once an appalling sound greeted the ears of the women and children in the center; it was a cry from their defenders—a cry for powder! "Our powder is giving out!" they exclaimed. "Have you any? Bring us some, or we can fight no longer."

A woman of the party had a good supply. She spread her apron on the ground, poured her powder into it, and going round from soldier to soldier, as they stood behind the trees, bade each who needed powder put down his hat, and poured a quantity upon it. Thus she went round the line of defense till her whole stock, and all she could obtain from others, was distributed. At last the savages gave way, and, pressed by their foes, were driven off the ground. The victorious whites returned to those for whose safety they

10

had ventured into the wilderness. Inquiries were made as to who had been killed, and one, running up, cried, " Where is the woman that gave us the powder? I want to see her! " " Yes! yes!—let us see her! " responded another and another; " without her we should have been all lost! " The soldiers ran about among the women and children, looking for her and making inquiries. Others came in from the pursuit, one of whom, observing the commotion, asked the cause, and was told.

" You are looking in the wrong place," he replied.

" Is she killed? Ah, we were afraid of that! " exclaimed many voices.

" Not when I saw her," answered the soldier. " When the Indians ran off, she was *on her knees in prayer* at the root of yonder tree, and there I left her."

There was a simultaneous rush to the tree—and there, to their great joy, they found the woman safe and still on her knees in prayer. Thinking not of herself, she received their applause without manifesting any other feeling than gratitude to Heaven for their great deliverance.

An eminent divine whose childhood was passed upon our New England frontier, during the period of the Revolution, narrated to the writer many years since, the story of his mother's life while her husband was absent in the patriot army. Their small farm was on the sterile hill-side, and with the utmost pains, barely yielded sufficient for the wants of the lone wife and her three little ones. There was no house within five miles, and the whole region around was stripped of its male inhabitants, such was the patriotic ardor of the people.

All the labors in providing for the household fell upon the mother. She planted and hoed the corn, milked the cow and tended the farm, at the same time not neglecting the inside duties of the household, feeding and clothing the children, nursing them when sick and instructing them in the rudiments of education.

"I call to mind, though after the lapse of eighty years," said the venerable man, "the image of my mother as distinctly as of yesterday, and she moves before me as she did in my childhood's home among those bleak hills—cheerful and serene through all, though even with my young eyes I could see that a brooding sorrow rested upon her spirit. I remember the day when my father kissed my brothers and me, and told us to be good boys, and help mother while he was gone: I remember too, that look upon my mother's face as she watched him go down the road with his musket and knapsack.

"When evening came, that day, and she had placed us in our little beds, I saw her kneeling and praying in a low tone, long and fervently, and heard her after she had pleaded that victory might crown our arms, intercede at the throne of grace for her absent husband and the father of her children.

"Then she rose and kissed us good-night, and as she bent above us I shall never forget till my latest hour the angelic expression upon her face. Sorrow, love, resignation, and holy trust were blended and beamed forth in that look which seemed to transfigure her countenance and her whole bearing.

"During all those trying years while she was so patiently toiling to feed and clothe us, and bearing the burdens and privations of her lonely lot, never did she omit the morning and evening prayer for her country and for the father of her children.

" One day we saw her holding an open letter in her hand and looking pale and as if she were about to faint. We gathered about her knees and gazed with wondering eyes, silently into her sad and care-worn face, for even then we had been schooled to recognize and respect the sorrows of a mother. Two weeks before that time, a battle had been fought in which father had been severely wounded. The slow mail of those days had only just brought this sad intelligence. As we stood beside her she bent and clasped us to her heart, striving to hide the great tears that coursed down her wasted cheeks.

" We begged her not to cry and tried to comfort her with our infantile caresses. At length we saw her close her eyes and utter a low prayer. Ere her lips had ceased to intercede with the Father of mercies, a knock was heard at the door and one of the neighboring settlers entered. He had just returned from the army and had come several miles on foot from his home, expressly to tell us that father was rapidly recovering from his wounds. It seemed as if he were a messenger sent from heaven in direct answer to the silent prayers of a mother, and all was joy and brightness in the house."

The patriot father returned to his family at the close of the war with the rank of Captain, which he had nobly won by his bravery in the battle's van. The sons grew up and became useful and honored citizens of a Republic which their father had helped to make free; and ever during their lives they fondly cherished the memory of the mother who had taught them so many examples of brave self-denial and pious devotion.

And still as we scan the pages of Revolutionary history, or revive the oral evidence of family tradition, the names and deeds of these brave and good women fill the eye and multiply in the memory. Through the fires, the frosts, the rains, the suns of one hundred years, they come back to us *now*, in the midst of our great national jubilee, vivid as with the life of yesterday. That era, which they helped to make glorious, is " with the years that are beyond the flood."

" Another race shall be, and other palms are won ; "

but never, while our nation or our language endures, shall the memory of those names and deeds pass away. In every succeeding year that registers the history of the Republic which they contributed to build, brighter and brighter shall grow the record of the Patriot Women of the Revolution.

CHAPTER VII.

IN regarding or in enjoying an end already accomplished by others, we are too apt to pass by the means through which that end was reached. America of to-day represents a grand result. We see that our land is great, rich, and powerful; we see that the flag waves from ocean to ocean, over a people furnished with all the appliances of civilization, and happy in their enjoyment; we are conscious that all this has come from the toils and the sufferings of many men and of many women who have lived and loved before us, and passed away, leaving behind them their country growing greater and richer, happier and more powerful, for what they have borne and done. But our views of the means by which that mighty end was reached are apt to be altogether too vague and general. While we are enjoying what others have worked to attain, let us not selfishly and forgetfully pass by the toils, the struggles, the firm endurance of those who went before us and accomplished this vast aggregate of results.

Each stage in the process by which these results were wrought out, had its peculiar trials, its special service. Looking back to that far-off past, and in the light of our own knowledge and conceptions, we find it almost impossible to decide which stage was encompassed with the deadliest dangers, the severest labors, the keenest sorrows, the largest list of discomforts. But certainly to woman, the breaking up of her eastern home, and the removal to the far west, was not the least burdensome and trying.

No characteristic of woman is more remarkable than the strength of her local associations and attachments. In making the home she learns to love it, and this feeling seems to be often strongest when the surroundings are the bleakest, the rudest, and the most comfortless. The Highlander and the Switzer pine amid the luxuriant scenes of tropical life, when their thoughts revert to the smoky shieling or to the rock-encompassed *chalet* of their far-off mountains. Such, too, doubtless, was the clinging fondness with which the women regarded their rude cabins on the frontier of the Atlantic States. They had toiled and fought to make these rude abodes the homes for those dearest to them; here children, the first-born of the Republic, had been nurtured; here, too, were the graves of the first fathers and mothers of America. Humble and comfortless as those dwelling-places would have seemed to the men and women of to-day, they were dear to the wives and mothers of colonial times.

Comprehending, as we may, this feeling, and knowing the peculiar difficulties of long journeys in those days, into a wild and hostile country, we can understand why the westward march of emigration and settlement was so slow during the first one hundred and fifty or sixty years of our history. New England had, it is true, been largely subjugated and reclaimed; a considerable body of emigrants, wedge-like, were driving slowly up through the Mohawk Valley towards Niagara; a weak, thin line, was straggling with difficulty across the Alleghanies in Pennsylvania, towards the Ohio, and a more compact and confident battalion in Virginia, was pushing into Kentucky. But how scattered and feeble that picket-line compared to the army which was soon to follow it.

For a season, and while the British were trying to force their yoke on the reluctant colonists, the westward movement had a check. The danger was in the rear. His old home in the east was threatened, and the pioneer turned about and faced the rising sun, until the danger was past and he could pursue his journey.

The close of the Revolutionary struggle gave a new impulse to the westward march of the American people, which had been arrested for the time being by the War of Independence.

The patriot soldiers found themselves, upon the advent of peace, impoverished in fortune; but with high hopes and stout hearts they immediately set about repairing the ravages of the long war. Nurtured in the rugged school of danger and hardship, they had ceased to regard the West with dread. Curiosity, blended with the hope of bettering their condition, turned their faces to that " fresh, unbounded, magnificent wilderness." Accustomed to camp life and scenes of exciting interest, the humdrum days at the old homestead became distasteful. The West was the hunter's paradise. The soil held beneath it the potency of harvests of extraordinary richness, and the soldier who had faced the disciplined battalions of Great Britain recked little of the prowling red man.

During the Revolution, the women, left alone by their husbands and fathers, who were with the army, were more than ever thrown on their own resources. They tilled the farm, reared their swarthy and nimble broods of children, and sent the boys in blue and buff all they could spare from their slender store. During all this trying period they were fitting themselves for that new life in the western wilds which had been marked out for them by the hand of an overruling Providence.

And yet, hard and lonely as the lives of these devoted women must have been in their eastern homes, and bright as their imaginations may have pictured the richness of the West, it must have given them many a pang when the husband and father told them that the whole family must be removed at once from their beloved homestead, which they or their fathers had redeemed from the wilderness after so many years of toil. We may imagine the resolution that was required to break up the old attachments which bind women to their homes and firesides.

It must have required a heroic courage to do this for the purpose of seeking a new home, not only among strangers, but among wild beasts and savages. But the fathers and mothers a hundred years ago possessed a spirit which rose above the perils of their times. They went forward, unhesitatingly, in their long and toilsome journeys westward, driving their slow-footed oxen and lumbering-wagons hundreds of miles, over ground where no road was; through woods infested with bears and wolves, panthers and warlike tribes of Indians; settling in the midst of those dangerous enemies, and conquering them all.

The army of pioneers, like the skirmishers who had preceded them, moved forward in three columns; the northernmost passed through New York State; the middle column moved westward through Pennsylvania; the southernmost marched through Virginia. Within ten years after the treaty of Versailles, the three columns had met in Ohio and Kentucky, and spreading out over that beautiful region, were fighting with nature and savage men to subjugate both and bring them within the bounds of civilization. No more sublime spectacle has ever greeted the eye of the historian than the march of that army. Twenty or thirty thousand men and women, bearing, like the Israelites of old, their ark across the desert and waste places— that ark which bore the blessings of civilization and religion within its holy shrine! Aged matrons, nursing mothers, prattling infants, hoary patriarchs, and strong veterans fresh from the fields of their country's glory, marching to form a mighty empire in the wilderness!

In this present age of rapid and easy transition from place to place, it is difficult to form a just conception of the tediousness, hardships, and duration of those early emigrations to the West. The difference in conveyance is that between a train of cars drawn by a forty-ton locomotive and a two-horse wagon, without springs, and of the most lumbering and primitive construction. This latter was the best conveyance that the emigrant could command. A few were so fortunately situated on the banks of rivers that they could float down with the current in flat-boats, while their cattle were being driven along the shore; or, if it was necessary to ascend toward the head-waters of a river, they could work their way up-stream with setting-poles. But most of the emigrants traveled with teams. Some of those who went part of the way in boats had to begin or end their journey in wagons. The vehicles which they provided on such occasions for land carriage were curiosities of wheel-craft—I speak of the Jersey wagons.

The old-fashioned Jersey wagon has, years ago, given place to more showy and flexible vehicles; but long before such were invented the Jersey wagon was an established institution, and was handed down, with the family name, from father to son. It was the great original of the modern emigrant wagon of the West; but as I have elsewhere pictured its appearance upon the arrival of a band of pioneers at their final destination, it is unnecessary to enter here upon any further description.

The spring of the year was the season usually selected for moving, and during many weeks previous to the appointed time, the emigrants had been actively providing against the accidents and discomforts of the road. When all was ready, the wagon was loaded, the oxen yoked and hooked to the neap; the women and children took their places on the summit of the huge load, the baby in its mother's lap, the youngest boy at his grandmother's feet, and off they started. The largest boy walked beside and drove the team, the other boys drove the cows, the men trudged behind or ahead, and the whole cavalcade passed out of the great gate, the grandmother peering through her spectacles, and the mother smiling through her tears and looking back more than once at the home which she had made but was now to leave for ever.

In this manner the earlier emigrants went forward, driving their heavily laden wagon by day and sleeping at night by the camp. After they had passed the region of roads and bridges they had to literally hew their way; cutting down bushes, prying their wagon out of bog-holes, building bridges or poling themselves across streams on rafts. But, in defiance of every obstacle, they pressed forward.

Neither rivers nor mountains stayed the course of the emigrant. Guiding his course by the sun, and ever facing the West, he went slowly on. When that luminary set, his parting rays lit the faces of the pioneer family, and when it rose it threw their long shadows before them on the soft, spongy turf of the forest glades. Sweating through the undergrowth; climbing over fallen trees; sinking knee-deep in marshes; at noon they halted to take a rest in the shade of the primeval forest, beside a brook, and there eat their mid-day meal of fried pork and corn cakes, which the women prepared; then on again, till the shadows stretched far back toward their old homes.

Sometimes a storm burst upon them, and the women and children huddled beneath the cart as the thunderbolts fell, shivering the huge trunks of the forest monarchs; and the lightning crimsoned the faces of the forlorn party with its glare. Then the heavens cleared; the sun came out; and the ox-cart went rumbling and creaking onward. No doubt the first days of that weary tramp had in them something of pleasurable excitement; the breezes of spring fanned the brows of the wayfarers, and told of the health and freedom of woodland life; the magnificence of the forest, the summits of the mountains, tinged with blue, the sparkling waters of lake and stream, must have given joy to even the most stolid of these households. But emotions of this description soon became strangers to their souls.

But the emigrants ere long found that the wilderness had lost the charms of novelty. Sights and sounds that were at first pleasing, and had lessened the sense of discomfort, soon ceased to attract attention. Their minds, solely occupied with obstacles, inconveniences, and obstructions, at every step of the way, became sullen, or, at least, indifferent.

To the toils and discomforts incident to their journey were often added casualties and great personal risks. An unlucky step might wrench an ankle; the axe might glance from a twig and split a foot open; and a broken leg, or a severed artery, is a frightful thing where no surgeon can be had. Exposure to all the changes of the weather—sleeping upon the damp ground, frequently brought on fevers; and sickness, at all times a great calamity, was infinitely more so to the pioneer. It must have been appalling in the woods. Many a mother has carried her wailing, languishing child in her arms, to lessen the jolting of the wagon, without being able to render it the necessary assistance. Many a family has paused on the way to gather a leafy couch for a dying brother or sister. Many a parent has laid in the grave, in the lonely wilderness, the child they should meet no more till the morning of the resurrection. Many a heart at the West has yearned at the thought of the treasured one resting beneath the spreading tree. After-comers have stopped over the little mound, and pondered upon the rude memorial carved in the bark above it; and those who had sustained a similar loss have wrung their hands and wept over it, for their own wounds were opened afresh.

Among the chapters of accident and casualty which make up the respective diaries of the families who left their eastern homes after the Revolution and joined the ranks of the Western immigrants there is none more interesting than that of Mrs. Jameson. She was the child of wealthy parents, and had been reared in luxury in the city of New York. Soon after peace was declared she was married to Edward Jameson, a brave soldier in the war, who had nothing but his stout arms and intrepid heart to battle with the difficulties of life. Her father, dying soon after, his estate was discovered to have been greatly lessened by the depreciation in value which the war had produced. Gathering together the remains of what was once a large fortune, the couple purchased the usual outfit of the emigrants of that period and set out to seek their fortunes in the West.

All went well with them until they reached the Alleghany River, which they undertook to cross on a raft. It was the month of May; the river had been swollen by rains, and when they reached the middle of the stream, the part of the raft on which Mr. Jameson sat became detached, the logs separated, and he sank to rise no more. The other section of the raft, containing Mrs. Jameson, her babe of eight months, and a chest of clothing and household gear, floated down-stream at the mercy of the rapid current.

Bracing herself against the shock, Mrs. Jameson managed to paddle to the side of the river from which she had just before started. She was landed nearly a

PERILOUS CROSSING OF THE ALLEGHANY RIVER.

mile below the point where had been left the cattle, and also the ox-cart in which their journey had been hitherto performed, and which her husband expected to carry over the river on the raft, returning for them as soon as his wife and babe had been safely landed on the western bank. The desolate mother succeeded in mooring the remains of the raft to the shore; then clasping her babe to her bosom, followed the bank of the river till she reached the oxen and cart, which she drove down to the place where she landed, and by great exertions succeeded in hauling the chest upon the bank. Her strength was now exhausted, and, lying down in the bottom of the cart, she gave way to grief and despair.

Her situation may be easily imagined: alone in the forest, thirty miles from the nearest settlement, her husband torn from her in a moment, and her babe smiling as though he would console his mother for her terrible loss. In her sad condition self-preservation would have been too feeble a motive to impel her to make any further effort to save herself; but maternal love—the strongest instinct in a woman's heart— buoyed her up and stimulated her to unwonted exertions.

The spot where she found herself was a dense forest, stretching back to a rocky ledge on the east, and terminated on the north by an alluvial meadow nearly bare of trees. Along the banks of the river was a thick line of high bushes and saplings, which served as a screen against the observations of savages passing up and down the river in their canoes. The woods were just bursting into leaf; the spring-flowers filled the air with odor, and chequered the green foliage

and grass; the whole scene was full of vernal freshness, life, and beauty. The track which the Jamesons
had followed was about midway between the northern
and southern routes generally pursued by emigrants,
and it was quite unlikely that others would cross the
river at that point. The dense jungle that skirted the
river bank was an impediment in the way of reaching
the settlements lower down, and there was danger of
being lost in the woods if the unfortunate woman
should start alone.

"On this spot," she said, "I must remain till some
one comes to my help."

The first two years of her married life had been
spent on a farm in Westchester County, New York,
where she had acquired some knowledge of farming
and woodcraft, by assisting her husband in his labors,
or by accompanying him while hunting and fishing.
She was strong and healthy; and quite unlike her
delicate sisters of modern days, her lithe frame was
hardened by exercise in the open air, and her face
was tinged by the kisses of the sun.

Slowly recovering from the terrible anguish of her
loss, she cast about for shelter and sustenance. The
woods were swarming with game, both large and
small, from the deer to the rabbit, and from the wild
turkey to the quail. The brooks were alive with trout.
The meadow was well suited for Indian corn, wheat,
rye, or potatoes. The forest was full of trees of every
description. To utilize all these raw materials was
her study.

A rude hut, built of boughs interlaced, and covered
thickly with leaves and dry swamp grass, was her first
work. This was her kitchen. The cart, which was

covered with canvas, was her sleeping-room. A shot-gun, which she had learned the use of, enabled her to keep herself supplied with game. She examined her store of provisions, consisting of pork, flour, and Indian meal, and made an estimate that they would last eight months, with prudent use. The oxen she tethered at first, but afterwards tied the horns to one of their fore feet, and let them roam. The two cows having calved soon after, she kept them near at hand by making a pen for the calves, who by their bleating called their mothers from the pastures on the banks of the river. In the meadow she planted half an acre of corn and potatoes, which soon promised an amazing crop.

Thus two months passed away. In her solitary and sad condition she was cheered by the daily hope that white settlers would cross her track or see her as they passed up and down the river. She often thought of trying to reach a settlement, but dreaded the dangers and difficulties of the way. Like the doe which hides her fawn in the secret covert, this young mother deemed herself and her babe safer in this solitude than in trying unknown perils, even with the chance of falling in with friends. She therefore contented herself with her lot, and when the toils of the day were over, she would sit on the bank and watch for voyagers on the river. Once she heard voices in the night on the river, and going to the bank she strained her eyes to gaze through the darkness and catch sight of the voyagers; she dared not hail them for fear they might be Indians, and soon the voices grew fainter in the distance, and she heard them no more. Again, while sitting in a clump of bushes on the bank

11

one day, she saw with horror six canoes with Indians, apparently directing their course to the spot where she sat. They were hideously streaked with war-paint, and came so near that she could see the scalping knives in their girdles. Turning their course as they approached the eastern shore they silently paddled down stream, scanning the banks sharply as they floated past. Fortunately they saw nothing to attract their attention; the cart and hut being concealed by the dense bushes, and there being no fire burning.

Fearing molestation from the Indians, she now moved her camp a hundred rods back, near a rocky ledge, from the base of which flowed a spring of pure water. Here, by rolling stones in a circle, she made an enclosure for her cattle at night, and within in it built a log cabin of rather frail construction; another two weeks was consumed in these labors, and it was now the middle of August.

At night she was at first much alarmed by the howling of wolves, who came sniffing round the cart where she slept. Once a large grey wolf put its paws upon the cart and poked its nose under the canvas covering, but a smart blow on the snout drove it yelping away. None of the cattle were attacked, owing to the bold front showed to these midnight intruders. The wolf is one of the most cowardly of wild beasts, and will rarely attack a human being, or even an ox, unless pressed by hunger, and in the winter. Often she caught glimpses of huge black bears in the swamps, while she was in pursuit of wild turkeys or other game; but these creatures never attacked her, and she gave them a wide berth.

One hot day in August she was gathering berries

on the rocky ledge beside which her house was situated, when seeing a clump of bushes heavily loaded with the finest blackberries, she laid her babe upon the ground, and climbing up, soon filled her basket with the luscious fruit. As she descended she saw her babe sitting upright and gazing with fixed eyeballs at some object near by; though what it was she could not clearly make out, on account of an intervening shrub. Hastening down, a sight met her eyes that froze her blood. An enormous rattlesnake was coiled within three feet of her child, and with its head erect and its forked tongue vibrating, its burning eyes were fixed upon those of the child, which sat motionless as a statue, apparently fascinated by the deadly gaze of the serpent.

Seizing a stick of dry wood she dealt the reptile a blow, but the stick being decayed and brittle, inflicted little injury on the serpent, and only caused it to turn itself towards Mrs. Jameson, and fix its keen and beautiful, but malignant eyes, steadily upon her. The witchery of the serpent's eyes so irresistibly rooted her to the ground, that for a moment she did not wish to remove from her formidable opponent.

The huge reptile gradually and slowly uncoiled its body; all the while steadily keeping its eye fixed on its intended victim. Mrs. Jameson could only cry, being unable to move, "Oh God! preserve me! save me, heavenly Father!" The child, after the snake's charm was broken, crept to her mother and buried its little head in her lap.

We continue the story in Mrs. Jameson's own words:—

"The snake now began to writhe its body down a

fissure in the rock, keeping its head elevated more than a foot from the ground. Its rattle made very little noise. It every moment darted out its forked tongue, its eyes became reddish and inflamed, and it moved rather quicker than at first. It was now within two yards of me. By some means I had dissipated the charm, and, roused by a sense of my awful danger, determined to stand on the defensive. To run away from it, I knew would be impracticable, as the snake would instantly dart its whole body after me. I therefore resolutely stood up, and put a strong glove on my right hand, which I happened to have with me. I stretched out my arm; the snake approached slowly and cautiously towards me, darting out its tongue still more frequently. I could now only recommend myself fervently to the protection of Heaven. The snake, when about a yard distant, made a violent spring. I quickly caught it in my right hand, directly under its head; it lashed its body on the ground, at the same time rattling loudly. I watched an opportunity, and suddenly holding the animal's head, while for a moment it drew in its forked tongue, with my left hand I, by a violent contraction of all the muscles in my hand, contrived to close up effectually its jaws!

"Much was now done, but much more was to be done. I had avoided much danger, but I was still in very perilous circumstances. If I moved my right hand from its neck for a moment, the snake, by avoiding suffocation, could easily muster sufficient power to force its head out of my hand; and if I withdrew my hand from its jaws, I should be fatally in the power of its most dreaded fangs. I retained, therefore, my hold with both my hands; I drew its body between my

feet, in order to aid the compression and hasten suffocation. Suddenly, the snake, which had remained
quiescent for a few moments, brought up its tail, hit
me violently on the head, and then darted its body
several times very tightly around my waist. Now
was the very acme of my danger. Thinking, therefore, that I had sufficient power over its body, I
removed my right hand from its neck, and in an
instant drew my hunting-knife. The snake, writhing
furiously again, darted at me; but, striking its body
with the edge of the knife, I made a deep cut, and
before it could recover its coil, I caught it again by
the neck; bending its head on my knee, and again
recommending myself fervently to Heaven, I cut its
head from its body, throwing the head to a great
distance. The blood spouted violently in my face;
the snake compressed its body still tighter, and I
thought I should be suffocated on the spot, and laid
myself down. The snake again rattled its tail and
lashed my feet with it. Gradually, however, the
creature relaxed its hold, its coils fell slack around
me, and untwisting it and throwing it from me as far
as I was able, I sank down and swooned upon the
bank.

" When consciousness returned, the scene appeared
like a terrible dream, till I saw the dead body of my
reptile foe and my babe crying violently and nestling
in my bosom. The ledge near which my cabin was
built was infested with rattlesnakes, and the one I
had slain seemed to be the patriarch of a numerous
family. From that day I vowed vengeance against
the whole tribe of reptiles. These creatures were in
the habit of coming down to the spring to drink, and

I sometimes killed four or five in a day. Before the summer was over I made an end of the whole family."

In September, two households of emigrants floating down the river on a flatboat, caught sight of Mrs. Jameson as she made a signal to them from the bank, and coming to land were pleased with the country, and were persuaded to settle there. The little community was now swelled to fifteen, including four women and six children. The colony throve, received accessions from the East, and, surviving all casualties, grew at last into a populous town. Mrs. Jameson was married again to a stalwart backwoodsman and became the mother of a large family. She was always known as the "Mother of the Alleghany Settlement."

Not a few of the pioneer women penetrated the West by means of boats. The Lakes and the River Ohio were the water-courses by which the advance guard of the army of emigrants was enabled to reach the fertile regions adjacent thereto. This mode of travel, while free from many of the hindrances and hardships of the land routes, was subject to other casualties and dangers. Storms on the lakes, and snags and shoals on the rivers, often made the pioneers regret that they had left the forests for the waters. The banks of the rivers were infested with savages, who slaughtered and scalped the men and carried the women and children into a captivity which was worse than death. The early annals of the West are full of the sad stories of such captivities, and of the women who took part in these terrible scenes.

The following instances will be interesting to the reader:

In the latter part of April, 1784, one Mr. Rowan,

with his own and five other families, set out from
Louisville, in two flat-bottomed boats, for the Long
Falls of Green River. Their intention was to descend
the Ohio to the mouth of Green River, then ascend
that stream to their place of destination. At that
time there were no settlements in Kentucky within
one hundred miles of Long Falls, afterwards called
Vienna.

Having driven their cattle upon one of the boats
they loaded the other with their household goods,
farming implements, and stores. The latter was provided with covers under which the six families could
sleep, with the exception of three of the men who
took charge of the cattle boat.

The first three days of their journey were passed
in ease and gaiety. Floating with the current and
using the broad oars only to steer with, they kept their
course in the main channel where there was little danger of shoals and snags. The weather was fine and
the scenery along the banks of the majestic river had
that placid beauty that distinguishes the country
through which the lower Ohio rolls its mighty mass of
waters on their way to the Mississippi. These halcyon
days of the voyage were destined, however, to be soon
abruptly terminated. They had descended the river
about one hundred miles, gliding along in peace and
fancied security; the women and children had retired
to their bunks, and all of the men except those who
were steering the boat were composing themselves to
sleep, when suddenly the placid stillness of the night
was broken by a fearful sound which came from the
river far below them. The steersmen at first supposed it was the howling of wolves. But as they

neared the spot from which the sound proceeded, on rounding a bend in the river, they saw the glare of fires in the darkness; the sounds at the same time re- doubled in shrillness and volume, and they knew then that a large body of Indians were below them and would almost inevitably discover their boats. The numerous fires on the Illinois shore and the peculiar yells of the savages led them to believe that a flat- boat which preceded them had been captured and that the Indians were engaged in their cruel orgies of torture and massacre. The two boats were immedi- ately lashed together, and the best practical arrange- ments were made for defending them. The men were distributed by Mr. Rowan to the best advantage in case of an attack; they were seven in number. The boats were neared to the Kentucky shore, keeping off from the bank lest there might be Indians on that shore also. When they glided by the uppermost fire they entertained a faint hope that they might escape unperceived. But they were discovered when they had passed about half of the fires and commanded to halt. They however remained silent, for Mr. Rowan had given strict orders that no one should utter any sound but that of the rifle; and not that until the In- dians should come within reach. The savages united in a most terrific yell, rushed to their canoes and pur- sued them. They floated on in silence—not an oar was pulled. The enemy approached the boats within a hundred yards, with a seeming determination to board them.

Just at this moment Mrs. Rowan rose from her seat, collected the axes and placed one by the side of each man, where he stood with his gun, touching him on the knee with the handle of the axe as she leaned it up beside him against the edge of the boat, to let him know it was there. She then retired to her seat, retaining a hatchet for herself.

None but those who have had a practical acquaintance with Indian warfare, can form a just idea of the terror which their hideous yelling is calculated to inspire. When heard that night in the mighty solitude through which those boats were passing, we are told that most of the voyagers were panic-stricken and almost nerveless until Mrs. Rowan's calm resolution and intrepidity inspired them with a portion of her own undaunted spirit. The Indians continued hovering on their rear and yelling, for nearly three miles, when awed by the inference which they drew from the silence of the party in the boat, they relinquished farther pursuit.

Woman's companionship and influence are nowhere more necessary than on the long and tedious journey of the pioneer to the West. Man is a born rover. He sails over perilous seas and beneath unfamiliar constellations. He penetrates the trackless forest and scales the mountains for gain or glory or out of mere love of motion and adventure. A life away from the fetters and conventionalities of civilized society also has its charms to the manly heart. The free air of the boundless wilderness acts on many natures as a stimulus to effort, but it seems also to breed a spirit of unrest. "I will not stay here! whither shall I go?" Thus the spirit whispers to itself. Motion, only motion! Onward! ever onward! The restless foot of the pioneer has reached and climbed the mountains. He pauses but a moment to gaze at the valley and presses forward. The valley reached and he must cross the river, and now the unbounded expanse of the plain spreads before him. Traversing this after many weary days he stands beneath a mightier mountain-range towering above him. Up! up! Struggling upward but ever onward he has reached the snowy summit and gazes upon wider valleys lit by a kinglier sun and spanned by kindlier skies; and far off he sees sparkling in the evening light another and grander ocean on whose shores he must pause. Thus by various motives and impulses the line which bounds the area of civilized society is constantly being extended.

But all through this tumult of the mind and heart, through this rush of motion and life there is heard another voice. Soft and penetrating it sounds in the hour of calm and stillness and tells of happiness and repose. As in the beautiful song one word is its burden, Home! Home! Sweet Home! where the lonely heart and toil-worn feet may find rest. That voice must have its answer, that aspiration must be reached by the aid of woman. It is she, and only she that makes the home. Around her as a beaming nucleus are attracted and gather the thousand lesser lights of the fireside. She is the central figure of the domestic group, and where she is not, there is no home. Man may explore a continent, subjugate nature and conquer savage races, but no permanent settlement can be made nor any new empire formed without the alliance of woman.

She must therefore be the companion of the restless rover on his westward march, in order that the secret cravings of his soul may be at last satisfied in that home of happiness and rest, which woman alone can form.

Nothing will better illustrate the restless and indomitable spirit that inspires the western pioneer, and at the same time display the constant companionship and tireless energy of woman, than the singular history of a family named Moody. The emigrant ancestors of this family lived and died in eastern Massachusetts, where after arriving from England, in 1634, they first settled. In 1675, two of the daughters were living west of the Connecticut river. A grand-daughter of the emigrant was settled near the New York boundary line in 1720. *Her* daughter marrying a Dutch farmer of Schoharie made her home in the valley of the Mohawk during the French and Indian wars and the Revolution. In 1783, although an aged woman, she moved with her husband and family to Ohio, where she soon after died, leaving a daughter who married a Moody, a far away cousin, and moved first into Indiana and finally into Illinois, where she and her husband died leaving a son, J. G. Moody, who inherited the enterprising spirit of his predecessors, and, marrying a female relative who inherited the family name and spirit, before he was of age resumed the family march towards the Pacific.

The first place where the family *halted* was in the territory of Iowa. Here they lived for ten years tilling a noble farm on the Des Moines river. Then they sold their house and land, and pushed one hundred miles further westward. Here again new toils and triumphs awaited them. With the handsome sum derived from the sale of their farm on the Des Moines, they were enabled to purchase an extensive domain of both prairie and woodland. In ten years they had a model farm, and the story of their successful labors attracted other settlers to their neighborhood. A large price tempted them and again they disposed of their farm.

We have traced genealogically the successive stages in the history of this pioneer family for the purpose of noting, not merely the cheerfulness with which so many generations of daughters accompanied their husbands on their westward march, but the energy which they displayed in making so many homes in the waste places, and preparing the way for the less bold and adventurous class of settlers who follow where the pioneer leads.

The family, after disposing of their second Iowa farm, immediately took up their line of march for Nebraska, where they bought and cultivated a large tract of land on one of the tributaries of the Platte. In due time the current of emigration struck them. A favorable offer for their house and cattle ranche was speedily embraced, and again they took up their line of march which extended this time into the heart of the Rocky Mountains, in Colorado, of which State they were among the earliest settlers.

Here Mr. Moody died; but his widow with her large family successfully maintained her cattle and sheep ranche till a rich gold mine was discovered upon her land. A sale was soon effected of both the mine and the ranche. In two weeks after the whole family, mother, sons, and daughters were *en route* to California, where their long wanderings terminated. There they are now living and enjoying the rich fruits of their energy and enterprise, proving for once the falsity of the proverb that " a rolling stone gathers no moss."

The women of this family are types of a class—soldiers, scouts, laborers, nurses in the " Grand Army," whose mission it is to reclaim the waste places and conquer uncivilized man.

If they fight, it is only for peace and safety. If they destroy, it is only to rebuild nobler structures in the interest of civilization. If they toil and bleed and suffer, it is only that they may rest on their arms, at last, surrounded by honorable and useful trophies, and look forward to ages of home-calm which have been secured for their posterity.

CHAPTER VIII.

HOMESTEAD-LIFE IN THE BACKWOODS AND ON THE PRAIRIE.

THE first stage in pioneer-life is nomadic : a half-score of men, women, and children faring on day after day, living in the open air, encamping at night beside a spring or brook, under the canopy of the forest, it is only when they reach their place of destination, that the germ of a community fixes itself to the soil, and rises obedient to those laws of social and civil order which distinguish the European colonist from the Asiatic nomad.

The experiences of camp life form the initial steps to the thorough backwoods education which a woman must at length acquire, to fit her for the duties and trials incident to all remote settlements. Riding, driving, or tramping on, now through stately groves, now over prairies which lose themselves in the horizon, now fording shallow streams, or poling themselves on rafts across rivers, skirting morasses or wallowing through them, and climbing mountains, as they breathe the fresh woodland air and catch glimpses of a thousand novel scenes and encounter the dangers or endure the hardships of this first stage in their pilgrimage, they learn those first hard lessons which stand them in such good stead when they have settled in their permanent abodes in the heart of the wilderness which it is the work of the pioneer to subdue.

To the casual observer there is an air of romance and wild enjoyment in this journey through that magnificent land. Many things there doubtless are to give zest and enjoyment to the long march of the pioneer and his family. The country through which they pass deserves the title of "the garden of God." The trees of the forest are like stately columns in some verdurous temple ; the sun shines down from an Italian sky upon lakes set like jewels flashing in the beams of light, the sward is filled with exaggerated velvet, through whose green the purple and scarlet gleams of fruit and flowers appear, and everything speaks to the eye of the splendor, richness, and joy of wild nature. Traits of man in this scene are favorite themes for the painter's art. The fire burning under the spreading oak or chestnut, the horses, or oxen, or mules picketed in the vistas, Indian wigwams and squaws with children watching curiously the pioneer household sitting by their fire and eating their evening meal; this is the picture framed by the imagination of a poet or artist; but this is but a superficial sketch,—a mere glimpse of one of them any thousand phases of the long and weary journey. The reality is quite another thing.

The arrival of the household at their chosen seat marks the second stage in backwoods-life, a stage which calls for all the powers of mind and body, tasks the hands, exercises the ingenuity, summons vigilance, and awakens every latent energy. Woman steps at once into a new sphere of action, and hand in hand, shoulder to shoulder, with her stronger but not more resolute companion, enters on that career which looks to the formation of communities and states. It is the household which constitutes the primal atom, the aggregation whereof makes the village, town, or city; the state itself rests upon the household finally, and the household is what the faithful mother makes it.

The toilsome march at length ended, we see the great wagon, with its load of household utensils and farming implements, bedsteads walling up the sides, a wash-tub turned up to serve as a seat for the driver, a broom and hoe-handle sticking out behind with the handles of a plough, pots and kettles dangling below, bundles of beds and bedding enthroning children of all the smaller sizes, stopping at last " for good," and the whole cortege of men, women, and boys, cattle, horses, and hogs, resting after their mighty tramp.

Shelter and food are the first wants of the settler; the log-cabin rises to supply the one; the axe, the plough, the spade, the hoe, prepare the other.

The women not seldom joined in the work of felling

trees and trimming logs to be used in erecting the cabins.

Those who have never witnessed the erection of log-cabins, would be surprised to behold the simplicity of their mechanism, and the rapidity with which they are put together. The axe and the auger are often the only tools used in their construction, but usually the drawing-knife, the broad-axe, and the crosscut-saw are added.

The architecture of the body of the house is sufficiently obvious, but it is curious to notice the ingenuity with which the wooden fireplace and chimney are protected from the action of the fire by a lining of clay, to see a smooth floor formed from the plain surface of hewed logs, and a door made of boards split from the log, hastily smoothed with the drawing-knife, united firmly together with wooden pins, hung upon wooden hinges, and fastened with a wooden latch. Not a nail nor any particle of metal enters into the composition of the building—all is wood from top to bottom, all is done by the woodsman without the aid of any mechanic. These primitive dwellings are by no means so wretched as their name and rude workmanship would seem to imply. They still frequently constitute the dwelling of the farmers in new settlements; they are often roomy, tight, and comfortable. If one cabin is not sufficient, another and another is added, until the whole family is accommodated, and thus the homestead of a respectable farmer often resembles a little village. The dexterity of the backwoodsman in the use of the axe is also remarkable, yet it ceases to be so regarded when we reflect on the variety of uses to which this implement is applied, and that in

WAGON TRAIN ON THE PRAIRIE.   Page 173.

fact it enters into almost all the occupations of the pioneer, in clearing land, building houses, making fences, providing fuel; the axe is used in tilling his fields; the farmer is continually obliged to cut away the trees that have fallen in his enclosure, and the roots that impede his plough; the path of the surveyor is cleared by the axe, and his lines and corners marked by this instrument; roads are opened and bridges made by the axe, the first court houses and jails are fashoned of logs with the same tool. In labor or hunting, in traveling by land or water, the axe is ever the companion of the backwoodsman.

Most of these cabins were fortresses in themselves, and were capable of being defended by a family for several days. The thickness of the walls and numerous loop-poles were sometimes supplemented by a clay covering upon the roof, so as to resist the fiery arrows of the savages. Sometimes places of concealment were provided for the women and children beneath the floor, with a closely fitting trap door leading to it. Such a place of refuge was provided by Mrs. Graves, a widow who lost her husband in Braddock's retreat. In a large pit beneath the floor of the cabin every night she laid her children to sleep upon a bed of straw, and there, replacing one of the floor logs, she passed the weary hours in darkness, seated by the window which commanded a view of the clearing through which the Indians would have to approach. When her youngest child required nursing she would lift the floor-log and sit on the edge of the opening until it was lulled to sleep, and then deposit the nursling once more in its secret bed.

Once, while sitting without a light, knitting, before

12

the window, she saw three Indians approaching stealthily. Retreating to the hiding place beneath the floor, she heard them enter the cabin, and, having struck a light, proceed to help themselves to such eatables as they found in the pantry. After remaining for an hour in the house, and appropriating such articles as Indians most value, viz., knives, axes, etc., they took their departure.

More elaborate fortresses were often necessary, and, for purposes of mutual defence in a country which swarmed with Indians, the settlers banded together and erected stations, forts, and block-houses.

*A *station* may be described as a series of cabins built on the sides of a parallelogram and united with palisades, so as to present on the outside a continuous wall with only one or two doors, the cabin doors opening on the inside into a common square.

A fort was a stockade enclosure embracing cabins, etc., for the accommodation of several families. One side was formed by a range of cabins separated by divisions or partitions of logs; the walls on the outside were ten or twelve feet high, with roofs sloping inward. Some of these cabins were provided with puncheon-floors, i. e., floors made of logs split in half and smoothed, but most of the floors were earthen. At the angles of these forts were built the block-houses, which projected about two feet beyond the outer walls of the cabins and stockade; these upper stories were about eighteen feet, or two inches every way larger than the under one, leaving an opening at the commencement of the second story, to prevent the enemy from making a lodgment under the walls.

These block-houses were devised in the early days

* DeHass.

of the first settlements made in our country, and furnished rallying points for the settlers when attacked by the Indians. On the Western frontier they were enlarged and improved to meet the military exigencies arising in a country which swarmed with savages.

* In some forts, instead of block-houses, the angles were furnished with bastions; a large folding gate, made of thick slabs nearest the spring, closed the forts; the stockade, bastion, cabin, and block-house walls were furnished with port-holes at proper heights and distances. The whole of the outside was made completely bullet-proof; the families belonging to these forts were so attached to their own cabins on their farms that they seldom moved into the forts in the spring until compelled by some alarm, i. e., when it was announced by some murder that Indians were in the settlement.

We have described thus in detail the fortified posts established along the frontier for the purpose of showing that the life of the pioneer woman, from the earliest times, was, and now is, to a large extent, a military one. She was forced to learn a soldier's habits and a soldier's virtues. Eternal vigilance was the price of safety, and during the absence of the male members of the household, which were frequent and sometimes protracted, the women were on guard-duty, and acted as the sentinels of their home fortresses. Watchful against stratagem as against violent attack, they passed many a night all alone in their isolated cabins, averting danger with all a woman's fertility of resource, and meeting it with all the courage of a man.

On one occasion a party of Indians approached a solitary log-house with the intention of murdering the

---

* Doddridge's Notes.

inmates. With their usual caution, one of their number was sent forward to reconnoiter, who, discovering the only persons within to be a woman, two or three children, and a negro man, rushed in by himself and seized the negro. The woman caught up the axe and with a single blow laid the savage warrior dead at her feet, while the children closed the door, and, with ready sagacity, employed themselves fastening it. The rest of the Indians came up and attempted to force an entrance, but the negro and the children kept the door closed, and the intrepid mother, having no effective weapon, picked up a gun-barrel which had neither stock nor lock and pointed it at the savages through the apertures between the logs. The Indians, deceived by the appearance of a gun, and daunted by the death of their companion, retired.

The station, the fort, and the block-house were the only refuge of the isolated settlers when the Indians became bolder in their attacks.

When the report of the four-pounder, or the ringing of the fort bell, or a volley of musketry sounded the alarm, the women and children hurried to the fortification. Sometimes, while threading the mazes of the forest, the hapless mother and her children would fall into an ambush. Springing from their cover, the prowling savages would ply their tomahawks and scalping knives amid the shrieks of their helpless victims, or bear them away into a captivity more cruel than death.

One summer's afternoon, while Mrs. Folsom, with her babe in her arms, was hasting to Fort Stanwig in the Black River Country, New York, after hearing the alarm, she caught sight of a huge Indian lying behind

a log, with his rifle leveled apparently directly at her.
She quickly sprang to one side and ran through the
woods in a course at right angles with the point of
danger, expecting every moment to be pierced with a
rifle ball. Casting a horror-stricken glance over her
shoulder as she ran, she saw her husband hastening on
after her, but directly under the Indian's rifle. Shriek-
ing loudly, she pointed to the savage just in time to
warn her husband, who stepped behind a tree as the
report of the rifle rang through the forest. In an instant he drew a bead upon the lurking foe, who fell
with a bullet through his brain.

Before the family could reach the fort a legion of
savages, roused by the report of the rifles, were on
their trail. The mother and child fled swiftly towards
their place of refuge, which they succeeded in reaching
without harm; but the brave father, while trying to
keep the savages at bay, was shot and scalped almost
under the walls of the fort.

Ann Bush, another of these border heroines, was
still more unfortunate than Mrs. Folsom. While she
and her husband were fleeing for safety to one of the
stations on the Virginia borders, they were overtaken
and captured by the Indians, who shot and scalped
her husband; and although she soon escaped from
captivity, yet in less than twelve months after, while
again attempting to find refuge in the same station,
she was captured a second time, with an infant in her
arms. After traveling a few hours the savages bent
down a young hickory, sharpened it, seized the child,
scalped it and spitted it upon the tree; they then
scalped and tomahawked the mother and left her for
dead. She lay insensible for many hours; but it was

the will of Providence that she should survive the shock. When she recovered her senses she bandaged her head with her apron, and, wonderful to tell, in two days staggered back to the settlement with the dead body of her infant.

The transitions of frontier life were often startling and sad. From a wedding to a funeral, from a merry-making to a massacre, were frequent vicissitudes. One of these shiftings of the scene is described by an actor and eye-witness as follows:

"Father had gone away the day before and mother and the children were alone. About nine o'clock at night we saw two Indians approaching. Mother immediately threw a bucket of water on the fire to prevent them from seeing us, made us lie on the floor, bolted and barred the door, and posted herself there with an axe and rifle. We never knew why they desisted from an attack or how father escaped. In two or three days all of us set out for Clinch Mountain to the wedding of Happy Kincaid, a clever young fellow from Holston, and Sally McClure, a fine girl of seventeen, modest and pretty, yet fearless. We knew the Shawnees were about; that our fort and household effects must be left unguarded and might be destroyed; that we incurred the risk of a fight or an ambuscade, a capture, and even death, on the route; but in those days, and in that wild country, folks did not calculate consequences closely, and the temptation to a frolic, a wedding, a feast, and a dance till daylight and often for several days together, was not to be resisted. Off we went. Instead of the bridal party, the well spread table, the ringing laughter, and the sounding feet of buxom dancers, we found a pile of ashes and six or seven ghastly corpses tomahawked and scalped." Mrs. McClure, her infant, and three other children, including Sally, the intended bride, had been carried off by the savages. They soon tore the poor infant from the mother's arms and killed and scalped it, that she might travel faster. While they were scalping this child, Peggy McClure, a girl twelve years old, perceived a sink-hole immediately at her feet and dropped silently into it. It communicated with a ravine, down which she ran and brought the news to the settlement. The same night Sally, who had been tied and forced to lie down between two warriors, contrived to loosen her thongs and make her escape. She struck for the canebrake, then for the river, and to conceal her trail resolved to descend it. It was deep wading, and the current was so rapid she had to fill her petticoat with gravel to steady herself. She soon, however, recovered confidence, returned to shore, and finally reached the still smoking homestead about dark next evening. A few neighbors well armed had just buried the dead; the last prayer had been said, when the orphan girl stood before them.

Yielding to the entreaties of her lover, who was present, and to the advice and persuasion of her friends, the weeping girl gave her consent to an immediate marriage ; and beside the grave of the household and near the ruins of the cabin they were accordingly made one.

These perilous adventures were episodes, we should remember, in a life of extraordinary labor and hardship. The luxuries and comforts of older communities were unknown to the settlers on the border-line, either in New England two centuries ago or in the West

within the present generation.   Plain in every way
was the life of the borderer—plain in dress, in manners,
in equipage, in houses.   The cabins were furnished in
the most primitive style.   Blocks or stumps of trees
served for chairs and tables.   Bedsteads were made
by laying rows of saplings across two logs, forming a
spring-bed for the women and children, while the men
lay on the floor with their feet to the fire and a log
under their heads for a pillow.

The furniture of the cabin in the West, for several
years after the settlement of the country, consisted of
a few pewter dishes, plates, and spoons, but mostly
of wooden bowls, trenchers, and noggins; if these last
were scarce, gourds and hard-shell squashes made up
the deficiency; the iron pots, knives, and forks were
brought from the East, with the salt and iron on pack-
horses.   The articles of furniture corresponded very
well with the articles of diet.   "Hog and hominy"
was a dish of proverbial celebrity; Johnny cake or
pone was at the outset of the settlement the only form
of bread in use for breakfast or dinner; at supper,
milk and mush was the standard dish; when milk
was scarce the hominy supplied its place, and mush
was frequently eaten with sweetened water, molasses,
bear's oil, or the gravy of fried meat.

In the display of furniture, delft, china, or silver
were unknown; the introduction of delft-ware was
considered by many of the backwoods people as a
wasteful innovation; it was too easily broken, and the
plates dulled their scalping and clasp knives.

The costume of the women of the frontier was
suited to the plainness of the habitations where they
lived and the furniture they used.   Homespun, linsey-

woolsey and buckskin were the primitive materials out of which their everyday dresses were made, and only on occasions of social festivity were they seen in braver robes. Rings, broaches, buckles, and ruffles were heir-looms from parents or grand-parents.

But this plainness of living and attire was a preparation for, and almost necessary antecedent of hardihood, endurance, courage, patience, qualities which made themselves manifest in the heroic acting of these women of the border. With such a state of society we can readily associate assiduous labor, a battling with danger in its myriad shapes, a subjugation of the hostile forces of nature, and a developing of a strange and peculiar civilization.

Here we see woman in her true glory, not a doll to carry silks and jewels, not a puppet to be dandled by fops, an idol of profane adoration reverenced to-day, discarded to-morrow, admired but not respected, desired but not esteemed, ruling by passion not affection, imparting her weakness not her constancy, to the sex she should exalt—the source and marrow of vanity. We see her as a wife partaking of the cares and guiding the labors of her husband and by domestic diligence spreading cheerfulness all around for his sake; sharing the decent refinements of civilization without being injured by them; placing all her joy, all her happiness in the merited approbation of the man she loves; as a mother, we find her affectionate, the ardent instructress of the children she has reared from infancy and trained up to thought and to the practice of virtue, to meditation and benevolence and to become strong and useful men and women.

" Could there be happiness or comfort in such

dwellings and such a state of society. To those who
are accustomed to modern refinement the truth appears like fable. The lowly occupants of log cabins were
often among the most happy of mankind. Exercise
and excitement gave them health, they were practi-
cally equal; common danger made them mutually dependent; brilliant hopes of future wealth and distinction led them on, and as there was ample room for all,
and as each new comer increased individual and general security, there was little room for that envy, jeal-
ousy, and hatred which constitutes a large portion of
human misery in older societies. Never were the
story, the joke, the song, and the laugh better enjoyed
than upon the hewed blocks or puncheon-stools around
the roaring log-fire of the early western settler. The
lyre of Apollo was not hailed with more delight in
primitive Greece than the advent of the first fiddler
among the dwellers of the wilderness, and the polished
daughters of the East never enjoyed themselves half
so well moving to the music of a full band upon the
elastic floor of their ornamented ball-room, as did the
daughters of the western emigrants keeping time to
the self-taught fiddler on the bare earth or puncheon
floor of the primitive log cabin: the smile of the polished beauty is the wave of the lake where the breeze
plays gently over it, and her movement the gentle
stream which drains it; but the laugh of the log cabin
is the gush of nature's fountain and its movement the
leaping water."

Amid the multifarious toils of pioneer-life, woman
has often proved that she is the last to forget the
stranger that is within the gates. She welcomes the
coming as she speeds the parting guest.

Let us suppose travelers caught in a rain storm, who reach at last one of these western homes. There is a roof, a stick chimney, drenched cattle crowding in beneath a strawy barrack, and some forlorn fowls huddling under a cart. The log-house is a small one, though its neat corn-crib and chicken-coop of slender poles bespeaks a careful farmer. No gate is seen, but great bars which are let down or climbed over, and the cabin has only a back door.

Within, everything ministers to the useful; nothing to the beautiful. Flitches of bacon, dried beef, and ham depend from the ceiling; pots and kettles are ranged in a row in the recess on one side the fire-place; and above these necessary utensils are plates and heavy earthen nappies. The axe and gun stand together in one corner.

The good woman of the house is thin as a shadow, and pinched and wrinkled with hard labor. Little boys and girls are playing on the floor like kittens.

A free and hospitable welcome is given to the travelers; their wet garments are ranged for drying on those slender poles usually seen above the ample fire-place of a log-cabin in the West, placed there for the purpose of drying sometimes the week's wash when the weather is rainy, sometimes whole rows of slender circlets of pumpkins for next spring's pies, or festoons of sliced apples.

The good woman, after busying herself in those little offices which evince a desire to make guests welcome, puts an old cloak on her head and flies out to place tubs, pails, pans, and jars under the pouring eaves, intimating that as soap was scarce, she "must try and catch rain water anyhow."

The " old man" has the shakes, so the woman has
all to do; throws more wood on the fire and fans it
with her apron; cuts rashers of bacon, runs out to the
hen-coop and brings in new-laid eggs; mixes a johnny-
cake and sets it in a pan upon the embers.

While the supper is cooking the rain subsides to a
sprinkle, and the travelers look at the surroundings of
this pioneer household.

The cabin stands in a prairie, skirted by a forest.
A stream gurgles by. The prairie is broken with
patches of corn and potatoes, which are just emerging
from the rich black mould. Pig-pens, a barn, and
corn-houses, a half-dozen sheep in an enclosure, cows
and calves and oxen in a barn-yard, a garden patch,
and hen-coops, and stumps of what were once mighty
trees, tell the story of the farmer's labors; and the
cabin, with all its appurtenances and surroundings,
show how much the good woman has contributed to
make it the abode of rustic plenty, all provided by the
unaided toil of this pioneer couple.

They had come from the East ten years before, and
their cabin was the initial point from which grew up a
numerous settlement. Other cabins sent up their
smoke in the prairie around them. A school-house
and church had been built, and a saw-mill was at work
on the stream near by, and surveyors for a railroad
had just laid out a route for the iron horse.

Two little boys come in now, skipping from school,
and at the same time the good woman, who is all
patience and civility, announces supper. Sage-tea,
johnny-cake, fried eggs, and bacon, seasoned with sun-
dry invitations of the hostess to partake freely, and
then the travelers are in a mood for rest.

The sleeping arrangements are of a somewhat per-
plexing character. These are one large bed and a
trundle bed; the former is given up to the travelers,
the trundle bed suffices for the little ones; the hostess
prepares a cotton sheet partition for the benefit of
those who choose to undress, and then begins to prepare herself for the rest which she stands sorely in
need of. She and her good man repose upon the
floor, with buffalo robes for pillows, and with their feet
to the fire.

The hospitality of the frontier woman is bounded
only by their means of affording it. Come when you
may, they welcome you; give you of their best while
you remain, and regret your departure with simple
and unfeigned sincerity. If you are sick, all that
sympathy and care can devise is done for you, and all
this is from the heart.

Homestead-life, and woman's influence therein, is
modified to some extent by the different races that
contributed their quotas to the pioneer army. The
early French settlements in our western States furnish
a picture somewhat different from those of the emigrants of English blood: a patriarchal state of society,
self-satisfied and kindly, with bright superficial features, but lacking the earnest purpose and restless
aggressive energy of the Anglo-American, whose very
amusements and festivals partook of a useful character.

Those French pioneer-women made thrifty and
industrious housewives, and entered, with all the
gaiety and enthusiasm of their race, into all the
merry-makings and social enjoyments peculiar to
those neighborhoods. On festive occasions, the bloom-

ing damsels wound round their foreheads fancy-colored handkerchiefs, streaming with gay ribbons, or plumed with flowers. The matrons wore the short jacket or petticoat. The foot was left uncovered and free, but on holidays it was adorned with the light moccasin, brilliant with porcupine quills, shells, beads, and lace.

A faithful picture of life in these French settlements possesses an indescribable charm, such as that conveyed by the perusal of Longfellow's Acadian Romance of "Evangeline," when we see in a border settlement the French maiden. wife, and widow.

Different types, too, of homestead-life are of course to be looked for in different sections. On the ocean's beach, on the shores of the inland seas, on the banks of great rivers, in the heart of the forest, on the rugged hills of New England, on southern Savannas, on western prairies, or among the mountains beyond, the region, the scenery, the climate, the social laws may be diverse, yet homestead-life on the frontier, widely varying as it does in its form and outward surroundings, is in its spirit everywhere essentially the same. The sky that bends over all, and the sun that sheds its light for all, are symbols of the oneness of the animating principle in the home where woman is the bright and potent genius.

We have spoken of the western form of homestead-life because the frontier-line of to-day lies in the occident. But in each stage of the movement that carried our people onward in their destined course from ocean to ocean, the wife and the mother were centers from which emanated a force to impel forward, and to fix firmly in the chosen abode those organisms of society which forms the molecular atoms out of which, by the laws of our being, is built the compact structure of civilization.

In approximating towards some estimate of woman's peculiar influence in those lonely and far-off western homes, we must not fail to take into account the humanizing and refining power which she exerts to soften the rugged features of frontier-life. Different classes of women all worked in their way towards this end.

" The young married people, who form a considerable part of the pioneer element in our country, are simple in their habits, moderate in their aspirations, and hoard a little old-fashioned romance—unconsciously enough—in the secret nooks of their rustic hearts. They find no fault with their bare loggeries; with a shelter and a handful of furniture, they have enough." If there is the wherewithal to spread a warm supper for the " old man " when he comes in from work, the young wife forgets the long, solitary, wordless day and asks no greater happiness than preparing it by the help of such materials and utensils as would be looked at with utter contempt in the comfortable kitchens of the East.

They have youth, hope, health, occupation, and amusement, and when you have added " meat, clothes, and fire," what more has England's queen ? "

We should, however, remember that there is another large class of women who, for various reasons, have left comfortable homes in older communities, and risked their happiness and all that they have in enterprises of pioneer life in the far West. What wonder that they should sadly miss the thousand old familiar means and appliances ! Some utensil or implement necessary to their husbandry is wanting or has been lost or broken, and cannot be replaced. Some comfort or luxury to which she has been used from childhood is lacking, and cannot be furnished. The multifarious materials upon which household art can employ itself are reduced to the few absolute essentials. These difficulties are felt more by the woman than the man. To quote the words of a writer who was herself a pioneer housewife in the West:

"The husband goes to his work with the same axe or hoe which fitted his hand in his old woods and fields; he tills the same soil or perhaps a far richer and more hopeful one; he gazes on the same book of nature which he has read from his infancy and sees only a fresher and more glowing page, and he returns home with the sun, strong in heart and full of self-congratulation on the favorable change in his lot. Perhaps he finds the home bird drooping and disconsolate. She has found a thousand difficulties which her rougher mate can scarcely be taught to feel as evils. She has been looking in vain for any of the cherished features of her old fireside. What cares he if the time-honored cupboard is meagerly represented by a few oak boards lying on pegs called shelves. His tea equipage shines as it was wont, the biscuits can hardly stay on the brightly glistening plates. His bread never was better baked. What does he want with the great old-fashioned rocking chair? When he is tired he goes to bed, for he is never tired till bed-time. The sacrifices in moving West have been made most largely by women."

It is this very dearth of so many things that once made her life easy and comfortable which throws her back upon her own resources. Here again is woman's strength. Fertile in expedients, apt in device, an artisan to construct and an artist to embellish, she proceeds to supply what is lacking in her new home. She has a miraculous faculty for creating much out of little, and for transforming the coarse into the beautiful. Barrels are converted into easy chairs and washstands; spring beds are manufactured with rows of slender, elastic saplings; a box covered with muslin stuffed with hay serves for a lounge. By the aid of considerable personal exertion, while she adds to the list of useful and necessary articles, she also enlarges the circle of luxuries. An hour or two of extra work now and then enables her to hoard enough to buy a new looking-glass, and to make from time to time small additions to the showy part of the household.

After she has transformed the rude cabin into a cozy habitation, she turns her attention to the outside surroundings. Woodbine and wild cucumber are trailed over the doors and windows; little beds of sweet-williams and marigolds line the path to the clearing's edge or across the prairie-sward to the well; and an apple or pear tree is put in here and there. In all these works, either of use or embellishment, if not done by her own hand she is at least the moving spirit. Thus over the rugged and homely features of her lot she throws something of the magic of that ideal of which the poet sings:

> " Nymph of our soul and brightener of our being :
> She makes the common waters musical—
> Binds the rude night-winds in a silver thrall,
> Bids Hybla's thyme and Tempe's violet dwell
> Round the green marge of her moon-haunted cell."

It is the thousand nameless household offices performed by woman that makes the home: it is the home which moulds the character of the children and makes the husband what he is. Who can deny the vast debt of gratitude due from the present generation of Americans to these offices of woman in refining and ameliorating the rude tone of frontier life? It may well be said that the pioneer women of America have made the wilderness bud and blossom like the rose. Under their hands even nature itself, no longer a wild, wayward mother, turns a more benign face upon her children. A land bright with flowers and bursting with fruitage testifies to the labors and influence of those who embellish the homestead and make it attractive to their husbands and children.

A traveler on the vast prairies of Kansas and Nebraska will often see cabins remote from the great thoroughfares embowered in vines and shrubbery and bright with beds of flowers. Entering he will discern the rugged features of frontier life softened in a hundred ways by the hand of woman. The steel is just as hard and more serviceable after it is polished, and the oak-wood as strong and durable when it is trimmed and smoothed. The children of the frontier are as hardy and as manly though the gentle voice of woman schools their rugged ways and her kind hand leads them through the paths of refinement and moulds them in the school of humanity.

CHAPTER IX.

SOME REMARKABLE WOMEN.

O F all the tens of thousands of devoted women
who have accompanied the grand army of pioneers into the wilderness, not one but that has been
either a soldier to fight, or a laborer to toil, or a ministering angel to soothe the pains and relieve the sore
wants of her companions. Not seldom has she acted
worthily in all these several capacities, fighting, toiling, and ministering by turns. If a diary of the events
of their pioneer-lives had been kept by each of these
brave and faithful women, what a record of toil and
warfare and suffering it would present. How many
different types of female character in different spheres
of action it would show—the self-sacrificing mother,
the tender and devoted wife, the benevolent matron,
the heroine who blenched not in battle! Unnumbered
thousands have passed beautiful, strenuous and brave
lives far from the scenes of civilization, and gone down
to their graves leaving only local, feeble voices, if any,
to celebrate their praises and to-day we know not the
place of their sepulcher. Others have had their
memories embalmed by the pens of faithful biograph-
ers, and a few also have left diaries containing a record
of the wonderful vicissitudes of their lives.

Woman's experience of life in the wilderness is never
better told than in her own words. More impressible
than man, to passing events; more susceptible to pain

(195)

and pleasure; enjoying and sorrowing more keenly
than her sterner and rougher mate, she possesses often
a peculiarly graphic power in expressing her own
thoughts and feelings, and also in delineating the
scenes through which she passes.

A woman's diary of frontier-life, therefore, possesses an intrinsic value because it is a faithful story,
and at the same time one of surpassing interest, in
consequence of her personal and active participation
in the toils, sufferings, and dangers incident to such a
life.

Such a diary is that of Mrs. Williamson which in
the quaint style of the olden time relates her thrilling
experience in the wilds of Pennsylvania. We see her
first as an affectionate, motherless girl accompanying
her father to the frontier, assisting him to prepare a
home for his old age in the depths of the forest and
enduring with cheerful resolution the manifold hardships and trials of pioneer-life, and finally closing her
aged parent's eyes in death. Then we see her as a
wife, the partner of her husband's cares and labors,
and as a mother, the faithful guardian of her sons;
and again as a widow, her husband having been torn
from her arms and butchered by a band of ruthless
savages. After her sons had grown to be sturdy men
and had left her to make homes for themselves, she
shows herself the strong and self-reliant matron of
fifty still keeping her outpost on the border, and culti-
vating her clearing by the assistance of two negroes.
At last after a life of toil and danger she is attacked
by a band of savages, and defends her home so bravely
that after making her their captive they spare her life
and in admiration of her courage adopt her into their

tribe. She dissembles her reluctance, humors her savage captors and forces herself to accompany them on their bloody expeditions wherein she saves many lives and mitigates the sufferings of her fellow-captives.

The narrative of her escape we give in her own quaint words.

"One night the Indians, very greatly fatigued with their day's excursion, composed themselves to rest as usual. Observing them to be asleep, I tried various ways to see whether it was a scheme to prove my intentions or not, but, after making a noise, and walking about, sometimes touching them with my feet, I found there was no fallacy. My heart then exulted with joy at seeing a time come that I might, in all probability be delivered from my captivity; but this joy was soon dampened by the dread of being discovered by them, or taken by any straggling parties; to prevent which, I resolved, if possible, to get one of their guns, and, if discovered, to die in my defense, rather than be taken. For that purpose I made various efforts to get one from under their heads (where they always secured them), but in vain.

"Frustrated in this my first essay towards regaining my liberty, I dreaded the thought of carrying my design into execution: yet, after a little consideration, and trusting myself to the divine protection, I set forward, naked and defenceless as I was; a rash and dangerous enterprise! Such was my terror, however, that in going from them, I halted and paused every four or five yards, looking fearfully toward the spot where I had left them, lest they should awake and miss me; but when I was about two hundred yards from them, I mended my pace, and made as much haste as I could to the foot of the mountains; when on sudden I was struck with the greatest terror and amaze, at hearing the wood-cry, as it is called, they make when any accident happens them. However, fear hastened my steps, and though they dispersed, not one happened to hit upon the track I had taken. When I had run near five miles, I met with a hollow tree, in which I concealed myself till the evening of the next day, when I renewed my flight, and next night slept in a canebrake. The next morning I crossed a brook, and got more leisurely along, returning thanks to Providence, in my heart, for my happy escape, and praying for future protection. The third day, in the morning, I perceived two Indians armed, at a short distance, which I verily believed were in pursuit of me, by their alternately climbing into the highest trees, no doubt to look over the country to discover me. This retarded my flight for that day; but at night I resumed my travels, frightened and trembling at every bush I passed, thinking each shrub that I touched, a savage concealed to take me. It was moonlight nights till near morning, which favored my escape. But how shall I describe the fear, terror and shock that I felt on the fourth night, when, by the rustling I made among the leaves, a party of Indians, that lay round a small fire, nearly out, which I did not perceive, started from the ground, and seizing their arms, ran from the fire among the woods. Whether to move forward, or to rest where I was, I knew not, so distracted was my imagination. In this melancholy state, revolving in my thoughts the now inevitable fate I thought waited on me, to my great astonishment and joy, I was relieved by a parcel of swine that made towards the place where I guessed the savages to be; who, on seeing the hogs, conjectured that their alarm had been occasioned by them, and directly returned to the fire, and lay down to sleep as before. As soon as I perceived my enemies so disposed of, with more cautious step and silent tread, I pursued my course, sweating (though the air was very cold) with the fear I had just been relieved from. Bruised, cut, mangled and terrified as I was, I still, through divine assistance, was enabled to pursue my journey until break of day, when, thinking myself far off from any of those miscreants I so much dreaded, I lay down under a great log, and slept undisturbed until about noon, when, getting up, I reached the summit of a great hill with some difficulty; and looking out if I could spy any inhabitants of white people, to my unutterable joy I saw some, which I guessed to be about ten miles distance. This pleasure was in some measure abated, by my not being able to get among them that night; therefore, when evening approached I again re-commended myself to the Almighty, and composed my weary mangled limbs to rest. In the morning I continued my journey towards the nearest cleared lands I had seen the day before; and about four o'clock in the afternoon I arrived at the house of John Bell."

Mrs. Daviess was another of these women who, like Mrs. Williamson, was a born heroine, of whom there were many who acted a conspicuous part in the territorial history of Kentucky. Large and splendidly formed, she possessed the strength of a man with the gentle loveliness of the true woman. In the hour of peril, and such hours were frequent with her, she was firm, cool, and fertile of resource; her whole life, of which we give only a few episodes, was one continuous succession of brave and noble deeds. Both she and Mrs. Williamson appear to have been real instances of the poet's ideal:

> "A perfect woman nobly planned
> To warn, to comfort, and command."

* Her husband, Samuel Daviess, was an early settler at Gilmer's Lick, in Lincoln County, Kentucky. In the month of August, 1782, while a few rods from his house, he was attacked early one morning by an Indian, and attempting to get within doors he found that his house was already occupied by the other Indians. He succeeded in making his escape to his brother's station, five miles off, and giving the alarm was soon on his way back to his cabin in company with five stout, well armed men.

Meanwhile, the Indians, four in number, who had entered the house while the fifth was in pursuit of Mr. Daviess, roused Mrs. Daviess and the children from their beds and gave them to understand that they must go with them as prisoners. Mrs. Daviess occupied as long a time as possible in dressing, hoping that some relief would come. She also delayed the Indians nearly two hours by showing them one article of clothing and then another, explaining their uses and expatiating on their value.

While this was going on the Indian who had been in pursuit of her husband returned with his hands stained with pokeberries, waving his tomahawk with violent gestures as if to convey the belief that he had killed Mr. Daviess. The keen-eyed wife soon dis-

---

* Collins' Historical Sketches.

covered the deception, and was satisfied that her husband had escaped uninjured.

After plundering the house, the savages started to depart, taking Mrs. Daviess and her seven children with them. As some of the children were too young to travel as rapidly as the Indians wished, and discovering, as she believed, their intention to kill them, she made the two oldest boys carry the two youngest on their backs.

In order to leave no trail behind them, the Indians traveled with the greatest caution, not permitting their captives to break a twig or weed as they passed along, and to expedite Mrs. Daviess' movements one of them reached down and cut off with his knife a few inches of her dress.

Mrs. Daviess was accustomed to handle a gun and was a good shot, like many other women on the frontier. She contemplated as a last resort that, if not rescued in the course of the day, when night came and the Indians had fallen asleep, she would deliver herself and her children by killing as many of the Indians as she could, believing that in a night attack the rest would fly panic-stricken.

Mr. Daviess and his companions reaching the house and finding it empty, succeeded in striking the trail of the Indians and hastened in pursuit. They had gone but a few miles before they overtook them. Two Indian spies in the rear first discovered the pursuers, and running on overtook the others and knocked down and scalped the oldest boy, but did not kill him. The pursuers fired at the Indians but missed. The latter became alarmed and confused, and Mrs. Daviess taking advantage of this circumstance jumped into a sink-hole with her infant in her arms. The Indians fled and every child was saved.

Kentucky in its early days, like most new countries, was occasionally troubled with men of abandoned character, who lived by stealing the property of others, and after committing their depredations, retired to their hiding-places, thereby eluding the operation of the law. One of these marauders, a man of desperate character, who had committed extensive thefts from Mr. Daviess, as well as from his neighbors, was pursued by Daviess and a party whose property he had taken, in order to bring him to justice.

While the party were in pursuit, the suspected individual, not knowing that any one was pursuing him, came to the house of Daviess, armed with his gun and tomahawk,—no person being at home but Mrs. Daviess and her children. After he had stepped into the house, Mrs. Daviess asked him if he would drink something; and having set a bottle of whiskey upon the table, requested him to help himself. The fellow not suspecting any danger, set his gun by the door, and while he was drinking Mrs. Daviess picked it up, and placing herself in the doorway had the weapon cocked and leveled upon him by the time he turned around, and in a peremptory manner ordered him to take a seat or she would shoot him. Struck with terror and alarm, he asked what he had done. She told him he had stolen her husband's property, and that she intended to take care of him herself. In that condition she held him prisoner until the party of men returned and took him into their possession.

These are only a few out of many similar acts which show the character of Mrs. Daviess. She became

STRATAGEM OF MRS. DAVIESS IN CAPTURING A KENTUCKY ROBBER.   Page 202.

noted all through the frontier settlements of that region during the troublous times in which she lived, not only for her courage and daring, but for her shrewdness in circumventing the stratagems of the wily savages by whom her family were surrounded. Her oldest boy inherited his mother's character, and promised to be one of the most famous Indian fighters of his day, when he met his death at the hands of his savage foes in early manhood.

If Mrs. Williamson and Mrs. Daviess were representative women in the more stormy and rugged scenes of frontier life, Mrs. Elizabeth Estaugh may stand as a true type of the gentle and benevolent matron, brightening her forest home by her kindly presence, and making her influence felt in a thousand ways for good among her neighbors in the lonely hamlet where she chose to live.

Her maiden name was Haddon; she was the oldest daughter of a wealthy and well educated but humbleminded Quaker of London. She was endowed by nature with strength of mind, earnestness, energy, and with a heart overflowing with kindness and warmth of feeling. The education bestowed upon her, was, after the manner of her sect, a highly practical one, such as might be expected to draw forth her native powers by careful training of the mind, without quenching the kindly emotions by which she was distinguished from her early childhood.

At the age of seventeen she made a profession of religion, uniting herself with the Quakers. During her girlhood William Penn visited the house of her father, and greatly interested her by describing his adventures with the Indians in the wilds of Pennsylvania. From that hour her thoughts were directed towards the new world, where so many of her sect had emigrated, and she longed to cross the ocean and take up her abode among them. She pictured to herself the toils and privations of the Quaker-pioneers in that new country, and ardently desired to join them and share their labors and dangers, and alleviate their sufferings by charitably dispensing a portion of that wealth which she was destined to possess.

Her father sympathized with her views and aims, and was at length induced to buy a large tract of land in New Jersey, where he proposed to go and settle in company with his daughter Elizabeth, and there carry out the plans which she had formed. His affairs in England took such a turn that he decided to remain in his native land.

This was a sad disappointment to Elizabeth. She had arrived at the conviction that among her people in the new world was to be her sphere of duty; she felt a call thither which she could not disregard ; and when her father, who was unwilling that the property should lie unimproved, offered the tract of land in New Jersey to any relative who would settle upon it, she gladly availed herself of the proffer, and begged that she might go herself as a pioneer into that far-off wilderness.

It was a sore trial for her parents to part with their beloved daughter; but her character was so stable, and her convictions of duty so unswerving, that at the end of three months and after much prayer, they consented tearfully that Elizabeth should join "the Lord's people in the new world."

Arrangements were accordingly made for her departure, and all that wealth could provide or thoughtful affection devise, was prepared, both for the long voyage across that stormy sea and against the hardships and trials in the forest home which was to be hers. In the spring of 1700 she set sail, accompanied by a poor widow of good sense and discretion, who had been chosen to act as her friend and housekeeper, and two trustworthy men-servants, members of the Society of Friends.

Among the many extraordinary manifestations of strong faith and religious zeal connected with the early settlement of this country, few are more remarkable than this enterprise of Elizabeth Estaugh. Tenderly reared in a delightful home in a great city, where she had been surrounded with pleasing associations from infancy, and where as a lovely young lady she was the idol of the circle of society in which she moved, she was still willing and desirous at the call of religious duty, to separate herself from home, friends, and the pleasures of civilization, and depart to a distant clime and a wild country. Hardly less remarkable and admirable was the self-sacrificing spirit of her parents in giving up their child in obedience to the promptings of her own conscience. We can imagine the parting on the deck of the vessel which was spreading its sails to bear this sweet missionary away from her native land and the beloved of her old home. Angelic love beams and sorrow darkles from the serene countenances of the father, and mother, and daughter, and yet no tear is shed on either side. The vessel drops down the harbor, and the family stand on the wharf straining their eyes to catch the last look from the departing maiden, who leans on the bulwark and answers the silent and sorrowful faces with a heavenly smile of love and pity. Even during the long and tedious voyage Elizabeth never wept. Her sense of duty controlled every other emotion of her soul, and she maintained her martyr-like cheerfulness and serenity to the end.

That part of New Jersey where the Haddon tract lay was at that period an almost unbroken wilderness. Scarcely more than twenty years had then elapsed since the twenty or thirty cabins had been built which formed the germ-settlement out of which grew the city of Brotherly Love, and nine miles of dense forest and a broad river separated the maiden and her household from the people in the hamlet across the Delaware.

The home prepared for her reception stood in a clearing of the forest, three miles from any other dwelling. She arrived in June, when the landscape was smiling in youthful beauty, and it seemed to her as if the arch of heaven was never before so clear and bright, the carpet of the earth never so verdant. As she sat at her window and saw evening close in upon her in that broad forest home, and heard for the first time the mournful notes of the whippoorwill, and the harsh scream of the jay in the distant woods, she was oppressed with a sense of vastness, of infinity, which she never before experienced, not even on the ocean. She remained long in prayer, and when she lay down to sleep beside her matron-friend, no words were spoken between them. The elder, overcome with fatigue, soon sank into a peaceful slumber; but the young enthusiast lay long awake, listening to the lone voice of the whippoorwill complaining to the night. Yet, notwithstanding this prolonged wakefulness, she arose early and looked out upon the lovely landscape. The rising sun pointed to the tallest trees with his golden finger, and was welcomed with a gush of song from a thousand warblers. The poetry in Elizabeth's soul, repressed by the severe plainness of her education, gushed up like a fountain. She dropped on her knees, and with an outburst of prayer, exclaimed fervently, " Oh, Father, very beautiful hast thou made this earth! How beautiful are thy gifts, O Lord!"

To a spirit less meek and brave, the darker shades of the picture would have obscured these cheerful gleams; for the situation was lonely, and the inconveniences innumerable. But Elizabeth easily triumphed over all obstacles, by practical good sense and by the quick promptings of her ingenuity. She was one of those clear, strong natures, who always have a definite aim in view, and who see at once the means best suited to the end. Her first inquiry was, what grain was best adapted to the soil of her farm; and being informed that rye would yield the best, " Then I shall eat rye bread," was the answer.

When winter came, and the gleaming snow spread its unbroken silence over hill and plain, was it not dreary then? It would have been dreary indeed to one who entered upon this mode of life for mere love of novelty, or a vain desire to do something extraordinary. But the idea of extended usefulness, which had first lured this remarkable girl into a path so unusual, sustained her through all her trials. She was too busy to be sad, and leaned too trustingly on her Father's hand to be doubtful of her way. The neighboring Indians soon loved her as a friend, for they always found her truthful, just, and kind. From their teachings she added much to her knowledge of simple medicines. So efficient was her skill, and so prompt her sympathy, that for many miles round, if man, woman, or child were alarmingly ill, they were sure to send for Elizabeth Haddon; and wherever she went, her observing mind gathered some hint for the improvement of farm or dairy. Her house and heart were both large, and as her residence was on the way to the Quaker meeting-house in Newtown, it became a place of universal resort to Friends from all parts of the country traveling that road, as well as an asylum for benighted wanderers.

Late one winter's evening a tinkling of sleigh-bells was heard at the entrance of the clearing, and soon the hoofs of horses were crunching the snow as they passed through the great gate towards the barn. The arrival of strangers was a common occurrence, for the home of Elizabeth Haddon was celebrated far and near as the abode of hospitality. The toil-worn or benighted traveler there found a sincere welcome, and none who enjoyed that friendly shelter and abundant cheer ever departed without regret. But now there was an unwonted stir in that well-ordered family; great logs were piled in the capacious fireplace, and hasty preparations were made as if to receive guests who were more than ordinarily welcome. Elizabeth, looking from the window, had recognized one of the strangers in the sleigh as John Estaugh, with whose preaching years before in London she had been deeply impressed, and ever since she had treasured in her memory many of his words. It was almost like a glimpse of her dear old English home to see him enter, and stepping forward with more than usual cordiality she greeted him, saying,

"Thou art welcome, friend Estaugh, the more so for being entirely unexpected."

"And I am glad to see thee, Elizabeth," he replied, with a friendly shake of the hand, "it was not until after I had landed in America that I heard the Lord had called thee hither before me; but I remember thy father told me how often thou hadst played the settler in the woods, when thou wast quite a little girl."

"I am but a child still," she replied, smiling.

"I trust thou art," he rejoined; "and as for those strong impressions in childhood, I have heard of many cases when they seemed to be prophecies sent from the Lord. When I saw thy father in London, I had even then an indistinct idea that I might sometime be sent to America on a religious visit."

"And hast thou forgotten, friend John, the ear of Indian corn which my father begged of thee for me? I can show it to thee now. Since then I have seen this grain in perfect growth; and a goodly plant it is, I assure thee. See," she continued, pointing to many bunches of ripe corn which hung in their braided husks against the wall of the ample kitchen; "all that, and more, came from a single ear, no bigger than the one thou didst give my father. May the seed sown by thy ministry be as fruitful!" "Amen," replied both the guests.

That evening a severe snow-storm came on, and all night the blast howled round the dwelling. The next morning it was discovered that the roads were rendered impassable by the heavy drifts. The home of

14

Elizabeth had already been made the center of a settlement composed mainly of poor families, who relied largely upon her to aid them in cases of distress. That winter they had been severely afflicted by the fever incident to a new settled country, and Elizabeth was in the habit of making them daily visits, furnishing them with food and medicines.

The storm roused her to an even more energetic benevolence than ordinary. Men, oxen, and sledges were sent out, and pathways were opened; the whole force of Elizabeth's household, under her immediate superintendence, joining in the good work. John Estaugh and his friend tendered their services joyfully, and none worked harder than they. His countenance glowed with the exercise, and a cheerful childlike outbeaming honesty of soul shone forth, attracting the kind but modest regards of the maiden. It seemed to her as if she had found in him a partner in the good work which she had undertaken.

When the paths had been made, Elizabeth set out with a sled-load of provisions to visit her patients, and John Estaugh asked permission to accompany her.

While they were standing together by the bedside of the aged and suffering, she saw her companion in a new and still more attractive guise. His countenance expressed a sincerity of sympathy warmed by rays of love from the Sun of mercy and righteousness itself. He spoke to the feeble and the invalid words of kindness and consolation, and his voice was modulated to a deep tone of tenderness, when he took the little children in his arms.

The following " first day," which world's people call the Sabbath, meeting was attended at Newtown by the whole family, and then John Estaugh was moved by the Spirit to speak words that sank into the hearts of his hearers. It was a discourse on the trials and temptations of daily life, drawing a contrast between this course of earthly probation, with its toils, sufferings, and sorrows, and that higher life, with its rewards to the faithful beyond the grave.

Elizabeth listened to the preacher with meek attention; he seemed to be speaking to her, for all the lessons of the discourse were applicable to herself. As the deep tones of the good man ceased to vibrate in her ears, and there was stillness for a full half hour in the house, she pondered over it deeply. The impression made by the young preacher seemed to open a new window in her soul; he was a God-sent messenger, whose character and teachings would lift still higher her life, and sanctify her mission with a holier inspiration.

A few days of united duties and oneness of heart made John and Elizabeth more thoroughly acquainted with each other than they could have been by years of ordinary fashionable intercourse.

They were soon obliged to separate, the young preacher being called to other meetings of his sect in New Jersey and Pennsylvania. When they bade each other farewell, neither knew that they would ever meet again, for John Estaugh's duty might call him from the country ere another winter, and his avocations in the new world were absorbing and continuous. With a full heart, but with the meekness characteristic of her sect, Elizabeth turned away to her daily round of good works with a new and holier zeal.

In May following they met again. John Estaugh,

in company with numerous other Friends, stopped at
her house to lodge while on their way to the quarterly
meeting at Salem. The next day a cavalcade started
from her hospitable door on horseback, for that was
before the days of wagons in Jersey.

John Estaugh, always kindly in his impulses, busied
himself with helping a lame and very ugly old woman,
and left his hostess to mount her horse as she could.
Most young women would have felt slighted; but in
Elizabeth's noble soul the quiet, deep tide of feeling
rippled with an inward joy. "He is always kindest
to the poor and neglected," thought she; "verily he
is a good youth."

She was leaning over the side of her horse, to
adjust the buckle of the girth, when he came up on
horseback and enquired if anything was out of order.
She thanked him, with slight confusion of manner,
and a voice less calm than her usual utterance. He
assisted her to mount, and they trotted along leisurely
behind the procession of guests, speaking of the soil
and climate of this new country, and how wonderfully
the Lord had here provided a home for his chosen
people. Presently the girth began to slip, and the
saddle turned so much on one side that Elizabeth was
obliged to dismount. It took some time to readjust
the girth, and when they again started, the company
were out of sight. There was brighter color than
usual in the maiden's cheeks, and unwonted radiance
in her mild, deep eyes.

After a short silence, she said, in a voice slightly
tremulous, "Friend John, I have a subject of importance on my mind, and one which nearly interests thee.
I am strongly impressed that the Lord has sent thee

to me as a partner for life. I tell thee my impression frankly, but not without calm and deep reflection, for matrimony is a holy relation, and should be entered into with all sobriety. If thou hast no light on the subject, wilt thou gather into the stillness and reverently listen to thy own inward revealings? Thou art to leave this part of the country to-morrow, and not knowing when I should see thee again, I felt moved to tell thee what lay upon my mind."

The young man was taken by surprise. Though accustomed to that suppression of emotion which characterizes his religious sect, the color came and went rapidly in his face, for a moment. But he soon became calmer, and replied, "This thought is new to me, Elizabeth, and I have no light thereon. Thy company has been right pleasant to me, and thy countenance ever reminds me of William Penn's title-page, '*Innocency with her open face.*' I have seen thy kindness to the poor, and the wise management of thy household. I have observed, too, that thy warm-heartedness is tempered with a most excellent discretion, and that thy speech is ever sincere. Assuredly, such is the maiden I would ask of the Lord as a most precious gift; but I never thought of this connection with thee. I came to this country solely on a religious visit, and it might distract my mind to entertain this subject at present. When I have discharged the duties of my mission, we will speak further."

"It is best so," rejoined the maiden, "but there is one thing disturbs my conscience. Thou hast spoken of my true speech; and yet, friend John, I have deceived thee a little, even now, while we conferred together on a subject so serious. I know not from what weakness the temptation came, but I will not hide it from thee. I allowed thee to suppose, just now, that I was fastening the girth of my horse securely; but, in plain truth, I was loosening the girth, John, that the saddle might slip, and give me an excuse to fall behind our friends; for I thought thou wouldst be kind enough to come and ask if I needed thy services."

They spoke no further upon this topic; but when John Estaugh returned to England in July, he pressed her hand affectionately, as he said, "Farewell, Elizabeth: if it be the Lord's will I shall return to thee soon."

The young preacher made but a brief sojourn in England. The Society of Friends in London appreciated his value as a laborer among them and would have been pleased to see him remain, but they knew how fruitful of good had been his labors among the brethren in the wilderness, and deemed it a wise resolution when he informed them that he should shortly return to America. Early in September he set sail from London and reached New York the following month. A few days after landing he journeyed on horseback to the dwelling where Elizabeth was awaiting him, and they were soon after married at Newtown Meeting according to the simple form of the Society of Friends. Neither of them made any change of dress for the occasion; there was no wedding feast; no priest or magistrate was present; in the presence of witnesses they simply took each other by the hand and solemnly promised to be kind and faithful to each other. The wedded pair then quietly returned to their happy home, prepared to resume together that life of good words and kind deeds which each had thus far pursued alone.

Thrice during the long period of their union did she cross the Atlantic to visit her aged parents, and not seldom he left her for a season when called to preach abroad. These temporary separations were hard for her to bear, but she cheerfully gave him up to follow in the path of his duty wherever it might lead him. Amid her cares and pleasures as a wife she neither grew self-absorbed nor, like many of her sex, bounded her benevolence within the area of the household. Her heart was too large, her charity too abounding, to do that, and her sense of duty to her fellow-men always dominated that narrow feeling which concentrates kindness on self or those nearest to one. While her husband performed his noble work in the care of souls, she pursued her career within the sphere where it was so allotted. As a housewife she was notable; to her might be applied the words of King Lemuel, in the Proverbs of Solomon, celebrating and describing the good wife, "and her works praised her in the gates." As a neighbor she was generous and sympathetic; she stretched out her hand to the poor and needy; she was at once a guardian and a minister of mercy to the settlement.

When, after forty years of happiness in wedlock, her husband was taken from her, she gave evidence of her appreciation of his worth in a preface which she published to one of his religious tracts entitled, "Elizabeth Estaugh's testimony concerning her beloved husband, John Estaugh." In this preface she says:

"Since it pleased Divine Providence so highly to

favor me with being the near companion to this dear worthy, I must give some small account of him. Few, if any, in a married state, ever lived in sweeter harmony than we did. He was a pattern of moderation in all things; not lifted up with any enjoyments, nor cast down at disappointments; a man endowed with many good gifts, which rendered him very agreeable to his friends, and much more to me, his wife, to whom his memory is most dear and precious."

Elizabeth survived her excellent husband twenty years, useful and honored to the last. The monthly meeting of Haddonfield, in a published testimonial, speaks of her thus:

" She was endowed with great natural abilities, which, being sanctified by the Spirit of Christ, were much improved; whereby she became qualified to act in the affairs of the church, and was a serviceable member, having been clerk to the woman's meeting nearly fifty years, greatly to their satisfaction. She was a sincere sympathizer with the afflicted; of a benevolent disposition, and in distributing to the poor, was desirous to do it in a way most profitable and durable to them, and, if possible, not to let the right hand know what the left did. Though in a state of affluence as to this world's wealth, she was an example of plainness and moderation. Her heart and house were open to her friends, whom to entertain seemed one of her greatest pleasures. Prudently cheerful and well knowing the value of friendship, she was careful not to wound it herself nor to encourage others in whispering supposed failings or weaknesses. Her last illness brought great bodily pain, which she bore with much calmness of mind and sweetness of spirit. She departed this life as one falling asleep, full of days, "like unto a shock of corn fully ripe.' "

The maiden name of this gentle and useful woman has been preserved in Haddonfield, thus appropriately commemorating her manifold services in the early days of the settlement of which she was the pioneer-mother.

CHAPTER X.

ROMANCE OF THE BORDER.

THE romance of border-life is inseparably associated with woman, being her natural attendant during her wanderings through the wilderness. A distinguished American orator has suggested that a series of novels might be written founded upon the true stories of the border-women of our country. Such a contribution to our literature has thus far been made only to a limited extent. The reason for this deficiency will be obvious on a moment's reflection. The *true stories* of the pioneer-wives and mothers are often as interesting as any work of fiction, and need no embellishment from the imagination of a writer, because they are crowded with incidents and situations as thrilling as those which form the staple out of which novels are fabricated ; love and adventure, hair-breadth escapes, heart-rending tragedies on the frontier, are thus woven into a narrative of absorbing and permanent interest, *permanent* because it is part of the history and biography of America. Some of the truest of these stories are those which are most deeply fraught with tenderness and romance. What is more calculated to move the mind and heart of man for example than a story of two lovers environed by some deadly danger, or of separation and reunion, or a love faithful unto death?

Many years ago a young pioneer traveling across the plains met a lady to whom he became attached, and after a short courtship they were united in marriage. A trip over the plains in those days was not one to be chosen for a honey-moon excursion but the pair bore their labors and privations cheerfully; perils and hardships only seemed to draw them closer together, and they were looking forward to a home on the Pacific slope where in plenty and repose they would be indemnified for the pains and fatigues of the journey. But their life's romance was destined, alas! to a sudden and mournful end. While crossing one of the rapid mountain streams their boat filled with water, and though the young man struggled manfully to gain the shore with his bride, the rush of the torrent bore them down and they sank to rise no more. An hour later their bodies were found locked together in a last embrace. The rough mountaineers had not the heart to unclasp that embrace but buried them by the side of the river in one grave.

The Indian was of course an important factor in the composition of these border romances. He was generally the villain in the plot of the story, and too often a successful villain whose wiles or open attacks were the means of separating two lovers. These tales have often a tragical catastrophe, but sometimes the *denouement* is a happy one, thanks to the courage and constancy of the heroine or hero.

* Among the adventurers whom Daniel Boone the famous hunter and Indian fighter of Kentucky, describes as having re-inforced his little colony was a young gentleman named Smith, who had been a major in the militia of Virginia, and possessed a full share of the gallantry and noble spirit of his native State. In the absence of Boone he was chosen, on account of his military rank and talent, to command the rude citadel which contained all the wealth of this patriarchal band, their wives, their children, and their herds. It held also an object particularly dear to this young soldier—a lady, the daughter of one of the settlers, to whom he had pledged his affections. It came to pass upon a certain day when a siege was just over, tranquillity restored, and the employment of husbandry resumed, that this young lady, with a lady companion, strolled out, as young ladies in love are very apt to do, along the bank of the Kentucky River.

Having rambled about for some time they espied a canoe lying by the shore, and in a frolic stepped into it, with the determination of visiting a neighbor on the opposite bank. It seems that they were not so well skilled in navigation as the Lady of the Lake who paddled her own canoe very dexterously; for instead of gliding to the point of destination they were whirled about by the stream, and at length thrown on a sand-bar from which they were obliged to wade to the shore. Full of the mirth excited by their wild adventure they hastily arranged their dresses and were proceeding to climb the bank, when three Indians rushed from a

* Potter's Life of Daniel Boone.

neighboring covert, seized the fair wanderers, and
forced them away. Their savage captors evincing no
sympathy for their distress, nor allowing them time
for rest or reflection, hurried them along during the
whole day by rugged and thorny paths. Their shoes
were worn off by the rocks, their clothes torn, and
their feet and limbs lacerated and stained with blood.
To heighten their misery one of the savages began to
make love to Miss ———, (the intended of Major S.)
and while goading her along with a pointed stick,
promised in recompense for her sufferings to make her
his squaw. This at once roused all the energies of her
mind and called its powers into action. In the hope that
her friends would soon pursue them she broke the twigs
as she passed along and delayed the party as much as
possible by tardy and blundering steps. The day and
the night passed, and another day of agony had nearly
rolled over the heads of these afflicted girls, when their
conductors halted to cook a hasty repast of buffalo
meat.

The ladies meanwhile were soon missed from the
garrison. The natural courage and sagacity of Smith
now heightened by love, gave him the wings of the
wind and the fierceness of the tiger. The light traces
of feminine feet led him to the place of embarkation;
the canoe was traced to the opposite shore; the deep
prints of the moccasin in the sand told the rest of the
story.

The agonized Smith, accompanied by a few of his
best woodsmen, pursued the spoil-encumbered foe.
The track once discovered they kept it with that unerring sagacity so peculiar to our hunters. The bended
grass, the disentangled briars, and the compressed

TWO KENTUCKY GIRLS CAPTURED BY INDIANS.

Page 290.

shrubs afforded the only, but to them the certain indication of the route of the enemy. When they had
sufficiently ascertained the general course of the retreat of the Indians, Smith quitted the trace, assuring
his companions that they would fall in with them at
the pass of a certain stream-head for which he now
struck a direct course, thus gaining on the foe who
had taken the most difficult paths.

Having arrived at the stream, they traced its course
until they discovered the water newly thrown upon
the rocks. Smith, leaving his party, now crept forward upon his hands and knees, until he discovered
one of the savages seated by a fire, and with a deliber-
ate aim shot him through the heart. The women
rushed towards their deliverer, and recognizing Smith,
clung to him in the transport of newly awakened joy
and gratitude; while a second Indian sprang towards
him with his tomahawk. Smith, disengaging himself
from the ladies, aimed a blow at his antagonist with
his rifle, which the savage avoided by springing aside,
but at the same moment the latter received a mortal
wound from another hand. The other and only remaining Indian fell in attempting to escape. Smith with
his interesting charge returned in triumph to the fort
where his gallantry no doubt was repaid by the sweet-
est of all rewards.

The May flower, or trailing arbutus, has been aptly
styled our national flower. It lifts its sweet face in
the desolate and rugged hillside, and flourishes in the
chilly air and earth of early spring. So amid the
rude scenes of frontier-life, love and romance peep
out, and courtship is conducted in log cabins and even
in more untoward places.

A tradition of the early settlement of Auburn, New York, relates that while Captain Hardenberg, the stout young miller, was busy with his sacks of grain in his little log-mill, he was unexpectedly assaulted and over-whelmed with the arrows not of the savages but of love. The sweet eyes as well as the blooming health and courage of the daughter of Roeliffe Brinkerhoff who had been sent by her father to the mill, made young Hardenberg capitulate, and during the hour while she was waiting for the grist he managed thor-oughly to assure her of the state of his affections; the courtship thus well begun resulted soon after in a wedding.

The imagination of the poet garnering the anecdotes and early traditions of the frontier around which lin-gers an aroma of love, has clothed them with new life, adorned them with bright colors, endowed them with fresh and vernal perfume and then woven them into a wreath with the magic art of poesy. From out of a group of stern features on Plymouth rock, graven with the deep lines of austere and almost cruel duty, the sweet face of Rose Standish looks winningly at us. The rugged captain of the Pilgrim band wooes Priscilla Mullins, through his friend John Alden, and finds too late that love does not prove fortunate when made by proxy; and Evangeline, maid, wife and widow comes back to us in beauty and sorrow from the far Acadian border. These romances of our eastern country have been fortunate in having a poet to make them immor-tal. But the West is equally fruitful in incidents which furnish material, and only lack the poet or novelist to work them up into enduring form.

The western country seems naturally fitted in many

ways for love and romance. In that region the mind is uncramped and unfettered by the excessive schooling and over-training which prevails in the older settlements of the East. The heart beats more freely and warmly when its current is unchecked by conventionalities. Life is more intense in the West. The transitions of life are more frequent and startling. Both men and things are continually changing. In such a society impulse governs largely: the cooler and more selfish faculties of man's nature are less dominant. When we add to these conditions, the changes, hardships, and enforced separations of the frontier as frequent concomitants, we have exactly a state of society which is fruitful in romantic incidents—brides torn from their husband's embrace and hurried away; but restored as suddenly and strangely; two faithful lovers parted forever or re-united miraculously; and thrilling scenes in love's melodrama acted and re-acted on different stages but always with startling effect.

The effects of the romantic incidents in the lives of our pioneer women are also heightened by the extraordinary freshness and ever-changing scenery of the wilderness. Nature there spreads out like a mighty canvas: the forest, the mountains, and the prairies show clear and distinct through the crystal air so that peak and tree and even the tall blades of grass are outlined with a microscopic nearness. Over this vivid surface bison are browsing, and antelopes gambolling; plumed warriors flit by on their ponies, as the pioneer-men and women with wagons, oxen and horses are moving westward. This is the scene where love springs spontaneously out of the close companionship which danger enforces.

The story of the Chase family is an illustration of the adage that truth is often stranger than fiction, and might readily furnish the groundwork upon which the genius of some future Cooper could construct an American romance of thrilling interest.

The stage whereon this drama of real life was acted lay in that rich, broad expanse between the Arkansas and the South Platte Rivers. The time, 1847. The principal actors were the Chase family, consisting of old Mr. Chase, his wife, sons, and grandsons, Mary, his daughter, LaBonté and Kilbuck two famous hunters and mountaineers, Antoine a guide and Arapahoe Indians.

The scene opens with a view of three white-tilted Conestoga wagons or " prairie schooners," each drawn by four pair of oxen rumbling along through a plain enameled with the verdure and many tinted flowers of spring. The day is drawing to its close, and the rays of the sinking sun throw a mellow light over a waving sea of vernal herbage. The wagons are driven by the sons of Mr. Chase and contain the women and the household goods of the family. Behind the great swaying " schooners " walk the men with shouldered rifles, and a troup of mounted men have just galloped up to bid adieu to the departing emigrants. From out this group, the mild face of Mary Chase beams with a parting smile in response to rough but kindly farewells of these her old friends and neighbors. The last words of warning and God-speed are spoken by the mounted men, who gallop away and leave them making their first stage on a journey which will carry them northward and westward more than two thousand miles from their old home in Missouri.

And now the sun has set, and still in the twilight
the train moves on, stopping as the darkness falls, at a
rich bottom, where the loose cattle, starting some hours
before them, have been driven and corralled. The
oxen are unyoked, the wagons drawn up, so as to
form the sides of a small square. A huge fire is kindled, the women descend and prepare the evening
meal, boiling great kettles of coffee, and baking corn-
cakes in the embers. The whole company stretch
themselves around the fire, and having finished their
repast, address themselves to sweet sleep, such as tired
voyagers over the plains can so well enjoy. The men
of the party are soon soundly slumbering; but the
women, depressed with the thoughts that they are
leaving their home and loved friends and neighbors,
perhaps forever, their hearts filled with forebodings of
danger and misfortune, cast only wakeful eyes upon
the darkened plain or up to the inscrutable stars that
are shining with marvelous brightness in the azure
firmament. Far into the night they wake and watch,
silently weeping until nature is exhausted, and a sleep,
troubled with sad dreams, visits them.

With the first light of morning the camp is astir,
and as the sun rises, the wagons are again rolling
along across the upland prairies, to strike the trail
leading to the south fork of the Platte. Slowly and
hardly, fifteen miles each day, they toil on over the
heavy soil. At night, while in camp, the hours are
beguiled by Antoine, their Canadian guide, who tells
stories of wild life and perilous adventures among the
hunters and trappers who make the prairies and
mountains their home. His descriptions of Indian
fights and slaughters, and of the sufferings and priva-
15

tions endured by the hunters in their arduous life,
fix the attention of the women of the party, and
especially of Mary Chase, who listens with greater
interest because she remembers that such was the life
led by one very dear to her—one long supposed to be
dead, and of whom, since his departure, fifteen years
before, she has heard not a syllable. Her imagination
now pictures him anew, as the most daring of these
adventurous hunters, and conjures up his figure
charging through the midst of yelling savages, or as
stretched on the ground, perishing of wounds, or of
cold and famine.

Among the characters that figure in Antoine's stories is a hunter named La Bonte, made conspicuous
by his deeds of hardihood and daring. At the first
mention of his name Mary's face is suffused with
blushes; not that she for a moment dreamed that it
could be her long lost La Bonte, for she knows that
the name is a common one, but because from associations which still linger in her memory, it recalled a
sad era in her former life, to which she could not
revert without a strange mingling of pleasure and
pain. She remembers the manly form of La Bonte
as she first saw him, and the love which sprang up
between them; and then the parting, with the hope of
speedy reunion. She remembers how two years
passed without tidings of her lover, when, one bitter
day, she met a mountaineer, just returned from the
far West to settle in his native State; and, inquiring
tremblingly after La Bonte, he told how he had met
his death from the Blackfeet Indians in the wild
gorges of the Yellowstone country.

Now, on hearing once more that name, a spring of

sweet and bitter recollections is opened and a vague hope is raised in her breast that the lover of her youth is still alive. She questions the Canadian, "Who was this La Bonte who you say was such a brave mountaineer?" Antoine replies, "He was a fine fellow—strong as a buffalo-bull, a dead shot, cared not a rush for the Indians, left a girl that he loved in Missouri, said the girl did not love him, and so he followed the trail to the mountains. He hasn't gone under yet; be sure of that," says the good natured guide, observing the emotion which Mary showed, and suspecting that she took a more than ordinary interest in the young hunter.

As the guide ceased to speak, Mary turns away and bursts into a flood of tears. The mention of the name of one whom she had long believed dead, and the recital of his praiseworthy qualities, awake the strongest feelings which she had cherished towards one whose loss she still bewails.

The scene now changes to the camp of a party of hunters almost within rifle-shot of the spot where the Chase family are sitting around their evening fire. There are three in this party: one is Kilbuck, so known on the plains, another is a stranger who has chanced to join them, the third is a hunter named *La Bonte*.

The conversation turning on the party encamped near them, the stranger remarks that their name is Chase. La Bonte looks up a moment from the lock of his rifle, which he is cleaning, but either does not hear, or, hearing, does not heed, for he resumes his work. "Traveling alone to the Platte valley," continues the stranger, "they'll lose their hair, sure." "I hope not,"

rejoins Kilbuck, " for there's a girl among them worth
more than that." " Where does she come from,
stranger," inquires La Bonte. " Down below Missouri,
from Tennessee, I hear." " And what's her name ? "
The colloquy is interrupted by the entrance into the
camp of an Arapahoe Indian. The hunters address
him in his own language. They learn from him that
a war-party of his people was out on the Platte-trail
to intercept the traders on their return from the North
Fork. He cautions them against crossing the divide,
as the braves, he says, are " a heap mad, and take
white scalp." The Indian, rewarded for his information with a feast of buffalo-meat, leaves the camp and
starts for the mountains. The hunters pursue their
journey the next day, traveling leisurely along, and
stopping where good grass and abundant game is
found, until, one morning, they suddenly strike a
wheel-track, which left the creek-bank and pursued a
course at right angles to it in the direction of the
divide. Kilbuck pronounces it but a few hours old,
and that of three wagons drawn by oxen. " These are
the wagons of old Chase," says the strange hunter:
" they're going right into the Rapahoe trap," cries
Kilbuck. " I knew the name of Chase years ago,"
says La Bonte in a low tone, " and I should hate the
worst kind to have mischief happen to any one that
bore it. This trail is fresh as paint, and it goes against
me to let these simple critters help the Rapahoes to
their own hair. This child feels like helping them
out of the scrape. What do you say, old hos ? " " I
think with you, my boy," replies Kilbuck, " and go in
for following the wagon-trail and telling the poor critters that there's danger ahead of them. " What's

your talk, stranger?" "I'm with you," answered the latter; and both follow quickly after La Bonte, who gallops away on the trail.

Returning now to the Chase family, we see again the three white-topped wagons rumbling slowly over the rolling prairie and towards the upland ridge of the divide which rose before them, studded with dwarf pines and cedar thickets. They are evidently traveling with caution, for the quick eye of Antoine, the guide, has discovered recent Indian signs upon the trail, and with the keenness of a mountaineer he at once sees that it is that of a war-party, for there were no horses with them and after one or two of the moccasin tracks there was the mark of a rope which trailed upon the ground. This was enough to show him that the Indians were provided with the usual lassoes of skin with which to secure the horses stolen on the expedition. The men of the party accordingly are all mounted and thoroughly armed, the wagons are moving in a line abreast, and a sharp lookout is kept on all sides. The women and children are all consigned to the interior of the wagons and the former also hold guns in readiness to take part in the defense should an attack be made. As they move slowly on their course no Indians make their presence visible and the party are evidently losing their fears if not their caution.

As the shadows are lengthening they reach Black Horse Creek, and corrall their wagons, kindle a fire, and are preparing for the night, when three or four Indians suddenly show themselves on the bluff and making friendly signals approach the camp. Most of the men are away attending to the cattle or collecting fuel, and only old Chase and a grandson fourteen years of age are in the camp. The Indians are hospitably received and regaled with a smoke, after which they gratify their curiosity by examining the articles lying around, and among others which takes their fancy the pot boiling over the fire, with which one of them is about very coolly to walk off, when old Chase, snatching it from the Indian's hands, knocks him down. One of his companions instantly begins to draw the buckskin cover from his gun and is about to take summary vengeance for the insult offered to his companion, when Mary Chase, courageously advancing, places her left hand on the gun which he is in the act of uncovering and with the other points a pistol at his breast.

Whether daunted by this bold act of the girl, or admiring her devotion to her father, the Indian, drawing back with a deep grunt, replaces the cover on his piece and motioning to the other Indians to be peaceable, shakes hands with old Chase, who all this time looks him steadily in the face.

The other whites soon return, the supper is ready, and all hands sit down to the repast. The Indians then gather their buffalo-robes about them and quickly withdraw. In spite of their quiet demeanor, Antoine says they mean mischief. Every precaution is therefore taken against surprise; the mules and horses are hobbled. the oxen only being allowed to run at large; a guard is set around the camp; the fire is extinguished lest the savages should aim by its light at any of the party; and all slept with rifles and pistols ready at their side.

The night, however, passes quietly away, and nothing disturbs the tranquility of the camp except the mournful cry of the prairie wolf chasing the antelope. The sun has now risen; they afe yoking the cattle to the wagons and driving in the mules and horses, when a band of Indians show themselves on the bluff and descending it approach the camp with an air of confidence. They are huge braves, hideously streaked with war-paint, and hide the malignant gleams that shoot from their snaky eyes with assumed smiles and expressions of good nature.

Old Chase, ignorant of Indian treachery and in spite of the warnings of Antoine, offering no obstruction to their approach, has allowed them to enter the camp. What madness! They have divested themselves of their buffalo-robes, and appear naked to the breech-clout and armed with bows and arrows, tomahawks, and scalping knives. Six or seven only come in at first, but others quickly follow, dropping in by twos and threes until a score or more are collected around the wagons.

Their demeanor, at first friendly, changes to insolence and then to fierceness. They demand powder and shot, and when they are refused begin to brandish their tomahawks. A tall chief, motioning to the band to keep back, now accosts Mr. Chase, and through Antoine as an interpreter, informs him that unless the demands of his braves are complied with he will not be responsible for the consequences; that they are out on the war-trail and their eyes red with blood so that they cannot distinguish between white man's and Utah's scalps; that the party and all their women and wagons are in the power of the Indian braves; and therefore that the white chief's best plan will be to make what terms he can ; that all they require is that they shall give up their guns and ammunition on the prairie and all their mules and horses, retaining only the medicine-buffaloes (the oxen) to draw their wagons. By this time the oxen have been yoked to the teams and the teamsters stand whip in hand ready for the order to start. Old Chase trembles with rage at the insolent demand. "Not a grain of powder to save my life," he yells ; "put out boys !" As he turns to mount his horse which stands ready saddled, the Indians leap upon the wagons and others rush against the men who make a brave fight in their defence. Mary, who sees her father struck to the ground, springs with a shrill cry to his assistance at the moment when a savage, crimson with paint and looking like a red demon, bestrides his prostrate body, brandishing a glittering knife in the air preparatory to plunging it into the old man's heart. All is wild confusion. The whites are struggling heroically against overpowering numbers. A single volley of rifles is heard and three Indians bite the dust. A moment later and the brave defenders are disarmed amid the shrieks of the women and the children and the triumphant whoops of the savages.

Mary, flying to her father's rescue, has been overtaken by a huge Indian, who throws his lasso over her shoulders and drags her to the earth, then drawing his scalping-knife he is about to tear the gory trophy from her head. The girl, rising upon her knees, struggles towards the spot where her father lies, now bathed in blood. The Indian jerks the lariat violently and drags her on her face, and with a wild yell rushes to complete the bloody work.

At that instant a yell as fierce as his own is echoed from the bluff, and looking up he sees La Bonte charging down the declivity, his long hair and the fringes of his garments waving in the breeze, his trusty rifle supported in his right arm, and hard after him Kilbuck and the stranger galloping with loud shouts to the scene of action. As La Bonte races madly down the side of the bluff, he catches sight of the girl as the ferocious savage is dragging her over the ground. A cry of horror and vengeance escapes his lips, as driving his spurs to the rowels into his steed he bounds like an arrow to the rescue. Another instant and he is upon his foe; pushing the muzzle of his rifle against the broad chest of the Indian he pulled the trigger, literally blowing out the savage's heart. Dropping his rifle, he wheels his trained horse and drawing a pistol from his belt he charges the enemy among whom Kilbuck and the stranger are dealing death-blows. The Indians, panic-stricken by the suddenness of the attack, turn and flee, leaving several of their number dead upon the field.

Mary, with her arms bound to her body by the lasso, and with her eyes closed to receive the fatal stroke, hears the defiant shout of La Bonte, and glancing up between her half-opened eyelids, sees the wild figure of the mountaineer as he sends the bullet to the heart of her foe. When the Indians flee, La Bonte, the first to run to her aid, cuts the skin-rope, raises her from the ground, looks long and intently in her face, and sees his never-to-be-forgotten Mary Chase. "What! can it be you, Mary?" he exclaims, gazing at the trembling maiden, who hardly believes her eyes as she returns his gaze and recognizes in her deliverer her former lover. She only sobs and clings closer to him in speechless gratitude and love.

Turning from these lovers reunited so miraculously, we see stretched on the battle-field the two grandsons of Mr. Chase, fine lads of fourteen or fifteen, who after fighting like men fall dead pierced with arrows and lances. Old Chase and his sons are slightly wounded, and Antoine shot through the neck and half scalped. The dead boys are laid tenderly beneath the prairie-sod, the wounds of the others are dressed, and the following morning the party continue their journey to the Platte. The three hunters guide and guard them on their way, Mary riding on horseback by the side of her lover.

For many days they pursued their journey, but with feelings far different from those with which they had made its earlier stages. Old Mr. Chase marches on doggedly and in silence; his resolution to seek a new home on the banks of the Columbia has been shaken more by the loss of his grandsons, than by the fatigues and privations incident to the march. The unbidden tears often steal down the cheeks of the women, who cast many a longing look behind them towards the southeastern horizon, far beyond whose purple rim lay their old home. The South Fork of the Platte has been passed, Laramie reached, and for a fortnight the lofty summits of the mountains which overhang the "pass" to California have been in sight; but when they strike the broad trail which would conduct them to their promised land in the valley of the Columbia, the party pause, gaze for a moment steadfastly at the mountain-summits, and then as if by a common impulse, the heads of the horses and oxen are faced to

the east, and men, women, and children toss their hats
and bonnets in the air, hurrahing lustily for home as
the huge wagons roll down along the banks of the
river Platte. The closing scene in this romantic
melodrama was the marriage of Mary and La Bonte,
in Tennessee, four months after the rescue of the
Chase family from the Indians.

The following "romance of the forest" we believe
has never before been published. The substance of it
was communicated to the writer by a gentleman who
received it from his grandfather, one of the early settlers of Michigan.

In the year 1762 the Great Pontiac, the Indian Na-
poleon of the Northwest, had his headquarters in a
small secluded island at the opening of Lake St. Clair.
Here he organized, with wonderful ability and secrecy,
a wide-reaching conspiracy, having for its object the
destruction of every English garrison and settlement
in Michigan. His envoys, with blood-stained hatchets,
had been despatched to the various Indian tribes of
the region, and wherever these emblems of butchery
had been accepted the savage hordes were gathering,
and around their bale-fires in the midnight pantomimes
of murder were concentrating their excitable natures
into a burning focus which would light their path to
carnage and rapine.

While these lurid clouds, charged with death and
destruction, were gathering, unseen, about the heads
of the adventurous pioneers, who had penetrated that
beautiful region, a family of eastern settlers, named
Rouse, arrived in the territory, and, disregarding the
admonitions of the officers in the fort at Detroit,
pushed on twenty miles farther west and planted

themselves in the heart of one of those magnificent oak-openings which the Almighty seems to have designed as parks and pleasure-grounds for the sons and daughters of the forest.

Miss Anna Rouse, the only daughter of the family, had been betrothed before her departure from New York State to a young man named James Philbrick, who had afterward gone to fight the French and Indians. It was understood that upon his return he was to follow the Rouse family to Michigan, where, upon his arrival, the marriage was to take place.

In a few months young Philbrick reached the appointed place, and in the following week married Miss Rouse in the presence of a numerous assemblage of soldiers and settlers, who had come from the military posts and the nearest plantations to join in the festivities.

All was gladness and hilarity; the hospitality was bounteous, the company joyous, the bridegroom brave and manly, and the bride lovely as a wild rose. When the banquet was ready the guests trooped into the room where it was spread, and even the sentinels who had been posted beside the muskets in the door-yard, seeing no signs of prowling savages, had entered the house and were enjoying the feast. Scarcely had they abandoned their post when an ear-piercing war-whoop silenced in a moment the joyous sound of the revelers. The soldiers rushed to the door only to be shot down. A few succeeded in recovering their arms, and made a desperate fight. Meanwhile the savages battered down the doors, and leaped in at the windows. The bridegroom was shot, and left for dead, as he was assisting to conceal his bride, and a gigantic warrior, seizing the latter, bore her away into the darkness. After a short but terrific struggle, the savages were driven out of the house, but the defenders were so crippled by their losses and by the want of arms which the enemy had carried away, that it was judged best not to attempt to pursue the Indians, who had disappeared as suddenly as they came.

When the body of the bridegroom was lifted up it was discovered that his heart still beat, though but faintly. Restoratives were administered, and he slowly came back to life, and to the sad consciousness that all that could make life happy to him was gone for ever.

The family soon after abandoned their new home and moved to Detroit, owing to the danger of fresh attacks from Pontiac and his confederates. Years rolled away; young Philbrick, as soon as he recovered from his wounds, took part in the stirring scenes of the war, and strove to forget, in turmoil and excitement, the loss of his fair young bride. But in vain. Her remembrance in the fray nerved his arm to strike, and steadied his eye to launch the bullet at the heart of the hated foes who had bereft him of his dearest treasure; and in the stillness of the night his imagination pictured her, the cruel victim of her barbarous captors.

Peace came in 1763, and he then learned that she had been carried to Canada. He hastened down the St. Lawrence and passed from settlement to settlement, but could gain no tidings of her. After two years, spent in unavailing search, he came back a sad and almost broken-hearted man.

Her image, as she appeared when last he saw her,

all radiant in youth and beauty, haunted his waking hours, and in his dreams she was with him as a visible presence. Months, years rolled away; he gave her up as dead, but he did not forget his long-lost bride.

One summer's day, while sitting in his cabin in Michigan, in one of those beautiful natural parks, where he had chosen his abode, he heard a light step, and, looking up, saw his bride standing before him, beautiful still, but with a chastened beauty which told of years of separation and grief.

Her story was a long one. When she was borne away from the marriage feast by her savage captor, she was seen by an old squaw, the wife of a famous chief who had just lost her own daughter, and being attracted by the beauty of Miss Rouse, she protected her from violence, and finally adopted her. Twice she escaped, but was recaptured. The old squaw afterwards took her a thousand miles into the wilderness, and watched her with the ferocious tenderness that the tigress shows for her young. At length, after nearly six years, her Indian mother died. She succeeded then in making her escape, traveled four hundred miles on foot, reached the St. Lawrence, and after passing through great perils and hardships, arrived at Detroit. There she soon found friends, who relieved her wants and conveyed her to her husband, whom she had remembered with fondness and loved with constancy during all the weary years of her captivity.

CHAPTER XI.

A HUNDRED ills brood over the cabin in the wilderness. Some are ever-present; others lie in wait, and start forth at intervals.

Labor, Solitude, Fear; these are the companions of woman on the border: to these come other visitants—weariness, and that longing, yearning, pining of the heart which the Germans so beautifully term *sehnsucht*—hunger, vigils, bodily pain and sickness, the biting cold, the drenching storm, the fierce heat, with savage eyes of man and beast glaring from the thicket. Then sorrow takes bodily shape and enters the house: loved ones are borne away—the child, or the father, or saddest of all, the mother; the long struggle is over, and the devoted woman of the household lays her wasted form beneath the grassy sod of the cabin yard.

Bereavement is hard to bear in even the houses where comfort, ease, and luxury surround the occupants, where friends and kinsfolk crowd to pour out sympathy and consolation. But what must it be in the rude cabin on the lonely border? The grave hollowed out in the hard soil of the little inclosure, the rough shell-coffin hewn with tears from the forest tree, the sorrowing household ranged in silence beside the form which will gladden the loneliness of that stricken

(239)

family no longer, and then the mourners turn away and go back to their homely toils.

If from the time of the landing we could recall the long procession of the actors and the events of border-life, and pass them before the eye in one great moving panorama, how somber would be the colors of that picture! All along the grand march what scenes of captivity, suffering, bereavement, sorrow, and in these scenes, woman the most prominent figure, for she was the constant actress in this great drama of woe!

The carrying away and the return of captives in war has furnished themes by which poets and artists in all ages have moved the heart of man. The breaking up of homes, the violent separations of those who are kindred by blood, and the sundering for ever of family ties were ordinary and every day incidents in the border-wars of our country: but the frequency of such occurrences does not detract from the mournful interest with which they are always fraught.

At the close of the old French and Indian War, Colonel Henry Bouquet stipulated with the Indian tribes on the Ohio frontier as one of the conditions of peace that they should restore all the captives which they had taken. This was agreed to, and on his return march he was met by a great company of settlers in search of their lost relatives. "Husbands found their wives and parents their children, from whom they had been separated for years. Women frantic between hope and fear, were running hither and thither, looking piercingly into the face of every child, to find their own, which, perhaps, had died—and then such shrieks of agony! Some of the little captives shrank from their own forgotten mothers, and hid in terror in the blankets of the squaws that had adopted them. Some that had been taken away young, had grown up and married Indian husbands or Indian wives, and now stood utterly bewildered with conflicting emotions. A young Virginian had found his wife ; but his little boy, not two years old when captured, had been torn from her, and had been carried off, no one knew whither. One day a warrior came in, leading a child. No one seemed to own it. But soon the mother knew her offspring and screaming with joy, folded her son to her bosom. An old woman had lost her granddaughter in the French war, nine years before. All her other relatives had died under the knife. Searching, with trembling eagerness, in each face, she at last recognized the altered features of her child. But the girl who had forgotten her native tongue, returned no answer, and made no sign. The old woman groaned, wept, and complained bitterly, that the daughter she had so often sung to sleep on her knees, had forgotten her in her old age. Soldiers and officers were alike overcome. 'Sing,' whispered Bouquet, 'sing the song you used to sing.' As the low, trembling tones began to ascend, the wild girl gave one sudden start, then listening for a moment longer, her frame shaking like an ague, she burst into a passionate flood of tears. That was sufficient. She was the lost child. All else had been effaced from her memory, but the music of the nursery-song. During her captivity she had heard it in her dreams."

Another story of the same character is that of Frances Slocum, the "Lost child of Wyoming," which though perhaps familiar to some of our readers, will bear repeating.

16

In the time of the Revolution the house of Mr. Slocum in the Wyoming valley, was attacked by a party
of Delawares. The inmates of the house, at the moment of the surprise, were Mrs. Slocum and four young
children, the eldest of whom was a son aged thirteen,
the second, a daughter aged nine, the third, Frances
Slocum, aged five, and a little son aged two and a
half.

The girl, aged nine years old, appears to have had
the most presence of mind, for while the mother ran
into a copse of wood near by, and Frances attempted
to secrete herself behind a staircase, the former seized
her little brother, the youngest above mentioned, and
ran off in the direction of the fort. True she could
not make rapid progress, for she clung to the child, and
not even the pursuit of the savages could induce her
to drop her charge. The Indians did not pursue her
far, and laughed heartily at the panic of the little girl,
while they could not but admire her resolution. Allowing her to make her escape, they returned to the
house, and after helping themselves to such articles as
they chose, prepared to depart.

The mother seems to have been unobserved by
them, although, with a yearning bosom, she had so disposed of herself that while she was screened from
observation she could notice all that occurred. But
judge of her feelings at the moment when they were
about to depart, as she saw her little Frances taken
from her hiding place, and preparations made to carry
her away into captivity. The sight was too much for
maternal tenderness to endure. Rushing from her
place of concealment, she threw herself upon her
knees at the feet of the captors, and with the most

earnest entreaties pleaded for the restoration of the child. But their bosoms were made of sterner stuff than to yield even to the most eloquent and affectionate entreaties of a mother, and with characteristic stoicism they prepared to depart. Deaf alike to the cries of the mother, and the shrieks of the child, Frances was slung over the shoulder of a stalwart Indian with as much indifference as though she were a slaughtered fawn.

The long, lingering look which the mother gave to her child, as her captors disappeared in the forest, was the last glimpse of her sweet features that she ever had. But the vision was for many a long year ever present to her fancy. As the Indian threw the child over his shoulder, her hair fell over her face, and the mother could never forget how the tears streamed down her cheeks, when she brushed it away as if to catch a last sad look of the mother from whom, her little arms outstretched, she implored assistance in vain.

These events cast a shadow over the remaining years of Mrs. Slocum. She lived to see many bright and sunny days in that beautiful valley—bright and sunny, alas! to her no longer. She mourned for the lost one, of whom no tidings, at least during her pilgrimage, could be obtained. After her sons grew up, the youngest of whom, by the way, was born but a few months subsequent to the events already narrated, obedient to the charge of their mother, the most unwearied efforts were made to ascertain what had been the fate of the lost sister. The forest between the Susquehanna and the Great Lakes, and even the most distant wilds of Canada, were traversed by the brothers in vain, nor could any information respecting her be derived from the Indians. Once, indeed, during an excursion of one of the brothers into the vast wilds of the West, a white woman, long ago captive, came to him in the hopes of finding a brother; but after many anxious efforts to discover evidences of relationship, the failure was as decisive as it was mutually sad.

There was yet another kindred occurrence, still more painful. One of the many hapless female captives in the Indian country becoming acquainted with the inquiries prosecuted by the Slocum family, presented herself to Mrs. Slocum, trusting that in her she might find her long lost mother. Mrs. Slocum was touched by her appearance, and fain would have claimed her. She led the stranger about the house and yards to see if there were any recollections by which she could be identified as her own lost one. But there was nothing written upon the pages of memory to warrant the desired conclusion, and the hapless captive returned in bitter disappointment to her forest home. In process of time these efforts were all relinquished as hopeless. The lost Frances might have fallen beneath the tomahawk or might have proved too tender a flower for transplantation into the wilderness. Conjecture was baffled, and the mother, with a sad heart, sank into the grave, as did also the father, believing with the Hebrew patriarch that the "child was not."

Long years passed away and the memory of little Frances was forgotten, save by two brothers and a sister, who, though advanced in the vale of life, could not forget the family tradition of the lost one. Indeed it had been the dying charge of their mother that they must never relinquish their exertions to discover Frances.

Fifty years and more had passed since the disappearance of little Frances, when news came to the surviving members of the bereaved family that she was still alive. She had been adopted into the tribe of the Miami Indians, and was passing her days as a squaw in the lodges of that people.

The two surviving brothers and their sister undertook a journey to see, and if possible, to reclaim, the long lost Frances. Accompanied by an interpreter whom they had engaged in the Indian country, they reached at last the designated place and found their sister. But alas! how changed! Instead of the fair-haired and laughing girl, the picture yet living in their imagination, they found her an aged and thorough-bred squaw in everything but complexion. She was sitting when they entered her lodge, composed of two large log-houses connected by a shed, with her two daughters, the one about twenty-three years old, and the other about thirty-three, and three or four pretty grandchildren. The closing hours of the journey had been made in perfect silence, deep thoughts struggling in the bosoms of all. On entering the lodge, the first exclamation of one of the brothers was,—" Oh, God! is that my sister!" A moment afterward, and the sight of her thumb, disfigured in childhood, left no doubt as to her identity. The following colloquy, conducted through the interpreter, ensued:

" What was your name when a child ?"

" I do not recollect."

" What do you remember ?"

"My father, my mother, the long river, the staircase under which I hid when they came."

"How came you to lose your thumb-nail?"

"My brother hammered it off a long time ago, when I was a very little girl at my father's house."

"Do you know how many brothers and sisters you had?"

She then mentioned them, and in the order of their ages.

"Would you know your name if you should hear it repeated?"

"It is a long time since, and perhaps I should not."

"Was it Frances?"

At once a smile played upon her features, and for a moment there seemed to pass over the face what might be called the shadow of an emotion, as she answered, "Yes."

Other reminiscences were awakened, and the recognition was complete. But how different were the emotions of the parties! The brothers paced the lodge in agitation. The civilized sister was in tears. The other, obedient to the affected stoicism of her adopted race, was as cold, unmoved, and passionless as marble.

The brothers and sister returned unable, after urgent and loving entreaties, to win back their tawny sister from her wilds. Her Indian husband and children were there; there was the free, open forest, and she clung to these; and yet the love of her kinsfolk for her, and her's for them, was not quenched.

Transporting ourselves far from the beautiful valley of Wyoming, where the grief-stricken mother will wake never more to the consciousness of the loss of

PARTED FOR EVER. Page 246.

her sweet Frances, we stand on the prairies of Kansas. The time is 1856. One of the settlers who, with his wife, was seeking to build up a community in the turmoil, which then made that beautiful region such dangerous ground, has met his death at the hands of a rival faction. We enter the widow's desolated home. A shelter rather than a house, with but two wretched rooms, it stands alone upon the prairie. The darkness of a stormy winter's evening was gathering over the snow-clad slopes of the wide, bare prairie, as, in company with a sympathizing friend, we enter that lonely dwelling.

In the scantily-furnished apartment into which we are shown, two or three women and as many children are crowding around a stove, for the night is bitter cold, and even the large wood-fire scarcely heated a space so thinly walled. Behind a heavy pine table, on which stands a flickering tallow-candle, and leaning against a half-curtained window on which the sleet and winter's blast beat drearily, sits a woman of some forty years of age, clad in a dress of dark, coarse stuff, resting her head on her hand, and seeming unmindful of all about her.

She was the widow of Thomas W. Barber, one of the victims of the Kansas war. The attenuated hand supporting the aching head, and half shielding the tear-dimmed eyes, the silent drops trickling down the wasted cheeks, told but too well the sad story.

"They have left me," she cried, "a poor, forsaken creature, to mourn all my days! Oh, my husband, my husband, they have taken from me all that I hold dear! one that I loved better than I loved my own life!"

Thomas W. Barber was a careful and painstaking

farmer, a kind neighbor, and an inoffensive, amiable man. His "untimely taking off" was indeed a sad loss to the community at large, but how much more to his wife! She had loved him with a love that amounted to idolatry. When he was returning from his daily toil she would go forth to meet him. When absent from home, if his stay was prolonged, she would pass the whole night in tears; and when ill, she would hang over his bed like a mother over her child. With a presentiment of evil, when he left his home for the last time, after exhausting every argument to prevent him from going, she had said to him, "Oh, Thomas! if you should be shot, I shall be left all alone, with no child and nothing in the wide world to fill your place!" This was their last parting.

The intelligence of his death was kept in mercy from her, through the kindness of friends, who hoped to break it to her gently. This thoughtful and sympathetic purpose was marred by the unthinking act of a young man, who had been sent with a carriage to convey her to the hotel where her husband's body lay. As he rode up he shouted, "Thomas Barber is killed!" His widow half-caught the dreadful words, and rushing to the door cried, "Oh, God! What do I hear?" Seeing the mournful and sympathetic faces of the bystanders, she knew the truth and filled the house with her shrieks. When they brought her into the apartment where her husband lay, she threw herself upon his corpse, and kissing the dead man's face, called down imprecations on the heads of those who had bereaved her of all she held dear.

The prairies of the great West resemble the ocean in more respects than in their level vastness, and the travelers who pass over them are like mariners who guide themselves only by the constellations and the great luminaries of heaven. The trail of the emigrant, like the track of the ship, is often uncrossed for days by others who are voyaging over this mighty expanse. Distance becomes delusive, and after journeying for days and failing to reach the foot-hills of the mountains, whose peaks have shone to his eyes in so many morning suns, the tired emigrant is tempted by the abounding richness of the country to pause. He is one hundred miles from the nearest settlement. Beside a stream he builds his cabin. He is like a voyager whose ship has been burned, leaving him in a strange land which he must conquer or die.

Such was the situation of that household on the prairie of Illinois, concerning whom is told a story full of mournful pathos. We should note, in passing on to our story, one of the dangers to which prairie-dwellers are exposed. They live two or three months every year in a magazine of combustibles. One of the peculiarities of the climate in those regions is the dryness of its summers and autumns. A drought often commences in August which, with the exception of a few showers towards the close of that month, continues, with little interruption, throughout the full season. The immense mass of vegetation with which the fertile soil loads itself during the summer is suddenly withered, and the whole earth is covered with combustible materials. A single spark of fire falling anywhere upon these plains at such a time, instantly kindles a blaze that spreads on every side, and continues its destructive course as long as it finds fuel, these

fires sweeping on with a rapidity which renders it
hazardous even to fly before them.

The flames often extend across a wide prairie and
advance in a long line; no sight can be more sublime
than to behold at night a stream of fire several miles
in breadth advancing across these plains, leaving behind
it a black cloud of smoke, and throwing before it a
vivid glare which lights up the whole landscape with
the brilliancy of noonday. A roaring and crackling
sound is heard like the rushing of the hurricane; the
flame, which, in general, rises to the height of about
twenty feet, is seen sinking and darting upward in
spires precisely as the waves dash against each other,
and as the spray flies up into the air; the whole
appearance is often that of a boiling and flaming sea
violently agitated. Woe to the farmer whose ripe
corn-field extends into the prairie, and who has care-
lessly suffered the tall grass to grow in contact with
his fences; the whole labor of a year is swept away in
a few hours.

More than sixty years since, and before the beautiful wild gardens of Illinois had been tilled by the hand
of the white man, an emigrant with his family came
thither from the East in search of a spot whereon to
make his home. One bright spring day his white-
topped wagon entered a prairie richer in its verdure
and more brilliant in its flowers, than any that had
yet met his eyes. At night-fall it halted beside a
clump of trees not far from a creek. On this site a
log-cabin soon rose and sent its smoke curling through
the overhanging boughs.

The only neighbors of the pioneers were the ram-
bling Indians. Their habitation was the center of a

vast circle not dwelt in, and rarely even crossed by white settlers; oxen, cows, and a dog were their only domestic animals. For many months after their cabin was built they depended on wild game and fruits for subsistence; the rifle of the father, and traps set by the boys, brought them an abundant supply of meat The wife and mother wrought patiently for those she loved. Her busy hands kept a well-ordered house by day, and at night she plied the needle to repair the wardrobe of her little household band. It was already growing scanty, and materials to replace it could only be procured at a distance, and means to procure it were limited. Patching and darning until their garments were beyond repair, she then supplied their place with skins stripped from the deer which the father had shot. Far into the night, by the flickering light of a single candle, this gentle housewife plied "her busy care," while her husband, worn out with his day's work, and her children, tired by their rambles, were slumbering in the single chamber of the cabin.

October came, and a journey to the nearest settlement for winter goods and stores, must be made. After due preparation the father and his eldest son started in the emigrant wagon, and expected to be absent many days, during which the mother and her children, with only the dog for their protection, looked hourly forth upon the now frost-embrowned prairie, and fondly hoped for their return.

Day after day passed, and no sign of life was visible upon the plain save the deer bounding over the sere herbage, or the wolf loping stealthily against the wind which bore the scent of his prey. A rising haze be-

gan to envelope the landscape, betokening the approach of the Indian summer,

> " The melancholy days had come,
>   The saddest of the year,"

and the desolation of nature found an answering mood
in the soul of that lone woman. One day she was
visited by a party of Indian warriors, and from them
she learned that there was a war between the tribes
through whose country the journey of her husband
lay. A boding fear for his safety took possession of
her, and after the warriors had partaken of her hospitality and departed, and night came, she laid her little
ones in their bed, and sat for hours on the threshold
of the cabin door, looking out through the darkness
and praying silently for the return of her loved ones.
The wind was rising and driving across the sky black
masses of clouds which looked like misshapen specters
of evil. The blast whistled through the leafless trees
and howled round the cabin. Hours passed, and still
the sorrowful wife and mother sat gazing into the
gloom as if her eyes would pierce it and lighten on
the wished-for object.

But what is that strange light which far to the north
gleams on the blackened sky? It was not the lightning's flash, for it was a steady brightening glow.
It was not the weird flash of the aurora borealis, but
a redder and more lurid sheen; nor was it the har-
binger of the rising sun which lit that northern sky.
From a tinge it brightens to a gleam, and deepened at
last into a broad glare. That lonely heart was over-
whelmed with the dreadful truth. The prairie is on
fire! Often had they talked of prairie fires as a spec-

tacle of grandeur. But never had she dreamed of
the red demon as an enemy to be encountered in
that dreadful solitude.

Her heart sank within her as she saw the danger
leaping toward her like some fiery and maddened
race-horse. Was there no escape ? Her children were
sweetly sleeping, and the faithful dog, her only guardian, was gazing as if with mute sympathy into her face.
Within an hour she calculates the conflagration would
be at her very door. All around her is one dry ocean
of combustibles. She cannot reach the tree-tops, and
if she could, to cling there would be impossible amid
those towering flames. The elements seemed to grow
madder as the fire approached; fiercer blew the blast,
intermitting for a moment only to gather fresh potency and mingle its own strength with that of the
flames. She still had a faint hope that a creek a few
miles away would be a barrier over which the blaze
could not leap. She saw by the broad light which
made even the distant prairie like noonday, the tops
of the trees that fringed the creek but for a few moments, and then they were swallowed up in that crimson furnace. Alas! the stream had been crossed by
the resistless flames, and her last hope died away.

Bewildered and half stupefied by the terrors of her
situation, she had not yet wakened her children. But
now no time was to be lost. Already in imagination
she felt the hot breath of her relentless foe. It was
with much difficulty that she awoke them and aroused
them to a sense of their awful danger. Hastily dressing them she encircled them in her arms and kissed
and fondled them as if for a last farewell. Now for the
first time she missed the dog, the faithful companion

and guardian of her solitude, and on whose aid she
still counted in the hour of supreme peril. She called
him loudly, but in vain. Turning her face northward
she saw one unbroken line of flame as far as the eye
could reach, and forcing its way towards her like an
infuriated demon, roaring, crackling, sending up columns of dun-colored smoke as it tore along over the
plain. A few minutes more and her fate would be
decided. Falling on her knees she poured out her
heart in prayer, supplicating for mercy and commend-
ing herself and her helpless babes to Almighty God.
As she rose calmed and stayed by that fervent supplication a low wistful bark fell on her ear; the dog
came bounding to her side; seizing her by the dress
as if he would drag her from the spot, he leaped away
from her, barking and whining, looking back towards
her as he ran. Following him a few steps and seeing
nothing, she returned and resumed her seat, awaiting
death beside her children.

Again the dog returned, pawing, whining, howling,
and trying in every way to attract her attention.
What could he mean? Then for the first time flashed
upon her the thought which had already occurred
to the sagacious instinct of the dumb brute! The
ploughed field! Yes, there alone was hope of safety!
Clasping the two youngest children with one arm she
almost dragged the eldest boy as she fled along the
trodden path, the dog going before them showing
every token of delight. The fire was at their heels,
and its hot breath almost scorched their clothes as
they ran. They gained the herbless ploughed field
and took their station in its center just as the flames
darted round on each side of them.

The exhausted mother, faint with the sudden deliverance, dropped on the ground among her helpless babes. Father of mercies! what an escape!

In a few moments the flames attacked the haystack, which was but a morsel to its fury, and then seizing the house devoured it more slowly, while the great volume of the fire swept around over the plain. Long did the light of the burning home blight the eye of the lone woman after the flames had done their worst on the prairie around her and gone on bearing ruin and devastation to the southern plains and groves.

The vigils and the terrors of that fearful night wrought their work on the lonely woman, and she sank into a trance-like slumber upon the naked earth, with her babes nestling in her lap and the dog, her noble guardian, crouching at her feet. She awoke with the first light of morning to the terrible realities from which for a few brief hours she had had a blessed oblivion. She arose as from a dream and cast a dazed look southward over a charred and blackened expanse stretching to the horizon, over which the smoke was hanging like a pall. Turning away, stunned by the fearful recollection, her eyes fell upon the smouldering ruins of her once happy home. She tottered with her chilled and hungry children towards the heap of smoking rafters and still glowing embers of the cabin, with which the morning breezes were toying as in merry pastime, and sat down upon a mound which stood before what had once been the door. Here, at least, was warmth, but whither should she go for shelter and food. There was no house within forty miles and the cruel flames had spared neither grain nor meat. There was no shelter but the canopy of heaven and no food but roots and half-burned nuts.

Wandering hither and thither under the charred and leafless trees, she picked up with her numb and nerveless fingers the relics of the autumn nuts or feebly dug in the frost-stiffened ground for roots. But these were rare; here and there she found a nut shielded by a decayed log, and the edible roots were almost hidden by the ashes of the grass. She returned to the fire, around which her innocent children had begun to frolic with childlike thoughtlessness. The coarse morsels which she gave them seemed for the moment to quiet their cravings, and the strange sight of their home in ruins diverted their minds. The mother saw with joy that they were amusing themselves with merry games and had no part in her bitter sorrows and fears. Long and earnestly did she bend her eyes on the wide, black plains to see if she could discern the white-topped wagon moving over that dark expanse. Noon came and passed but brought not the sight for which she yearned: only the brown deer gamboling and the prairie hen wheeling her flight over the scorched waste!

Night came with its cold, its darkness, its hunger, its dreadful solitude! The chilled and shelterless woman sat with the heads of her sleeping children pillowed in her lap, and listened to the howling of the starved wolves, the dog her only guardian. She had discovered a few ground-nuts, which she had divided among the children, reserving none for herself; she had stripped off nearly all her clothing in order to wrap them up warmly against the frosty air, and with pleasant words, while her head was bursting, she had soothed them to sleep beside the burning pile; and there, through the watches of the long night, she gazed fondly at them and prayed to the Father of mercies that they, at least, might be spared.

The night was dark: beyond the circle of the burning embers nothing could be discerned. At intervals, her blood was curdled by the long, mournful howl of the gaunt gray wolf calling his companions to their prey. The cold wind whistled around her thinly clad frame and chilled it to the core. As the night grew stiller a drowsiness against which she contended in vain, overcame her, her eyelids drooped, her shivering body swayed to and fro, until by the tumbling down of the embers she was again aroused, and would brace herself for another hour's vigil. At last the darkness became profoundly silent and even the wind ceased to whisper, the nocturnal marauders stole away, and night held her undisputed reign. Then came a heavy dreamless sleep and overpowered the frame of the watcher, chilled as it was, and faint with hunger, and worn with fatigue and vigils: she curled her shivering limbs around her loved ones and became oblivious to all.

It was the cry of her babes that waked her from slumber. The fire was slowly dying; the sun was looking down coldly from the leaden sky; slowly his beams were obscured by dark, sullen masses of vapor, which at last curtained the whole heavens. Rain! When she sat watching in the darkness, a few hours before, she thought nothing could make her condition worse. But an impending rain-storm which, thirty-six hours before, would have been hailed as merciful and saving, would now only aggravate their situation.

17

Darker and darker grew the sky. She must hasten
for food ere the clouds should burst. Her limbs were
stiff with cold, her sight was dim, and her brain reeled
as she rose to her feet and tottered to the grove to
search for sustenance to keep her wailing babes alive.
Her own desire for food was gone, but all exhausted
as she was she could not resist the pleadings of the
loved ones who hung upon her garments and begged
for food.

Gleaning a few more coarse morsels on the ground
so often searched, she tottered back to the spot which
still seemed home though naught of home was there.
Strange, racking pains wrung her wasted body, and
sinking down beside her children she felt as if her
last hour had come. Yes! she would perish there
beside those consecrated ashes with her little ones
around her. A drizzling rain was falling faster and
faster. The fire was dying and she pushed the brands
together, and gathered her trembling babes about her
knees, and between the periods of her agony told
them not to forget their mamma nor how they had
lost her; she gave the eldest boy many tender mes-
sages to carry to her husband and to her first born.
With wondering and tearful face he promised to do as
she desired, but begged her to tell him where she
would be when his father came and whether his little
brother would go with her and leave him all alone.

The rain poured down mercilessly and chilly blew
the blast. The embers hissed and blackened and shed
no more warmth on the suffering group. Keener and
heavier grew the mother's pangs, and there beside the
smoking ruins of her home, prone on the drenched
soil, with the pitiless sky bending above her, her help-

less children wailing around her writhing form, the
hapless woman gave birth to a little babe, whose eyes
were never opened to the desolation of its natal home.

Unconscious alike to the cries of the terror stricken
children and of the moaning caresses of her dumb
friend, that poor mother's eyes were only opened
on the dreadful scene when day was far advanced.
Through the cold rain, still pouring steadily down, the
twilight seemed to her faint eyes to be creeping over
the earth. Sweet sounds were ringing in her ears.
These were but dreams that deluded her weakened
mind and senses. She strove to rise, but fell back
and again relapsed into insensibility. Once again her
eyes opened. This time it was no illusion. The
eldest of the little watchers was shouting in her ear,
" Mother, I see father's wagon ! " There it was close
at hand. All day it had been slowly moving across
the blackened prairie. The turf had been softened
by the rain and the last few miles had been inconceiv-
ably tedious. The charred surface of the plain had
filled the heart of both father and son with terror,
which increased as they advanced.

When they were within a mile of the spot where
the cabin stood and could see no house, they both
abandoned the wagon, and leaving the animals to
follow as they chose, they flew shouting loudly as
they sped on till they stood over the perishing group.
They could not for the moment comprehend the dreadful calamity, but stared at the wasted faces of the
children, the infant corpse, the dying wife, the desolate home.

Cursing the day that he had been lured by the
festal beauty of those prairies, the father lifted the

dying woman in his arms, gazed with an agonized face upon her glassy eyes, and felt the faint fluttering in her breast that foretold the last and worst that could befall him. Slowly, word by word, with weak sepulchral voice, she told the dreadful story.

He slipped off his outer garments and wrapped them around her, and wiping off the rain-drops from her face drew her to his heart. But storm or shelter was all the same to her now, and the death-damp on her brow was colder than the pelting shower. He accused himself of her cruel murder and wildly prayed her forgiveness. From these accusations she vindicated him, besought him not to grieve for her, and with many prayers for her dear children and their father, she resigned her breath with the parting light of that sad autumnal day.

After two days and nights of weeping and watching, he laid her remains deep down below the prairie sod, beside the home which she had loved and made bright by her presence.

CHAPTER XII.

NO portion of our country has been the scene of more romantic and dangerous adventures than that region described under the broad and vague term the "Southwest." Texas, New Mexico, and Arizona, are vast, remote, and varied fields with which danger and hardship, wonder and mystery are ever associated. The country itself embraces great contrarieties of scenery and topography—the rich farm, the expansive cattle ranch, the broad lonely prairie watered by majestic rivers, the barren desert, the lofty plateau, the secluded mining settlement, and vast mountain ranges furrowed by torrents into black cañons where sands of gold lie heaped in inaccessible, useless riches.

The forms of human society are almost equally diverse. Strange and mysterious tribes, each with different characteristics, here live side by side. Vile mongrel breeds of men multiply to astonish the ethnologist and the moralist. Here roam the Comanches and the Apaches, the most remorseless and bloodthirsty of all the North American aboriginal tribes. Mexican bandits traverse the plains and lurk in the mountain passes, and American outlaws and desperadoes here find a refuge from justice.

As the Anglo-Saxon after fording the Sabine, the Brazos, and the Colorado River of Texas, advances westward, he is brought face to face with these differ-

ent races with whom is mixed in greater or less proportion the blood of the old Castilian conquerors.
Each of these races is widely alien from, and most of
them instinctively antagonistic to the North European
people.

Taking into view the immense distances to be traversed, the natural difficulties presented by the face of
the country, the remoteness of the region from civilization, and the mixed, incongruous and hostile character of the inhabitants, we might naturally expect that
its occupation by peaceful settlers,—by those forms
of household life in which woman is an essential element—would be indefinitely postponed.   But that energy and ardor which marks alike the men and the
women of our race has carried the family, that germ
of the state, over all obstacles and planted it in the
inhospitable soil of the most remote corners of this
region, and there it will flourish and germinate doubtless till it has uprooted every neighboring and noxious
product.

The northeastern section of this extensive country
is composed of that stupendous level tract known as
the " Llano Estacado," or " Staked Plain."   Stretching
hundreds of miles in every direction, this sandy plain,
treeless, arid, with only here and there patches of
stunted herbage, whitened by the bones of horses and
mules, and by the more ghastly skeletons of too adventurous travelers, presents an area of desolation
scarcely more than paralleled by the great African
Desert.

In the year 1846, after news had reached the States
that our troops were in peaceful occupation of New
Mexico, a party of men and women set out from the

upper valley of the Red River of Louisiana, with the intention of settling in the valley of the river Pecos, in the eastern part of the newly conquered territory. The company consisted of seven persons, viz: Mr. and Mrs. Benham and their child of seven years, Mr. and Mrs. Braxton and two sons of fifteen and eighteen years respectively.

They made rapid and comfortable progress through the valley of the Red River, and in two weeks reached the edge of the "Staked Plain," which they now made preparations to cross, for the difficulties and dangers of the route were not unknown to them. Disencumbering their pack-mules of all useless burdens and supplying themselves with water for two days, they pushed forward on their first stage which brought them on the evening of the second day to a kind of oasis in this desert where they found wood, water, and grass. From this point there was a stretch of ninety miles perfectly bare of wood and water, and with rare intervals of scanty herbage for the beasts. After this desolate region had been passed they would have a comparatively easy journey to their destination.

On the evening of the second day of their passage across this arid tract they had the misfortune to burst their only remaining water cask, and to see the thirsty sands drink up in a moment every drop of the precious liquid. They were then forty miles from the nearest water. Their beasts were jaded and suffering from thirst. The two men were incapacitated for exertion by slight sun-strokes received that day, and one of the boys had been bitten in the hand by a rattlesnake while taking from its burrow a prairie dog which he had shot.

The next day they pursued their march only with the utmost difficulty; the two men were barely able to sit on their horses, and the boy which had been bitten was faint and nerveless from the effect of the poison. The heat was felt very severely by the party as they dragged themselves slowly across the white expanse of sand, which reflected the rays of the sun with a painful glare into the haggard eyes of the wretched wanderers. Before they had made fifteen miles, or little more than one-third of the distance that would have to be accomplished before reaching water, the horses and mules gave out and at three o'clock in the afternoon the party dismounted and panting with heat and thirst stretched themselves on the sand. The sky above them was like brass and the soil was coated with a fine alkali deposit which rose in clouds at their slightest motion, filling their nostrils and eyes, and increasing the agonies they were suffering.

Their only hope was that they would be discovered by some passing train of hunters or emigrants. This hope faded away as the sun declined and nothing but the sky and the long dreary dazzling expanse of sand met their eyes.

The painful glare slowly softened, and with sunset came coolness; this was some slight mitigation to their sufferings; sleep too, promised to bring oblivion; and hope, which a merciful Providence has ordained to cast its halo over the darkest hours, told its flattering tale of possible relief on the morrow.

The air of that desert is pellucid as crystal, and the last beams of the sun left on the unclouded azure of the sky a soft glow, through which every thing in the western horizon was outlined as if drawn by some magic pencil. Casting their eyes in that direction the wretched wayfarers saw far away a dun-colored haze through which small black specks seemed to be moving. Growing larger and more distinct it approached them slowly over the vast expanse until its true nature was apparent. It was a cloud of dust such as a party of horsemen make when in rapid motion over a soil as fine and light as ashes. Was it friend or foe? Was it American cavalry or was it a band of Mexican guerrillas that was galloping so fiercely over that arid plain? These torturing doubts were soon solved. Skimming over the ground like swallows, six sunburnt men with hair as black as the crow's wing, gaily dressed, and bearing long lances, soon reined in their mustangs within twenty paces of the party and gazed curiously at them. One of the band then rode up and asked in broken English if they were "Americans:" having thus made a reconnoisance and seeing their helplessness, without waiting for a reply, he beckoned to his companions who approached and demanded the surrender of the party. Under other circumstances a stout resistance would have been made; but in their present forlorn condition they could do nothing.

Their guns, a part of their money, and whatever the unfortunate families had that pleased the guerrillas, was speedily appropriated, the throats of their horses and mules were cut, Mrs. Braxton and Mrs. Benham were seized, and in spite of their struggles and shrieks each of them was placed in front of a swarthy bandit, and then the Mexicans rode away cursing "Los Americanos," and barbarously leaving them to die of hunger and thirst.

After a four hours' gallop, the marauders reached

an adobe house on Picosa Creek, a tributary of the Rio Pecos. This was the headquarters of the gang, and here they kept relays of fresh horses, mustangs, fiery, and full of speed and bottom. Mrs. Benham and Mrs. Braxton were placed in a room by themselves on the second story, and the door was barricaded so that escape by that avenue was impossible; but the windows were only guarded by stout oaken bars, which the women, by their united strength, succeeded in removing. Their captors were plunged in a profound slumber, when Mrs. Benham and her companion dropped themselves out of the window, and succeeded in reaching the stable without discovery. Here they found six fresh horses ready saddled and bridled, the others on which the bandits had made their raid being loose in the enclosure.

It was a cruel necessity which impelled our brave heroines to draw their knives across the hamstrings of the tired horses, thus disabling them so as to prevent pursuit. Then softly leading out the six fresh mustangs, each of our heroines mounted one of the horses man-fashion and led the others lashed together with lariats; walking the beasts until out of hearing, they then put them to a gallop, and, riding all night, came, at sunrise, to the spot where their suffering friends lay stretched on the sand, having abandoned all hope.

After a brief rest, the whole party pushed rapidly forward on their journey, arriving that evening at a place of safety. Two days after, they reached the headwaters of the Pecos. Here they purchased a large adobe house, and an extensive tract, suitable both for grazing and tillage.

These events occurred early in the autumn. During the following winter the Mexicans revolted, and massacred Governor Bent and his military household. On the same day seven Americans were killed at Arroyo Hondo; a large Mexican force was preparing to march on Santa Fé, and for a time it seemed as if the handful of American soldiers would be driven out of the territory. This conspiracy was made known to the authorities by an American girl, who was the wife of one of the Mexican conspirators, and becoming, through her husband, acquainted with the plan of operations, divulged them to General Price in season to prevent a more general outbreak. As it was, the American settlers were in great danger.

The strong and spacious house in which the Benhams and Braxtons lived had formerly been used as a stockade and fortification against Indian attack. Its thick walls were pierced with loop-holes, and its doors, of double oak planks, were studded with wrought-iron spikes, which made it bullet-proof. A detachment of United States troops were stationed a short distance from their ranch, and the two families, in spite of the disturbed condition of the country, felt reasonably secure. The troops were withdrawn, however, after the revolt commenced, leaving the new settlers dependent upon their own resources for protection. Their cattle and horses were driven into the enclosure, and the inmates of the house kept a sharp lookout against hostile parties of marauders, whether Indian or Mexican.

Early on the morning of January 24th a mounted party of twelve Mexicans made their appearance in front of the enclosure, which they quickly scaled, and discharged a volley of balls, one of which passed through a loop-hole, and, entering Mr. Braxton's eye as he was aiming a rifle at the assailants, laid him dead at the feet of his wife. Mrs. Braxton, with streaming eyes, laid the head of her husband in her lap and watched his expiring throes with agony, such as only a wife and mother can feel when she sees the dear partner of her life and the father of her sons torn in an instant from her embrace. Seeing that her husband was no more, she dried her tears and thought only of vengeance on his murderers.

The number of the besieged was twelve at the start, viz: Mr. and Mrs. Braxton, Mr. and Mrs. Benham and their children, three Irish herders, and a half-breed Mexican and his wife, who were house servants. The death of Mr. Braxton had reduced their number to eleven. A few moments later the Mexican half-breed disappeared, but was not missed in the excitement of the defense.

The besieged returned with vigor the fire of their assailants, two of whom had already bit the dust. The women loaded the guns and passed them to the men, who kept the Mexicans at a respectful distance by the rapidity of their fire. Mrs. Benham was the first to mark the absence of Juan the Mexican half-breed, and, suspecting treachery, flew to the loft with a hatchet in one hand and a revolver in the other. Her suspicion was correct. Juan had opened an upper window, and, letting down a ladder, had assisted two of the attacking party to ascend, and they were preparing to make an assault on those below by firing through the cracks in the floor, when the intrepid woman despatched Juan with a shot from her revolver and clove the skull of another Mexican; the third leaped from the window and escaped.

As Mrs. Benham was about to descend from the loft, after drawing up the ladder and closing the window, she was met by the wife of the treacherous half-breed, who aimed a stroke at her breast with a *machete* or large knife, such as the Mexicans use. She received a flesh wound in the left arm as she parried the blow, and it was only with the mixed strength of Mrs. Braxton and one of the herders, who had now ascended to the loft, that the infuriated Mexican whom Mrs. Benham had made a widow, could be mastered and bound.

Three of the attacking party had now been killed and three others placed *hors de combat;* the remnant were apparently about to retire from the siege, when six more swarthy desperadoes, mounted on black mustangs, came galloping up and halted on a hill just out of rifle shot.

Mrs. Braxton and Mrs. Benham, looking through a field glass, at once recognized them as the band which had made them captives a few months before.

After a few moments of consultation one of the band, who appeared to be only armed with a bow and arrow, advanced towards the house waving a white flag. Within thirty paces of the door stood a large tree, and behind this the envoy, bearing the white flag, ensconced himself, and, striking a light, twanged his bow and sent a burning arrow upon the roof of the house, which, being dry as tinder, in a moment was in a blaze.

Both of the women immediately carried water to the roof and extinguished the flames. Another arrow, wrapped in cotton steeped in turpentine, again set the roof on fire, and as one of the intrepid matrons threw a bucket of water upon the blaze, the dastard stepped from behind the tree and sent a pistol ball through her right arm, but at the same moment received two rifle balls in his breast, and fell a corpse.

Mrs. Benham, for it was she who had been struck, was assisted by her husband to the ground floor, where her wound was examined and found to be fortunately not a dangerous one. A new peril, however, now struck terror to their hearts; the water was all exhausted. The fire began to make headway. Mrs. Braxton, calling loudly for water to extinguish it, and meeting no response, descended to the ground floor, where the defenders were about to give up all hope, and either resign themselves to the flames, or by emerging from the house, submit to massacre at the hands of the now infuriated foe. As Mrs. Braxton rolled her eyes hither and thither in search of some substitute for water, they fell on the corpse of her husband. His coat and vest were completely saturated with blood. It was only the sad but terrible necessity which immediately suggested to her the use to which these garments could be put. Shuddering, she removed them quickly but tenderly from the body, flew to the roof and succeeded, by these dripping and ghastly tokens of her widowhood, in finally extinguishing the flames.

The attack ceased at night-fall, and the Mexicans withdrew. The outbreak having been soon quelled by the United States forces, the territory was brought again into a condition of peace and comparative security.

At the close of the war in 1848, Mrs. Braxton married a discharged volunteer named Whitley, and having disposed of the late Mr. Braxton's interest in the New Mexican ranche, removed, in 1851, with her husband and family, to California, where they lived for two years in the Sacramento valley.

Whitley was possessed of one of those roving and adventurous spirits which is never happy in repose, and when he was informed by John Crossman, an old comrade, of the discovery of a rich placer which he had made during his march as a United States soldier across the territory of Arizona, at that time known as the Gadsden purchase, he eagerly formed a partnership with the discoverer, who was no longer in the army, and announced to his wife his resolution to settle in Arizona. She endeavored by every argument she could command to dissuade him from this rash step, but in vain, and finding all her representations and entreaties of no avail, she consented, though with the utmost reluctance, to accompany him. They accordingly sold their place and took vessel with their household goods, for San Diego, from which point they purposed to advance across the country three hundred miles to the point where Crossman had located his placer.

The territory of Arizona may be likened to that wild and rugged mountain region in Central Asia, where, according to Persian myth, untold treasures are guarded by the malign legions of Ahriman, the spirit of evil. Two of the great elemental forces have employed their destructive agencies upon the surface of the country until it might serve for an ideal picture of desolation. For countless centuries the water has seamed and gashed the face of the hills, stripping them of soil, and cutting deep gorges and cañons through the rocks. The water then flowed away or disappeared in the sands, and the sun came with its parching heat to complete the work of ruin. Famine and thirst stalk over those arid plains, or lurk in the waterless and gloomy cañons; as if to compensate for these evils, the soil of the territory teems with mineral wealth. Grains of gold glisten in the sandy *débris* of ancient torrents, and nuggets are wedged in the faces of the precipices. Mountains of silver and copper are waiting for the miner who is bold enough to venture through that desolate region in quest of these metals.

The journey from San Diego was made with pack-mules and occupied thirty days, during which nearly every hardship and obstacle in the pioneer's catalogue was encountered. When they reached the spot described by Crossman they found the place, which lay at the bottom of a deep ravine, had been covered with boulders and thirty feet of sand by the rapid torrents of five rainy seasons. They immediately commenced "prospecting." Mrs. Braxton had the good fortune to discover a large "pocket," from which Crossman and her husband took out in a few weeks thirty thousand dollars in gold. This contented the adventurers, and being disgusted with the appearance of the country, they decided to go back to California.

Instead of returning on the same route by which they came, they resolved to cross the Colorado river higher up and in the neighborhood of the Santa Maria. They reached the Colorado river after a toilsome march, but while searching for a place to pass over,

Crossman lost his footing and fell sixty feet down a precipice, surviving only long enough to bequeath his share of the treasure to his partner. Here, too, they had the misfortune to lose one of their four pack-mules, which strayed away. Pressing on in a north-westerly direction they passed through a series of deep valleys and gorges where the only water they could find was brackish and bitter, and reached the edge of the California desert. They had meanwhile lost another mule which had been dashed to pieces by falling down a cañon. Mr. Whitley's strength becoming exhausted his wife gave up to him the beast she had been riding, and pursued her way on foot, driving before her the other mule, which bore the gold-dust with their scanty supply of food and their only remaining cooking utensils. Their tents and camp furniture having been lost they had suffered much from the chilly nights in the mountains, and after they had entered the desert, from the rays of the sun. Before they could reach the Mohave river Mr. Whitley became insane from thirst and hunger, and nothing but incessant watchfulness on the part of his wife could prevent him from doing injury to himself. Once while she was gathering cactus-leaves to wet his lips with the moisture they contained, he bit his arm and sucked the blood. Upon reaching the river he drank immoderately of the water and in an hour expired, regaining his consciousness before death, and blessing his devoted wife with his last breath. Ten days later the brave woman had succeeded in reaching Techichipa in so wasted a condition that she looked like a specter risen from the grave. Here by careful nursing she was at length restored to health. The

18

gold-dust which had cost so dearly was found after a long search, beneath the carcass of the mule, twenty miles from Techichipa.

The extraordinary exploits of Mrs. Braxton can only be explained by supposing her to be naturally endowed with a larger share of nerve and hardihood than usually falls to the lot of her sex. Some influence, too, must be ascribed to the peculiarly wild and free life that prevails in the southwest. Living so much of the time in the open air in a climate peculiarly luxuriant and yet bracing, and environed with dangers in manifold guise, all the latent heroism in woman's nature is brought out to view, her muscular and nervous tissues are hardened, and her moral endurance by constant training in the school of hardship and danger, rests upon a strong and healthy physique. Upon this theory we may also explain the following incident which is related of another border-woman of the southwest.

* Beyond the extreme outer line of settlements in western Texas, near the head waters of the Colorado River, and in one of the remotest and most sequestered sections of that sparsely populated district, there lived in 1867, an enterprising pioneer by the name of Babb, whose besetting propensity and ambition consisted in pushing his fortunes a little farther toward the setting sun than any of his neighbors, the nearest of whom, at the time specified, was some fifteen miles in his rear.

The household of the borderer consisted of his wife, three small children, and a female friend by the name of L———, who, having previously lost her husband,

* Marcy's Border Reminiscences.

was passing the summer with the family. She was a veritable type of those vigorous, self-reliant border women, who encounter danger or the vicissitudes of weather without quailing.

Born and nurtured upon the remotest frontier, she inherited a robust constitution, and her active life in the exhilarating prairie air served to develop and mature a healthy womanly physique. From an early age she had been a fearless rider, and her life on the frontier had habituated her to the constant use of the horse until she felt almost more at home in the saddle than in a chair.

Upon one bright and lovely morning in June, 1867, the adventurous borderer before mentioned, set out from his home with some cattle for a distant market, leaving his family in possession of the ranch, without any male protectors from Indian marauders.

They did not, however, entertain any serious apprehensions of molestation in his absence, as no hostile Indians had as yet made their appearance in that locality, and everything passed on quietly for several days, until one morning, while the women were busily occupied with their domestic affairs in the house, the two oldest children, who were playing outside, called to their mother, and informed her that some mounted men were approaching from the prairie. On looking out, she perceived, to her astonishment, that they were Indians coming upon the gallop, and already very near the house. This gave her no time to make arrangements for defense; but she screamed to the children to run in for their lives, as she desired to bar the door, being conscious of the fact that the prairie warriors seldom attack a house that is closed, fearing, doubtless, that it may be occupied by armed men, who might give them an unwelcome reception.

The children did not, however, obey the command of their mother, believing the strangers to be white men, and the door was left open. As soon as the alarm was given, Mrs. L——— sprang up a ladder into the loft, and concealed herself in such a position that she could, through cracks in the floor, see all that passed beneath.

Meantime the savages came up, seized and bound the two children outdoors, and, entering the house, rushed toward the young child, which the terror-stricken mother struggled frantically to rescue from their clutches; but they were too much for her, and tearing the infant from her arms, they dashed it upon the floor; then seizing her by the hair, they wrenched back her head and cut her throat from ear to ear, putting her to death instantaneously.

Mrs. L———, who was anxiously watching their proceedings from the loft, witnessed the fiendish tragedy, and uttered an involuntary shriek of horror, which disclosed her hiding-place to the barbarians, and they instantly vaulted up the ladder, overpowered and tied her; then dragging her rudely down, they placed her, with the two elder children, upon horses, and hurriedly set off to the north, leaving the infant child unharmed, and clasping the murdered corpse of its mangled parent.

In accordance with their usual practice, they traveled as rapidly as their horses could carry them for several consecutive days and nights, only making occasional short halts to graze and rest their animals, and get a little sleep themselves, so that the unfortunate captives necessarily suffered indescribable tortures from harsh treatment, fatigue, and want of sleep and food. Yet they were forced by the savages to continue on day after day, and night after night, for many, many weary miles toward the "Staked Plain," crossing *en route* the Brazos, Wachita, Red, Canadian, and Arkansas Rivers, several of which were at swimming stages.

The warriors guarded their captives very closely, until they had gone so great a distance from the settlements that they imagined it impossible for them to make their escape and find their way home, when they relapsed their vigilance slightly, and they were permitted to walk about a little within short limits from the bivouacs; but they were given to understand by unmistakable pantomime that death would be the certain penalty of the first attempt to escape.

In spite of this, Mrs. L———, who possessed a firmness of purpose truly heroic, resolved to seize the first favorable opportunity to get away, and with this resolution in view, she carefully observed the relative speed and powers of endurance of the different horses in the party, and noted the manner in which they were grazed, guarded, and caught; and upon a dark night, after a long, fatiguing day's ride, and while the Indians were sleeping soundly, she noiselessly and cautiously crawled away from the bed of her young companions, who were also buried in profound slumber, and going to the pasture-ground of the horses, selected the best, leaped upon his back *à la garçon*, with only a lariat around his neck, and without saddle or bridle, quietly started off at a slow walk in the direction of the north star, believing that this course would lead her to the nearest white habitations. As soon as she had gone out of hearing from the bivouac, without detection or pursuit, she accelerated the speed of the horse into a trot, then to a gallop, and urged him rapidly forward during the entire night.

At dawn of day on the following morning she rose upon the crest of an eminence overlooking a vast area of bald prairie country, where, for the first time since leaving the Indians, she halted, and, turning round, tremblingly cast a rapid glance to the rear, expecting to see the savage blood-hounds upon her track; but, to her great relief, not a single indication of a living object could be discerned within the extended scope of her vision. She breathed more freely now, but still did not feel safe from pursuit; and the total absence of all knowledge of her whereabouts in the midst of the wide expanse of dreary prairie around her, with the uncertainty of ever again looking upon a friendly face, caused her to realize most vividly her own weakness and entire dependence upon the Almighty, and she raised her thoughts to Heaven in fervent supplication.

The majesty and sublimity of the stupendous works of the great Author and Creator of the Universe, when contrasted with the insignificance of the powers and achievements of a vivified atom of earth modeled into human form, are probably under no circumstances more strikingly exhibited and felt than when one becomes bewildered and lost in the almost limitless amplitude of our great North American " pampas," where not a single foot-mark or other trace of man's presence or action can be discovered, and where the solitary wanderer is startled at the sound even of his own voice.

The sensation of loneliness and despondency resulting from the appalling consciousness of being really and absolutely lost, with the realization of the fact that but two or three of the innumerable different points of direction embraced within the circle of the horizon will serve to extricate the bewildered victim from the awful doom of death by starvation, and in entire ignorance as to which of these particular directions should be followed, without a single road, trail, tree, bush, or other landmark to guide or direct—the effects upon the imagination of this formidable array of disheartening circumstances can be fully appreciated only by those who have been personally subjected to their influence.

A faint perception of the intensity of the mental torture experienced by these unfortunate victims may, however, be conjectured from the fact that their senses at such junctures become so completely absorbed and overpowered by the cheerless prospect before them, that they oftentimes wander about in a state of temporary lunacy, without the power of exercising the slightest volition of the reasoning faculties.

The inflexible spirit of the heroine of this narrative did not, however, succumb in the least to the imminent perils of the situation in which she found herself, and her purposes were carried out with a determination as resolute and unflinching as those of the Israelites in their protracted pilgrimage through the wilderness, and without the guidance of pillars of fire and cloud.

The aid of the sun and the broad leaves of the

pilot-plant by day, with the light of Polaris by night, enabled her to pursue her undeviating course to the north with as much accuracy as if she had been guided by the magnetic needle.

She continued to urge forward the generous steed she bestrode, who, in obedience to the will of his rider, coursed swiftly on hour after hour during the greater part of the day, without the least apparent labor or exhaustion.

It was a contest for life and liberty that she had undertaken, a struggle in which she resolved to triumph or perish in the effort: and still the brave-hearted woman pressed on, until at length her horse began to show signs of exhaustion, and as the shadows of evening began to appear he became so much jaded that it was difficult to coax or force him into a trot, and the poor woman began to entertain serious apprehensions that he might soon give out altogether and leave her on foot.

At this time she was herself so much wearied and in want of sleep that she would have given all she possessed to have been allowed to dismount and rest; but, unfortunately for her, those piratical quadrupeds of the plains, the wolves, advised by their carnivorous instincts that she and her exhausted horse might soon fall an easy sacrifice to their voracious appetites, followed upon her track, and came howling in great numbers about her, so that she dared not set her feet upon the ground, fearing they would devour her ; and her only alternative was to continue urging the poor beast to struggle forward during the dark and gloomy hours of the long night, until at length she became so exhausted that it was only with the utmost effort of her iron will that she was enabled to preserve her balance upon the horse.

Meantime the ravenous pack of wolves, becoming more and more emboldened and impatient as the speed of her horse relaxed, approached nearer and nearer, until, with their eyes flashing fire, they snapped savagely at the heels of the terrified horse, while at the same time they kept up their hideous concert like the howlings of ten thousand fiends from the infernal regions.

Every element in her nature was at this fearful juncture taxed to its greatest tension, and impelled her to concentrate the force of all her remaining energies in urging and coaxing forward the wearied horse, until, finally, he was barely able to reel and stagger along at a slow walk; and when she was about to give up in despair, expecting every instant that the animal would drop down dead under her, the welcome light of day dawned in the eastern horizon, and imparted a more cheerful and encouraging influence over her, and, on looking around, to her great joy, there were no wolves in sight.

She now, for the first time in about thirty-six hours, dismounted, and knowing that sleep would soon overpower her, and the horse, if not secured, might escape or wander away, and there being no tree or other object to which he could be fastened, she, with great presence of mind, tied one end of the long lariat to his neck, and, with the other end around her waist, dropped down upon the ground in a deep sleep, while the famished horse eagerly cropped the herbage around her.

She was unconscious as to the duration of her

slumber, but it must have been very protracted to have compensated the demands of nature, for the exhaustion induced by her prodigious ride.

Her sleep was sweet, and she dreamed of happiness and home, losing all consciousness of her actual situation until she was suddenly startled and aroused by the pattering sound of horses' feet, beating the earth on every side.

Springing to her feet in the greatest possible alarm, she found herself surrounded by a large band of savages, who commenced dancing around, flouting their war-clubs in terrible proximity to her head, while giving utterance to the most diabolical shouts of exultation.

Her exceedingly weak and debilitated condition at this time, resulting from long abstinence from food, and unprecedented mental and physical trials, had wrought upon her nervous system to such an extent that she imagined the moment of her death had arrived, and fainted.

The Indians then approached, and, after she revived, placed her again upon a horse, and rode away with her to their camp, which, fortunately, was not far distant. They then turned their prisoner over to the squaws, who gave her food and put her to bed; but it was several days before she was sufficiently recovered to be able to walk about the camp.

She learned that her last captors belonged to "Lone Wolf's" band of Kiowas.

Although these Indians treated her with more kindness than the Comanches had done, yet she did not for an instant entertain the thought that they would ever voluntarily release her from bondage; neither had she the remotest conception of her present locality, or of the direction or distance to any white settlement; but she had no idea of remaining a slave for life, and resolved to make her escape the first practicable moment that offered.

During the time she remained with these Indians a party of men went away to the north, and were absent six days, bringing with them, on their return, some ears of green corn. She knew the prairie tribes never planted a seed of any description, and was therefore confident the party had visited a white settlement, and that it was not over three days' journey distant. This was encouraging intelligence for her, and she anxiously bided her time to depart.

Late one night, after all had become hushed and quiet throughout the camp, and every thing seemed auspicious for the consummation of her purposes, she stole carefully away from her bed, crept softly out to the herd of horses, and after having caught and saddled one, was in the act of mounting, when a number of dogs rushed out after her, and by their barking, created such a disturbance among the Indians that she was forced, for the time, to forego her designs and crawl hastily back to her lodge.

On a subsequent occasion, however, fortune favored her. She secured an excellent horse and rode away in the direction from which she had seen the Indians returning to camp with the green corn. Under the certain guidance of the sun and stars she was enabled to pursue a direct bearing, and after three consecutive days of rapid riding, anxiety, fatigue, and hunger, she arrived upon the border of a large river, flowing directly across her track. The stream was swollen to the top of its banks; the water coursed like a torrent through its channel, and she feared her horse might not be able to stem the powerful current; but after surmounting the numerous perils and hardships she had already encountered, the dauntless woman was not to be turned aside from her inflexible purpose by this formidable obstacle, and she instantly dashed into the foaming torrent, and, by dint of encouragement and punishment, forced her horse through the stream and landed safely upon the opposite bank.

After giving her horse a few moments' rest, she again set forward, and had ridden but a short distance when, to her inexpressible astonishment and delight, she struck a broad and well-beaten wagon-road, the first and only evidence or trace of civilization she had seen since leaving her home in Texas.

Up to this joyful moment the indomitable inflexibility of purpose of our heroine had not faltered for an instant, neither had she suffered the slightest despondency, in view of the terrible array of disheartening circumstances that had continually confronted her, but when she realized the hopeful prospect before her of a speedy escape from the reach of her barbarous captors, and a reasonable certainty of an early reunion with people of her own sympathizing race, the feminine elements of her nature preponderated, her stoical fortitude yielded to the delightful anticipation, and her joy was intensified and confirmed by seeing, at this moment, a long train of wagons approaching over the distant prairie.

The spectacle overwhelmed her with ecstasy, and she wept tears of joy while offering up sincere and heartfelt thanks to the Almighty for delivering her from a bondage more dreadful than death.

She then proceeded on until she met the wagons in charge of Mr. Robert Bent, whom she entreated to give her food instantly, as she was in a state bordering upon absolute starvation. He kindly complied with her request, and after the cravings of her appetite had been appeased he desired to gratify his curiosity, which had been not a little excited at the unusual exhibition of a beautiful white woman appearing alone in that wild country, riding upon an Indian saddle, with no covering on her head save her long natural hair, which was hanging loosely and disorderly about her shoulders. Accordingly, he inquired of her where she lived, to which she replied, "In Texas." Mr. B. gave an incredulous shake of his head at this response, remarking at the same time that he thought she must be mistaken, as Texas happened to be situated some five or six hundred miles distant. She reiterated the assurance of her statement, and described to him briefly the leading incidents attending her capture and escape; but still he was inclined to doubt, believing that she might possibly be insane.

He informed her that the river she had just crossed was the Arkansas, and that she was then on the old Santa Fé road, about fifteen miles west of Big Turkey Creek, where she would find the most remote frontier house. Then, after thanking him for his kindness, she bade him adieu, and started away in a walk toward the settlements, while he continued his journey in the opposite direction.

On the arrival of Mr. Bent at Fort Zara, he called upon the Indian agent, and reported the circumstance

of meeting Mrs. L——, and, by a singular coinci-
dence, it so happened that the agent was at that very
time holding a council with the chiefs of the identical
band of Indians from whom she had last escaped, and
they had just given a full history of the entire affair,
which seemed so improbable to the agent that he was
not disposed to credit it until he received its confirma-
tion through Mr. Bent. He at once dispatched a man
to follow the woman and conduct her to Council Grove,
where she was kindly received, and remained for some
time, hoping through the efforts of the agents to gain
intelligence of the two children she had left with the
Comanches, as she desired to take them back to their
father in Texas; but no tidings were gained for a long
while.

The two captive children were afterwards ransomed
and sent home to their father.

It will readily be seen, by a reference to the map
of the country over which Mrs. L—— passed, that
the distance from the place of her capture to the point
where she struck the Arkansas river could not have
been short of about five hundred miles, and the greater
part of this immense expanse of desert plain she
traversed alone, without seeing a single civilized human
habitation.

It may well be questioned whether any woman
either in ancient or modern times ever performed such
a remarkable equestrian feat, and the story itself would
be almost incredible were we not in possession of so
many well authenticated instances of the hardihood
and powers of endurance shown by woman on the
frontiers of our country.